Life

STUDENT'S BOOK | INTERMEDIATE

NATIONAL GEOGRAPHIC
LEARNING

HELEN STEPHENSON
PAUL DUMMETT
JOHN HUGHES

Australia • Brazil • Mexico • Singapore • United Kingdom • United States

Contents

Unit	Grammar	Vocabulary	Real life (functions)	Pronunciation
1 **Culture and identity** pages 9–20	present simple and present continuous stative verbs question forms: direct questions question forms: indirect questions	word focus: *love* feelings wordbuilding: adjective and noun collocations	opening and closing conversations	direct questions short questions
VIDEO: Faces of India page 18 ▶ REVIEW page 20			
2 **Performing** pages 21–32	present perfect simple *already*, *just* and *yet* present perfect simple and past simple	musical styles emotions word focus: *kind* describing performances	choosing an event	weak forms intonation with *really, absolutely*, etc.
VIDEO: Taiko master page 30 ▶ REVIEW page 32			
3 **Water** pages 33–44	past simple and past continuous past perfect	describing experiences wordbuilding: adverbs word focus: *get*	telling stories	*d* and *t* after -*ed* endings *was* and *were*
VIDEO: Four women and a wild river page 42 ▶ REVIEW page 44			
4 **Opportunities** pages 45–56	predictions future forms	word focus: *job* and *work* education wordbuilding: prefix *re-* pay and conditions job requirements	making and responding to requests	weak and strong auxiliary verbs
VIDEO: Everest tourism changed Sherpa lives page 54 ▶ REVIEW page 56			
5 **Wellbeing** pages 57–68	modal verbs (1) first conditional: *if* + *will* *when, as soon as, unless, until, before*	a healthy lifestyle word focus: *so* restaurants	describing dishes	weak forms disappearing sounds
VIDEO: Dangerous dining page 66 ▶ REVIEW page 68			
6 **Mysteries** pages 69–80	purpose: *to ...* , *for ...* and *so that ...* certainty and possibility	word focus: *long* art wordbuilding: nouns and verbs -*ly* adverbs in the news	reacting to surprising news	weak form of *have* showing interest and disbelief
VIDEO: Encounters with a sea monster page 78 ▶ REVIEW page 80			

Listening	Reading	Critical thinking	Speaking	Writing
an extract from a TV programme about Native American culture two people doing a quiz about colours and their meaning	an article about cultural identity an article about globalization	examples	getting to know you my language course how international you feel first impressions	text type: a business profile writing skill: criteria for writing
three people talking about arts events a man talking about his dance academy	an article about listening to music an article about performance art	balance	new releases performing a survey on the arts arts events	text type: a review writing skill: linking ideas (1)
an extact from a radio programme about recreation in the water interviews about what happened next	an interview about underwater discoveries an article about an unforgettable experience	drawing conclusions	the first time what had happened learning a lesson it happened to me	text type: a blog post writing skill: interesting language
three people talking about their childhood ambitions three women talking about decisions	an article about the future of work an article about the economic boom in China	the author's view	predictions planning your work the perfect job requests	text type: a covering letter writing skill: formal style
an extract from a radio programme about healthy eating two people discussing the power of the mind	a news item about traditional dishes a news item about imaginary eating an article about modern lifestyles	writer's purpose	rules and regulations consequences modern life restaurant dishes	text type: a formal letter/email writing skill: explaining consequences
two people discussing an unusual photo a speaker at a conference talking about a mystery an extract from a radio programme about the Nasca lines	an article about flexible thinking an article about one of aviation's greatest mysteries	speculation or fact?	what's it for? speculating comparing ideas surprising news	text type: a news story writing skill: structuring a news story

Unit	Grammar	Vocabulary	Real life (functions)	Pronunciation
7 Living space pages 81–92	*used to*, *would* and past simple comparison: adverbs comparison: patterns	in the city wordbuilding: noun → adjective word focus: *as* and *like*	stating preferences and giving reasons	rising and falling intonation
VIDEO: The town with no wi-fi page 90 ▶ REVIEW page 92				
8 Travel pages 93–104	verb patterns: *-ing* form and *to* + infinitive present perfect continuous and simple How long?	holiday activities travel problems	dealing with problems	strong and weak forms
VIDEO: Questions and answers page 102 ▶ REVIEW page 104				
9 Shopping pages 105–116	passives articles and quantifiers	shopping (1) wordbuilding: compound adjectives shopping (2)	buying things	linking silent letters
VIDEO: Making a deal page 114 ▶ REVIEW page 116				
10 No limits pages 117–128	second conditional defining relative clauses	medicine word focus: *take* injuries	talking about injuries	sentence stress *and*
VIDEO: What does an astronaut dream about? page 126 ▶ REVIEW page 128				
11 Connections pages 129–140	reported speech reporting verbs	communications technology	telephone language	contrastive stress polite requests with *can* and *could*
VIDEO: Can you read my lips? page 138 ▶ REVIEW page 140				
12 Experts pages 141–152	third conditional *should have* and *could have*	wordbuilding: prefixes *in-*, *im-*, *un-* word focus: *go*	making and accepting apologies	*should have* and *could have* sentence stress
VIDEO: Shark vs. octopus page 150 ▶ REVIEW page 152				

COMMUNICATION ACTIVITIES page 153 ▶ GRAMMAR SUMMARY page 156 ▶ AUDIOSCRIPTS page 180

Listening	Reading	Critical thinking	Speaking	Writing
three people talking about different living arrangements podcast replies about house design	an article about what New York used to be like an article about a little town in Puerto Rico	descriptions	places advice a tourist destination choices	text type: a description of a place writing skill: organizing ideas
three people talking about travel tips people talking about their holidays an extract from a radio programme about a wildlife conservationist	an article about writers returning to their roots an article about tourism	close reading	holiday companions favourite activities going green travel problems	text type: a text message writing skill: informal style
market research interviews with three people who are shopping an extract from a radio programme about impulse buying	an article about two ways of going shopping an article about how to negotiate a price	testing a conclusion	shopping now and in the future souvenirs buying things	text type: customer feedback writing skill: clarity: pronouns
a podcast about the *Marathon des Sables* an extract from a TV preview show about bionic bodies	an article about life on another planet two stories about acts of endurance	reading between the lines	I'd love to live in … medicine inspirational people talking about injuries	text type: a personal email writing skill: linking ideas (2)
four conversations about the news four conversations about news headlines	an article about isolated tribes an article about community journalism	opinions	news stories personal communication apps telephone messages	text type: an opinion essay writing skill: essay structure
an interview with a farmer two stories about uncomfortable situations	a review of a book about Arctic expeditions an article about the samurai	relevance	decisions where did I go wrong? going back in time making and accepting apologies	text type: a website article writing skill: checking your writing

Life around the world – in 12 videos

Unit 12 Shark vs. octopus

What happens when a shark and an octopus meet.

Unit 2 Taiko master

The history of Taiko drumming from its origins in Japan to modern-day San Francisco.

Unit 6 Encounters with a sea monster

Three people tell their stories about what they saw in the water.

Canada

USA

UK

Spain

Morocco

Unit 7 The town with no wi-fi

Find out what life is like in the quiet zone of Green Bank.

Unit 11 Can you read my lips?

Rachel Kolb tells us about communicating as a deaf person.

Peru

Unit 8 Questions and answers

National Geographic Explorers from Spain, the UK, Peru and other countries talk about their roles and about objects that are important to them in their work.

Life videos

Unit 10 What does an astronaut dream about?

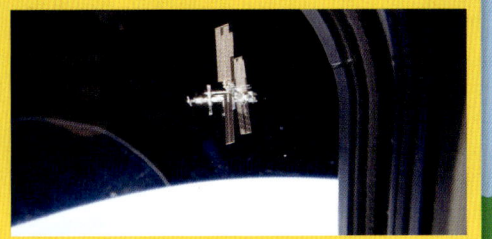

British astronaut Helen Sharman describes her experience of being on the Mir space station.

Unit 3 Four women and a wild river

Amber Valenti leads a kayak trip down the Amur River in Mongolia, Russia and China.

Russia

Unit 9 Making a deal

Learn how to bargain in Morocco.

Mongolia

Japan

China

Nepal

Unit 5 Dangerous dining

Find out why people eat the most dangerous fish on Earth – fugu.

India

Unit 1 Faces of India

Find out about Rajasthan through a focus on its people and faces.

Unit 4 Everest tourism changed Sherpa lives

Find out if Everest tourism has been a good or a bad thing for the local people.

7

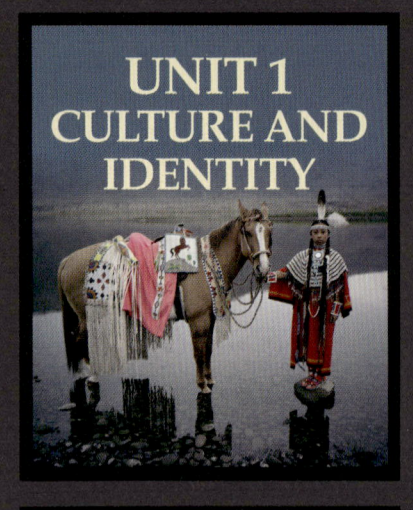

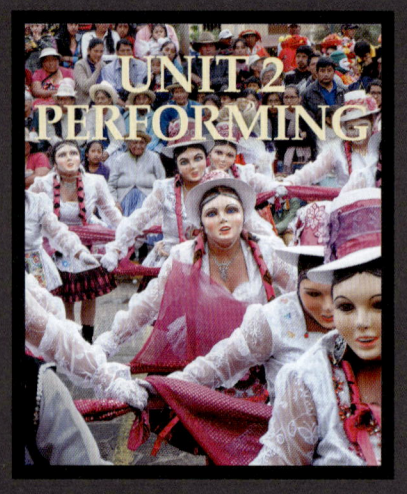

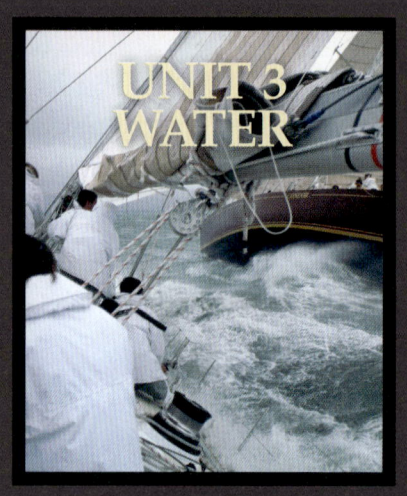

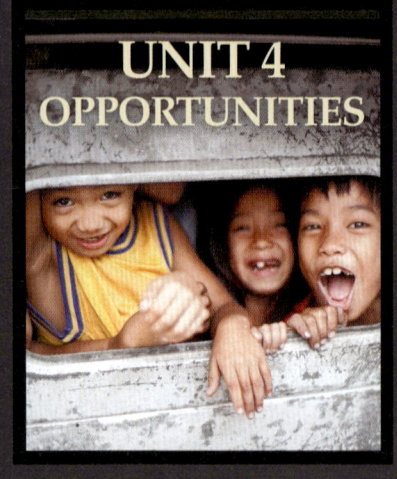

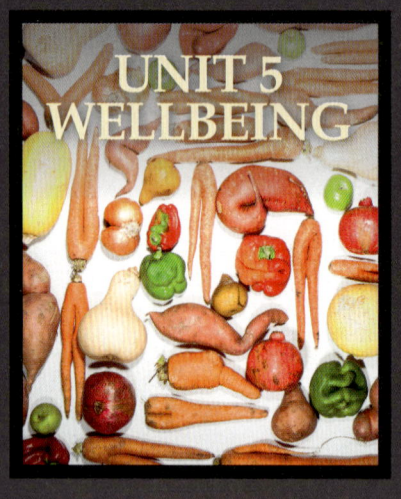

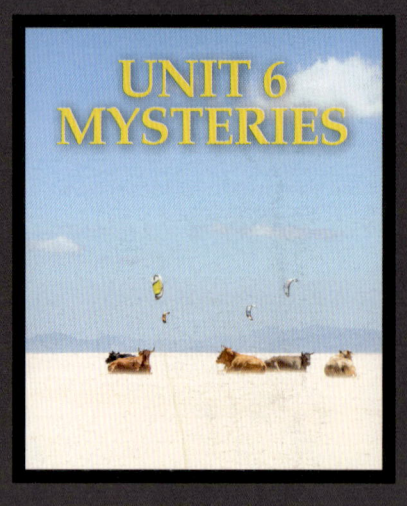

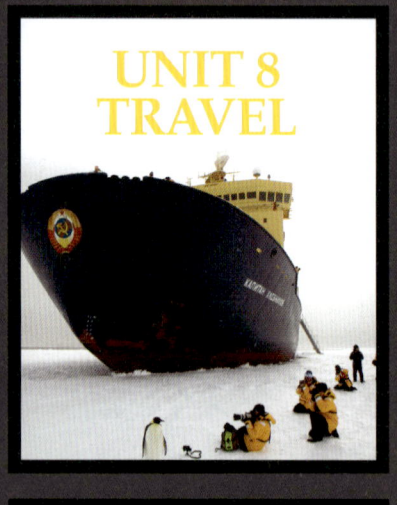

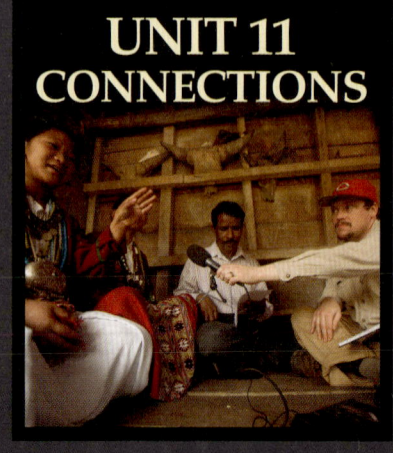

UNIT 1 CULTURE AND IDENTITY	UNIT 2 PERFORMING	UNIT 3 WATER
UNIT 4 OPPORTUNITIES	UNIT 5 WELLBEING	UNIT 6 MYSTERIES
UNIT 7 LIVING SPACE	UNIT 8 TRAVEL	UNIT 9 SHOPPING
UNIT 10 NO LIMITS	UNIT 11 CONNECTIONS	UNIT 12 EXPERTS

Unit 1 Culture and identity

Destiny Buck, of the Wanapum tribe of Native Americans, with her horse Daisy

FEATURES

10 How we see other cultures
How we think about cultural groups

12 Culture and colour
Do quizzes about colour

14 A world together
Find out what globalization really means

18 Faces of India
A video about the photographer Steve McCurry

1 Work in pairs. Look at the photo and the caption. Discuss the questions.
  1. Where's the girl from?
  2. What's she wearing? Everyday clothes or traditional clothes?
  3. The photo shows two things that are important in Native American culture. What do you think they are?

2 ▶1 Listen to an extract from a TV programme on world cultures. Check your ideas from Exercise 1.

3 ▶1 Listen to the extract again. Complete the sentences.
  1. People from all cultures need a sense of …
  2. Many Native American children learn to ride …
  3. Wearing the colours of our favourite team says 'We …'

4 Work in pairs. Do you belong to any of these groups? Tell your partner about them or any other groups you know about.

cultural societies	hobby groups
educational classes	online communities
family groups	sports clubs

my life ▸ GETTING TO KNOW YOU ▸ MY LANGUAGE COURSE ▸ HOW INTERNATIONAL YOU FEEL ▸ FIRST IMPRESSIONS
▸ A BUSINESS PROFILE

reading cultural identity • grammar present simple and present continuous • word focus love • speaking getting to know you

1a How we see other cultures

Reading

1 Look at the hats. Which part of the world do you think each one comes from?

2 Read the article and check your ideas from Exercise 1.

3 Read the article again. Find three reasons why we form general opinions of other cultural groups.

4 Work in pairs. How do films, news reports and TV shows influence our opinions of other cultural groups?

Grammar present simple and present continuous

> ▶ **PRESENT SIMPLE and PRESENT CONTINUOUS**
>
> **Present simple**
> I **live** in central London.
> [...] people **put** the things they meet in the world into groups.
>
> **Present continuous**
> He**'s wearing** one of those bush hats.
> I**'m looking** out of my window.
>
> For further information and practice, see page 156.

5 Look at the grammar box. Which verb form do we use for these things?
  1 things which are permanent or generally true
  2 things which are temporary or in progress at the time of speaking

6 Choose the correct option to complete the sentences.
  1 a *I work / I'm working* for a large cultural organization.
    b *I work / I'm working* extra hours. It's the busy season at work.
  2 a *We live / We're living* with my parents until our flat is ready.
    b *We live / We're living* just outside the city.
  3 a The kids *are / are being* naughty today. Sorry!
    b The kids *are / are being* usually very good.
  4 a *She has / She's having* an exam every week.
    b *She has / She's having* some problems with her school work.

How we see other cultures

▶ 2

My neighbour recently came back from holiday. I guess he was in Australia – he's wearing one of those bush hats with corks around it everywhere he goes. I'm curious about why we identify places by things like hats. I mean, baseball caps are certainly popular in the United States, but I'm looking out of my window (I live in central London) and nobody is wearing a bowler hat. And you don't see many Mexicans with sombreros or Vietnamese with straw hats in everyday life either.

The question is, why do we think about other national groups in this way? According to psychologists, it's because people put the things they meet in the world into groups. We do this for several reasons. First, it means that our brain doesn't work so hard because it doesn't need to analyse every new individual thing that we meet. Another reason is that when we understand (or think we understand) something, we can make predictions about it – we know what kind of behaviour to expect. Finally, it seems that we all love to feel good about ourselves and the group we belong to. This is easier when we put others into groups too.

So is it a good thing or a bad thing to have these general opinions? Perhaps the first and more important question is to ask ourselves if the things we believe about other groups are actually true. And in the case of hats, I don't think it is!

baseball cap

straw hat

bowler hat

sombrero

bush hat

10

7 Complete the pairs of sentences with the present simple and present continuous forms of the verbs.

1. a He _____ (not / feel) relaxed when he's on a plane.
   b He _____ (not / feel) very well at the moment.
2. a I _____ (come) from Scotland originally.
   b I _____ (come) – wait for me!
3. a I _____ (do) an evening class this year.
   b I _____ (do) my homework as soon as I get in from class.
4. a My friend _____ (look) for a new job in a different company.
   b My friend _____ (look) tired after she's been to the gym.

▶ **DYNAMIC and STATIVE VERBS**

Dynamic verbs
People put the things they meet in the world into groups.
Just a moment. I'm putting my hat and scarf on.

Stative verbs
We know what kind of behaviour to expect.
(not *are knowing*)

For further information and practice, see page 156.

---

8 Look at the grammar box. Choose the correct option to complete the rules.

1. Dynamic verbs *are / are not* used in both the continuous and simple form.
2. Stative verbs are not normally used in the *continuous form / simple form*.

9 Underline these stative verbs in the article.

| believe | belong | mean | need | seem |
| understand | wonder | | | |

10 Add the stative verbs from Exercise 9 to the table. Then add these verbs.

| contain | hate | like | love | prefer | realize |
| remember | sound | suppose | taste | | |

	Stative verbs
Thoughts and mental processes	know, _____, _____, _____, _____, _____, _____, _____, _____
The senses	hear, _____
Emotions	want, _____, _____, _____, _____, _____
Possession	have, _____, _____

11 Choose the correct option to complete the sentences.

1. Jake's on the phone. *He tells / He's telling* Pat about his holiday.
2. What *do you think / are you thinking* of my hat?
3. *Do you remember / Are you remembering* last summer?
4. *I hear / I'm hearing* you have a new job.
5. Maria's at the travel agent's. She *asks / is asking* the dates of the flight.
6. *I want / I'm wanting* to pass my exams first time.
7. Sorry, *I don't know / I'm not knowing* the answer.
8. *Do you make / Are you making* coffee? Great.

Word focus *love*

12 Work in pairs. Look at this extract from the article. Then look at how *love* is used in the sentences. When could you use each expression?

… *we all love to feel good about ourselves …*

1. I'd love to! Thanks.
2. I love walking in the rain.
3. Lots of love, Jenna
4. We love the summer.
5. Please give Oscar our love.
6. The story of two strangers who fall in love.
7. They are very much in love.
8. I'm loving it.

13 Work in pairs. Write two-line exchanges using the expressions in Exercise 12. Then act out your exchanges.

A: *Do you want to come for something to eat after class?*
B: **I'd love to!** *Thanks.*

Speaking my life

14 Work in pairs. Ask and answer questions using these stative verbs. Ask one follow-up question each time.

1. remember / first English class?
2. clubs / belong to?
3. how many languages / know?
4. hours sleep a night / need?
5. any food / hate?
6. prefer / tea or coffee?
7. food / love?

A: **Do you remember** *your first English class?*
B: **No, why? Do you?**

vocabulary feelings • listening colours and their meaning • grammar question forms • pronunciation questions • speaking my language course

1b Culture and colour

Vocabulary feelings

1 Work in pairs. How do you think the people described in the comments feel? Choose from these adjectives.

| angry | cheerful | happy | lucky | positive | sad |

1 He's feeling a bit blue today.
2 He just saw red!
3 He's in a black mood today.

2 Choose the correct option to complete the sentences. Then ask your partner the questions.

1 What are two things that make you *happiness / happy*?
2 When did you last have some good *luck / lucky*?
3 Can you tell me if you are *brave / bravery*?
4 What achievements are you *pride / proud* of?
5 Do you think *anger / angry* is a good thing?
6 Do you know who the most *power / powerful* person in the world is?

Listening

3 ▶3 Work in pairs. Do the quiz *Colours and their meaning*. Then listen and check your answers.

4 ▶3 Listen again and complete the table.

Colour	Place	Meaning
red	Western cultures Eastern cultures	1 2
yellow	3 4	knowledge 5
6	Japan	7 8
blue	9	death
green	10	environmentalism

5 Do these colours mean the same in your culture? What's your favourite colour?

Colours and their meaning

1 Look at the photo. Where are the women going?
  a to a birthday party
  b to a wedding

2 Does red mean different things in Eastern and Western cultures?
  a yes   b no

3 Where does yellow mean 'knowledge'?
  a China   b India

4 Which colour means 'happiness' in Japan?
  a orange   b pink

5 Do Mexicans wear blue at funerals?
  a yes   b no

6 Who uses green as their symbol?
  a environmentalists
  b the women's movement

Grammar question forms

> **QUESTION FORMS: DIRECT QUESTIONS**
>
> **Subject questions**
> Which colour **means** happiness in Japan?
> Who/What **uses** green as a symbol?
>
> **Other questions**
> Where **are** they **going**?
> What **does** yellow **mean**?
>
> For further information and practice, see page 156.

6 Look at the grammar box. Which type of question has the same subject–verb word order as affirmative sentences?

7 Look at the quiz in Exercise 3 again. Which questions are object questions? Which are subject questions?

8 Write questions for these answers. Begin with the words in brackets.

1. Mexicans wear blue at funerals. (who)
   Who wears blue at funerals?
2. Yellow means happiness in Egypt. (which colour)
3. Some people wear purple on International Women's Day. (what colour)
4. Picasso painted a white dove as a symbol of peace. (who)
5. Red means anger in many cultures. (what)
6. The United States president lives in the White House. (who)

9 Pronunciation direct questions

a ▶4 Listen to the questions from Exercise 8. Does the speaker's voice rise at the end of the questions? Or does it rise, then fall?

b ▶4 Listen again and repeat the questions.

> **QUESTION FORMS: INDIRECT QUESTIONS**
>
> Do you know what **yellow means**?
> Can you tell me who **uses** green as a symbol?
>
> For further information and practice, see page 156.

10 Look at the grammar box. What is the order of the subject and verb in indirect questions?

11 Write indirect questions for these direct questions. Begin with the words in brackets.

1. How many hours a week do you study English? (Can you tell me)
   Can you tell me how many hours a week you study English?
2. Why are you doing this course? (Can you tell me)
3. When does the course finish? (Do you know)
4. How many languages does the teacher speak? (Do you know)
5. Which other courses are you doing? (Can you tell me)
6. How many students are there in this class? (Do you know)

Speaking my life

12 Work in pairs. Ask and answer your questions from Exercise 11.

13 Complete these *blue* and *yellow* quiz questions with verbs or question words.

14 Work in two pairs within a group of four.

Pair A: Turn to page 153 and follow the instructions.

Pair B: Turn to page 154 and follow the instructions.

1. Where _____ the Blue-footed booby live?
2. _____ lives in the Blue House in South Korea?
3. _____ you know the name of the country where the Blue Nile begins?
4. _____ part of the USA is famous for Blues music?

1. Where _____ yellow taxi cabs from originally?
2. Which fruit _____ the Californian Yellow Fruit Festival celebrate?
3. _____ sport gives a yellow jersey to the winner?
4. Can you tell me where the house that inspired Van Gogh's 'Yellow House' painting _____ ?

my life ▶ GETTING TO KNOW YOU ▶ MY LANGUAGE COURSE ▶ HOW INTERNATIONAL YOU FEEL ▶ FIRST IMPRESSIONS ▶ A BUSINESS PROFILE

reading globalization • wordbuilding adjective + noun collocations • critical thinking examples • speaking how international you feel

1c A world together

Reading

1 Complete the definition of *globalization*. Use the same word twice.

Globalization is the idea that companies are now working in many different _____ and the culture of different _____ is becoming similar.

2 Read the article quickly. Which paragraph(s) talk(s) about business? Which talk(s) about culture?

3 Read the article again. Answer the questions.
   1 Which two recent experiences demonstrated globalized culture to the author? (paragraph 1)
   2 Which four things have increased the connections between countries? (paragraph 2)
   3 Which four things do some people think have a negative effect on other cultures? (paragraph 3)

4 Work in pairs. Does globalization affect you or someone you know? How?

Wordbuilding adjective + noun collocations

> **WORDBUILDING adjective + noun collocations**
>
> Some adjectives and nouns often go together.
> *national identity, vegetarian food*
>
> For further practice, see Workbook page 11.

5 Look at the wordbuilding box. Complete the sentences with these words. Then find the collocations in the article and check your answers.

| culture | market | view | identity | menu |
| thing | | | | |

1 Television is a good example of **popular** _____.
2 Nowadays companies have a **worldwide** _____ of customers.
3 My local café has a great **vegetarian** _____.
4 I think speaking foreign languages is a **good** _____.
5 Drinking tea is part of the English **national** _____.
6 I try to have a **positive** _____ of changes in my life.

6 Work in pairs. Think of at least one more collocation with each adjective in Exercise 5. Then ask and answer questions with the collocation.

Do you like vegetarian food?

Critical thinking examples

7 The author is trying to describe what globalization is. Which two types of globalization does she mention?

8 Giving examples is one way of helping to make a point. Underline examples of these things in the article.
   1 how popular culture moves from one country to another (paragraph 1)
   2 globalization in business (paragraph 2)
   3 how 'national cultures are strong' (paragraph 3)

9 How did the author's examples help you understand what globalization is?

10 Read the pairs of sentences. Underline the example sentences. Then write sentences of your own giving examples.
   1 You can eat great international food in my town. There are lots of Thai restaurants in particular.
   2 Internet TV gives you access to programmes from different countries. Brazilian soap operas are popular here now.
   3 There's lots to do in the evenings in my area. We've got a couple of great theatres.

Speaking my life

11 Work in pairs to prepare a survey on how 'international' other students' lives are. Use these ideas. Then work on your own and ask at least two other students your questions.

| clothes | food | movies | music | sports |
| technology | | | | |

Are any of your clothes made in other countries?
Which international foods do you eat/like?

12 Share the results of your survey with the class. Which international items are most common?

Unit 1 Culture and identity

A WORLD TOGETHER

BY ERLA ZWINGLE

▶ 5

We are in the middle of worldwide changes in culture. Popular culture is crossing from one country to another in ways we have never seen before. Let me give you some examples. One day, I'm sitting in a coffee shop in London having a cup of Italian espresso served by an Algerian waiter, listening to American music playing in the background. A few days later, I'm walking down a street in Mexico – I'm eating Japanese food and listening to the music of a Filipino band. In Japan, many people love flamenco. Meanwhile, in Europe, Japanese food is the latest in-thing. European girls decorate their hands with henna tattoos. It's the globalization of culture.

This globalization of culture follows on from the globalization of business. Modern industry now has a worldwide market. Businesses make their products in one country and sell them in another. Companies employ people on one continent to answer telephone enquiries from customers on a different continent.

It's true that buying and selling goods in different countries is not new. But nowadays, everything happens faster and travels further. In the past, there were camel trains, ships and railways. Then planes, telephones and television brought us closer together. Television had fifty million users after thirteen years, but the internet had the same number after only five years. Today the internet can connect us all in real time as together we watch the same news story as it happens, anywhere in the world.

How do people feel about globalization? It depends on where they live and how much money they have. Not everyone is happy about globalization. More than a fifth of all the people in the world now speak some English. Some people believe that there is a kind of 'cultural attack' from the English language, social media, and McDonald's and Starbucks. But I have a more positive view. I think that cultures are strong and countries don't need to lose their national identity. In India, there are more than four hundred languages and several different religions – and McDonald's serves mutton instead of beef and offers a vegetarian menu. In Shanghai, the television show *Sesame Street* teaches Chinese values and traditions. As one Chinese teacher said, 'We've got an American box with Chinese content in it.'

But there is one thing that is certain – globalization is here to stay. And if that means we'll understand each other better, that's a good thing.

my life ▶ GETTING TO KNOW YOU ▶ MY LANGUAGE COURSE ▶ HOW INTERNATIONAL YOU FEEL ▶ FIRST IMPRESSIONS ▶ A BUSINESS PROFILE

15

real life opening and closing conversations • pronunciation short questions

1d First impressions

Real life opening and closing conversations

'You never get a second chance to make a good first impression.'

- Dress appropriately. A dark blue suit is great for a business meeting, a red tie or scarf suggests power and energy.
- Be punctual, courteous and positive.
- Make sure you know the other person's name. Use it!
- Make the other person the focus of your attention. Sound interested! Ask questions!
- Know what you want to say and say it effectively!
- Don't forget to follow up on your meeting with a phone call or an email.

1 Read the seminar handout. Then work in groups and discuss these questions.

1. Do the colours and clothes mean the same thing in your country?
2. What does *to be punctual* mean in your country?
3. Do you use first names or surnames in your country?
4. Which advice is appropriate in your country? Which is not appropriate?

2 ▶6 Listen to two conversations at a business skills seminar in the UK. Four participants are role-playing 'first meetings'. Which advice in the seminar handout do they folllow? Tick the points.

3 ▶6 Look at the expressions for opening and closing conversations. Listen again and tick the expressions Paola, Colin, Lucy and Yuvraj use. Which pair of participants do you think gave the best performance?

4 Look at the expressions for opening and closing conversations again. Which expressions are the most formal?

▶ **OPENING AND CLOSING CONVERSATIONS**

Opening a conversation
May I introduce myself?
Allow me to introduce myself.
How do you do? My name's …
Hello, how are you. I'm …
It's a pleasure to meet you.
I'm very pleased to meet you.

Closing a conversation and moving on
Thanks for your time.
It's been good talking to you.
Let me give you my card.
Let's stay in touch.
Why don't I give you my card?
How about meeting again?

5 Pronunciation short questions

a ▶7 Listen to these exchanges. Notice how the speakers use short questions to show interest.

1. C: I mostly work on web adverts.
   P: Do you?
2. P: I'm in sales.
   C: Oh, are you?
3. L: Oh yes, my brother goes to *Get fit*.
   Y: Does he?
4. Y: It's nearly ready to open, in fact.
   L: Is it?

b Work in pairs. Practise the exchanges.

6 Practise the conversations from Exercise 2 with your partner. Look at the audioscript on page 180.

7 Imagine you are a participant at the business skills seminar. Complete the profile information card. Then do the seminar task. Use the expressions for opening and closing conversations to help you.

| Name |
| Company |
| Position |
| Responsibilities |
| Current projects you are involved in |

First Impressions
Task: You are at a networking event. Introduce yourself to as many people as you can and arrange to follow up useful contacts. You only have two minutes with each person.

networking (n) /ˈnetwɜːkɪŋ/ making useful business contacts

8 Work in pairs. Compare the information you found out about different people in Exercise 7.

my life ▶ GETTING TO KNOW YOU ▶ MY LANGUAGE COURSE ▶ HOW INTERNATIONAL YOU FEEL ▶ **FIRST IMPRESSIONS** ▶ A BUSINESS PROFILE

writing a business profile • writing skill criteria for writing

Unit 1 Culture and identity

1e About us

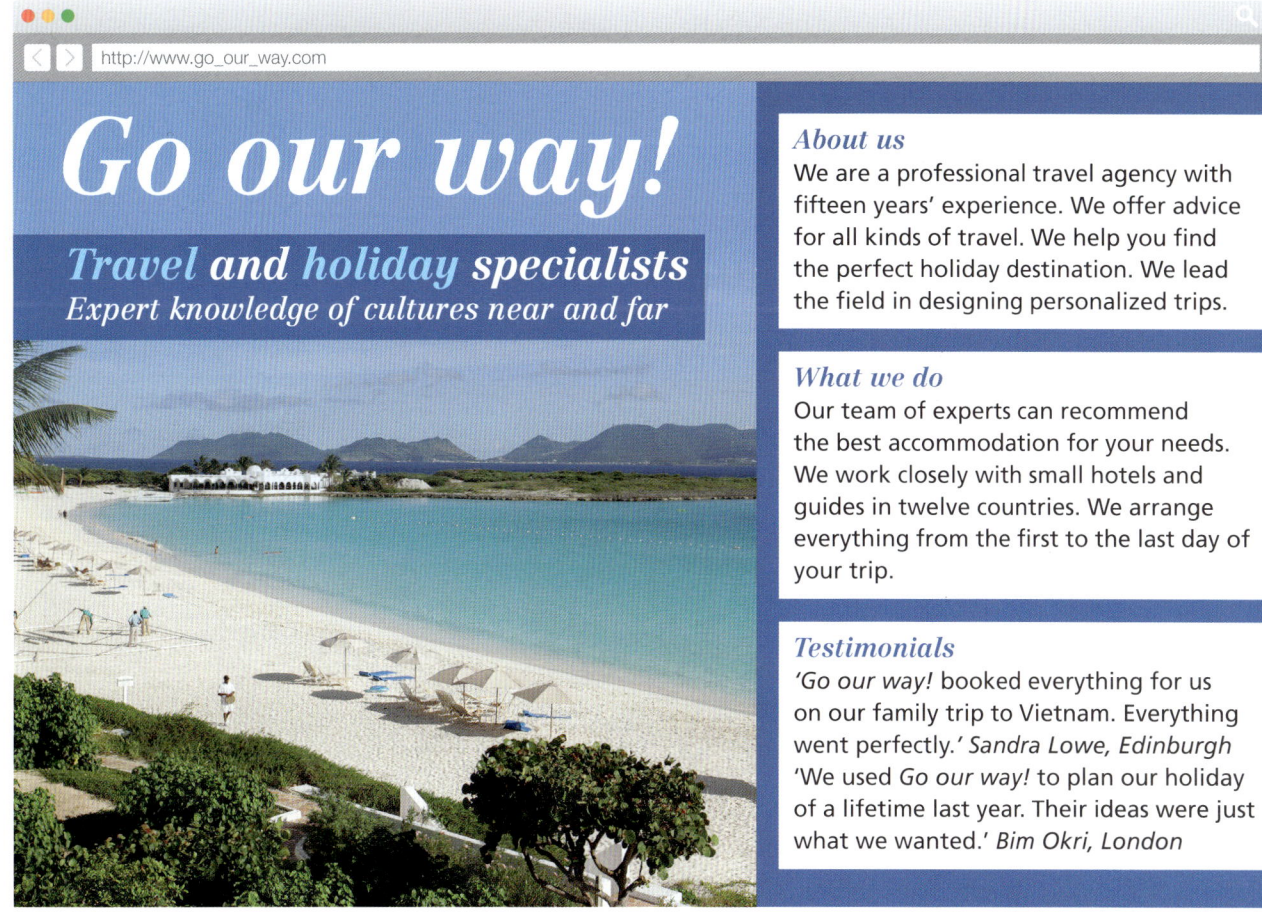

Go our way!
Travel and **holiday** specialists
Expert knowledge of cultures near and far

About us
We are a professional travel agency with fifteen years' experience. We offer advice for all kinds of travel. We help you find the perfect holiday destination. We lead the field in designing personalized trips.

What we do
Our team of experts can recommend the best accommodation for your needs. We work closely with small hotels and guides in twelve countries. We arrange everything from the first to the last day of your trip.

Testimonials
'*Go our way!* booked everything for us on our family trip to Vietnam. Everything went perfectly.' *Sandra Lowe, Edinburgh*
'We used *Go our way!* to plan our holiday of a lifetime last year. Their ideas were just what we wanted.' *Bim Okri, London*

Writing a business profile

1 Read the information about *Go our way!* Who (a–d) do you think would be interested in their services?

   a families with young children
   b groups of friends
   c business travellers
   d independent travellers

2 Writing skill criteria for writing

a Read the information again. Choose the correct option.

   1 text type: *website / letter*
   2 style: *neutral / formal / informal*
   3 reader: *current customers / possible customers*
   4 purpose: *to promote the company / to advertise a product*
   5 structure: *a sequenced text / separate sections of text*

b Which features of the text helped you decide your answers to Exercise 2a?

3 Underline these things in the text.
   1 travel vocabulary
   2 verbs that describe what the company does

4 Compete the sentences with some of the verbs you underlined in Exercise 3.
   1 Our telecommunications company can _____ of all your communication needs.
   2 Let our market researchers _____ the best strategy for your business.
   3 As a fast food company, we _____ the way in healthy food choices.
   4 Our personal banking advisors _____ you save money.

5 Work in groups. Imagine you run a small business together. Decide on your company name, field of work and some current projects.

6 Work on your own. Write a profile to promote your business. Use the *Go our way!* profile and the categories in Exercise 2 to help you.

7 Work in your groups again. Read your profiles and choose the one which best promotes your company. Think about the following points.

   • **accuracy** Spelling mistakes do not look professional!
   • **clarity** Does the reader understand exactly what your business does?

my life ▶ GETTING TO KNOW YOU ▶ MY LANGUAGE COURSE ▶ HOW INTERNATIONAL YOU FEEL ▶ FIRST IMPRESSIONS
▶ A BUSINESS PROFILE

1f Faces of India

A shepherd in Rajasthan, India

Unit 1 Culture and identity

Before you watch

1 Look at the photo and the caption. Describe the man's appearance. What does his expression tell you about him?

2 Key vocabulary

a Read the sentences. The words in bold are used in the video. Guess the meaning of the words.

1 The **shepherd** has two dogs to help him move the sheep.
2 I think the eyes are often a person's most interesting **feature**.
3 It takes days to get to Rajasthan as it's quite **remote**.
4 The local people dress in a very **particular** way.
5 My friend always **amuses** me with his funny stories.

b Match the words in bold in Exercise 2a with these definitions.

a part of the face
b far from other places, difficult to get to
c special, individual or different from others
d the job of looking after sheep
e to make someone laugh or to entertain someone

While you watch

3 1.1 Watch the first part of the video (0.00–0.28). Complete the information about Steve McCurry.

Steve McCurry is a ¹ .... His first job was working on a ² .... His ambition was to travel and see the ³ .... He's worked at National Geographic for about ⁴ .... years.

4 1.1 Watch the rest of the video and look closely at the people you see. Then work in pairs and describe the person you remember best from the video.

5 1.1 Watch the whole video again. Match the beginnings of the sentences (1–6) with the endings (a–f).

1 Rajasthan is home to
2 Rajasthan is
3 The people of Rajasthan are
4 Some nomads have the job of
5 Steve McCurry is
6 Steve McCurry is interested in

a a shy person.
b gentle and hospitable.
c meeting people.
d some nomadic shepherds.
e strange and wonderful.
f amusing people.

6 1.1 Can you remember what Steve McCurry says about photographing faces? Do you agree? Choose the correct option or watch the last section of the video (2.29 to the end) again.

It's *the eyes / strange features / the whole face* that tells the story.

After you watch

7 Vocabulary in context

a 1.2 Watch the clips from the video. Choose the correct meaning of the words and phrases.

b Answer the questions in your own words. Then work in pairs and compare your answers.

1 Can you think of two places where you feel at home?
2 What do you think is a good way to make a living?
3 Have you been anywhere that felt like another planet?
4 Have you seen anything or done anything which you could describe as 'kind of strange'?
5 What activities do people do which involve getting warmed up before they start?

8 Work in groups. Steve McCurry's photos in the video focus on the people and especially their faces to 'tell the story' of Rajasthan. Choose a place or a group of people you know. Plan a photoshoot of ten photos to tell the 'story'. Use these ideas to help you.

- What are the most important features of the group?
- Is appearance or activity more important?
- Do you need to include the place or just the people?

fortune teller (n) /ˈfɔːtʃuːn ˌtelə/ someone who predicts a person's future
hospitable (adj) /hɒsˈpɪtəbl/ friendly to visitors
nomad (n) /ˈnəʊmæd/ someone who moves from one place to another to live
snake charmer (n) /ˈsneɪk ˌtʃɑːmə/ someone who performs with snakes

19

UNIT 1 REVIEW AND MEMORY BOOSTER

Grammar

1 Complete the interview with a prize-winning travel writer from London at the prize-giving event.

1. Q: What _____ (this prize / mean) to you?
   A: Actually, I _____ (feel) very proud of myself. I never _____ (expect) to win prizes.
2. Q: When you sit down to write, how _____ (you / decide) what to write about?
   A: I _____ (not / know), really. Sometimes my readers _____ (send) me ideas.
3. Q: _____ (which places / interest) you?
   A: Oh, everywhere. Every culture _____ (have) something special about it.
4. Q: _____ (you / work) on anything at the moment?
   A: I _____ (do) some research for a new book and I also _____ (want) to finish some magazine articles.
5. Q: _____ (you / can / tell) me what the book's about?
   A: At the moment, I _____ (think) about either Brazil or Vietnam. I love both places.

2 Are the sentences about Zoe true (T) or false (F)?

1. She's surprised to win prizes for her books.
2. She usually writes about what her readers want.
3. She's writing some articles on Peru and Vietnam.

3 ≫ MB Work in pairs. Say which tense is used in each gap in Exercise 1 and explain why.

4 ≫ MB Work in pairs. Each person choose one dynamic and one stative verb from Exercise 1. Ask and answer questions using each verb.

I CAN
- ask and answer questions about things which are always and generally true, and routines (present simple)
- ask and answer questions about things happening now (present continuous)
- talk about possessions and states: thoughts and mental processes, etc. (stative verbs)
- use different question forms: direct and indirect questions

Vocabulary

5 Write the noun forms of these adjectives.

| angry | brave | cheerful | happy | lucky |
| powerful | proud | sad | | |

6 ≫ MB Work in pairs. Look at the adjectives in Exercise 5. How often do you feel like this? What kinds of situations make you feel this way?

I CAN
- talk about feelings and personal states

Real life

7 Look at the expressions (1–6). Do we use them to open (O) or close (C) conversations?

1. Hello, how are you? I'm …
2. How about meeting again?
3. How do you do? My name's …
4. Let me give you my card.
5. Let's stay in touch.
6. May I introduce myself?

8 Work in small groups. You are at an event for the travel industry. Act out conversations with different partners using a suitable expression to begin and end the conversation.

I CAN
- introduce myself in formal and informal situations
- open and close a conversation
- ask for and give personal information

Unit 2 Performing

Masked folk dancers and their audience, Ollantaytambo, Peru

FEATURES

22 Music today
How we listen to music today

24 Learning to dance
Why do we dance?

26 Living statues
Entertainment on the street

30 Taiko master
A video about a Japanese art form

1 Which word is the odd one out in each group? Why?

1 actor audience dance director
   dance – all the others are people
2 choreographer conductor musician play
3 concert dancer musical show
4 act comedian entertainer magician
5 band choir orchestra singer
6 ballet clown drama opera

2 ▶8 Listen to three people talking about different events. Tick the words in Exercise 1 they mention.

3 ▶8 Listen again. Which person is talking about the photo? What are the other two people talking about?

4 Work in pairs. Are you interested in the arts? Discuss these questions.

1 How often do you go to concerts, shows or the theatre?
2 What are your favourite types of events?
3 What traditional events in your country or region do you enjoy?
4 Do you like taking part in things or do you prefer being in the audience?

my life ▶ NEW RELEASES ▶ PERFORMING ▶ A SURVEY ON THE ARTS ▶ ARTS EVENTS ▶ A REVIEW

vocabulary musical styles • reading listening to music • grammar present perfect simple • speaking new releases

2a Music today

Vocabulary musical styles

1 Work in pairs. Discuss the questions. Do you like the same kind of music?

1 What's your favourite album?
2 Do you like all the tracks on it?
3 How do you usually listen to music?

2 ▶9 Listen to six music clips. Discuss the clips with your partner. Use some of these words.

catchy   cheerful   interesting   lively
repetitive   sad   tuneless   unusual

3 ▶9 Listen again. Which country do you think each clip is from? Write the number (1–6) next to the country.

blues – USA
bhangra – India
bossa nova – Brazil
Celtic – Ireland
charanga – Cuba
flamenco – Spain
Gnawaa – Morocco
Malagasy – Madagascar
punk – UK
reggae – Jamaica
taiko drumming – Japan
township jive – South Africa

Reading

4 Read the article from a magazine, *Music today*. What's the article about? Choose the correct option (a–c).

a the best live bands
b becoming a musician
c music and new technology

5 Read the article again. Discuss the questions.

1 Is it easy to find music stores in town centres? Why? / Why not?
2 Why are there more music websites nowadays?
3 How do we listen to music for free?
4 Why is it now easier to listen to international musicians?

6 Are any of the things in the article true for you? Tell your partner.

▶10

THE ONLINE *revolution*

The way we listen to and buy music has changed enormously in recent years. These days it's hard to find a music store in your local town centre – where have they all gone? The answer, of course, is online. The number of music websites has grown incredibly quickly since internet connections became faster and cheaper. But it's not only the way we buy music that's different, it's also what we buy. New vinyl records have been hard to find for years. And CD sales have fallen and MP3 sales are slowing down. In fact, thanks to musicians' websites and other streaming websites, we can now choose the music we listen to without actually buying it. These days our choice is much wider – bands and singers release their music online direct to the listeners and so it has become much easier to discover different kinds of music from all over the world. One thing that hasn't changed so much, however, is our love of live music. Bands still go on tour and play at festivals, giving their audiences often unforgettable experiences.

vinyl (n) /ˈvaɪnəl/ a kind of plastic used to make records

A musician plays a trumpet on a rooftop in Cyprus.

Grammar present perfect simple

▶ **PRESENT PERFECT SIMPLE**

CD sales **have fallen**.
One thing that **hasn't changed** is our love of live music.
Where **have** they **gone**?

For further information and practice, see page 158.

7 Look at the grammar box. How do we form the present perfect simple? Which verbs have irregular past participles?

8 Underline four more present perfect simple sentences in the article. Then choose the correct options in these sentences (a–d).

a We *know / don't know* exactly when the activities or situations started.
b The activities or situations started in the past. They *have / don't have* an effect on the present.
c The present perfect is used with *for / since* and the point of time when the activity started.
d The present perfect is used with *for / since* and a period of time.

9 Complete the text with the present perfect simple form of the verbs.

Digital downloads of albums ¹_____ (become) the most popular way to buy music in recent years, but not everybody ²_____ (lose) interest in vinyl records. Sales of vinyl records ³_____ (rise) significantly since 2007. Many buyers are younger fans who ⁴_____ (realize) that music sounds better on vinyl. The price of a typical pop CD ⁵_____ (not / go up) for a while, but some collectors ⁶_____ (pay) thousands of pounds for original vinyl records by early punk bands.

10 Complete the sentences with the present perfect simple form of these verbs.

| be | happen | not have | not hear | record | sell |

1 Fado singer Mariza _____ over a million records worldwide.
2 Charanga bands _____ part of Cuban culture since the 1940s.
3 Most people in the UK _____ any hoomii music.
4 Punk music _____ much success in recent years.
5 What _____ to MTV since Youtube began?
6 How many albums _____ your favourite band _____ ?

11 Are these expressions used with *for* or *since*? Write two lists.

1986   a couple of days   a few months
a while   ages   centuries   I was a child   July
last Monday   lunchtime   my last holiday
some time   the day before yesterday   years

12 Write the present perfect simple form of the verbs. Then complete the sentences so that they are true for you. Work in pairs and compare your sentences.

1 I _____ (not / listen) to _____ for ages.
2 I _____ (live) in this town for _____ .
3 I _____ (be) in my current job/class since _____ .
4 I _____ (know) my best friend since _____ .
5 I _____ (not / go) to _____ for months.
6 I _____ (have) my _____ since last year.

▶ **ALREADY, JUST and YET**

My nearest record store has **just** closed.
I haven't bought any music online **yet**.
I've **already** listened to some music sites.

For further information and practice, see page 158.

13 ▶ 11 Match the comments (1–4) with the responses (a–d). Complete the sentences with *already*, *just* and *yet*. Then listen and check.

1 Have you heard Shakira's new single?
2 Do you want to borrow the new James Bond DVD?
3 Have you seen the musical *Wicked* _____ ?
4 I've _____ bought tickets to see *Stomp* in London!

a No, thanks. I've _____ seen it. I saw it at the cinema.
b Yes, we have. It's even better than the film.
c Really? Is that show still running?
d No, not _____ . Is it as good as her last one?

Speaking my life

14 Work in pairs. Act out conversations as in Exercise 13. Use these ideas.

an album / a song / a track
a book / a magazine / comic
a musical / a show / a play / a concert / a film
an exhibition / a festival

A: *The new Adele album has **just** come out. Have you heard it **yet**?*
B: *No, **not yet**. What's it like?*

vocabulary emotions • listening a dance academy • grammar present perfect simple and past simple • speaking performing

2b Learning to dance

Vocabulary emotions

1 What kind of things can change your mood? Choose the correct option to complete the sentences.

1. That music is so cheerful – **it** always **puts me in a** *bad / good* **mood**.
2. That song's so sad. **I feel like** *crying / laughing* every time I hear it.
3. It's a really funny film. **I can't stop** *crying / laughing* when I think about it.
4. TV shows about people's problems **make me** *cry / smile*.
5. I love dancing because **it** *cheers me up / makes me feel sad*.

2 Work in pairs. Tell your partner what changes your moods. Use some of the expressions in bold in Exercise 1.

I don't go out dancing very often. But when I do, it puts me in a good mood.

Listening

3 Work in pairs. Discuss the questions.

1. What kind of dances are traditional in your region or country?
2. Have you ever been to a dance class or learned a dance?
3. Do you enjoy dancing?
4. Do you dance at special occasions? Which ones?
5. Is there a dance or kind of dance you'd like to be able to do?

4 ▶ 12 Listen to a dance teacher, Bruce Daley, talking about his career. Correct the factual errors in these sentences.

1. Daley opened the studio when he started dancing professionally.
2. A lot of young kids began coming when big TV shows started.
3. Two of his older students became professionals last year.
4. Once, a very happy young man came to class.

A dancer at Montreal's Palais des Congrès

5 ▶ 12 Listen again. Are the sentences true (T) or false (F)?

1. Daley runs dance classes for professional dancers.
2. His first students were older people.
3. Many people have found a new social life at his studio.
4. Traditional ballroom dancing has never been popular.
5. Daley has seen how dancing can change people's moods.
6. He's had two careers through dance.

6 Bruce Daley talks about the role of dancing in people's lives. Can you think of other activities people do to:

1. make them feel young? *keeping fit*
2. meet people?
3. have a social life?
4. change their mood?

Grammar present perfect simple and past simple

> ▶ **PRESENT PERFECT SIMPLE and PAST SIMPLE**
>
> *Dancing* **has been** *my life, really.*
> *And starting this school was the best thing I've ever done.*
> *My injuries* **ended** *my career as a dancer ten years ago.*
> *But opening the school* **gave** *me a new career as a teacher.*
>
> For further information and practice, see page 158.

7 Look at the grammar box. Circle the past simple verbs and underline the present perfect simple forms. Then choose the correct option to complete the rules.

1. We use the *present perfect simple / past simple* when we don't say when something happened.
2. We use the *present perfect simple / past simple* when we say – or it is clear from the situation – when something happened.

8 Underline the present perfect simple forms and circle the past simple verbs in the audioscript on page 180. Which ones have different past simple and past participle forms?

9 Look at the pairs of sentences. Explain why the two different verb forms are used.

1. a Anya Paseka danced professionally for years.
   b Anya Paseka has danced professionally for years.
2. a The students went to New York for a week.
   b The students have gone to New York for a week.
3. a The show was at the Theatre Royal all summer.
   b The show has been at the Theatre Royal all summer.

10 ▶ 13 Choose the correct options to complete the text. Then listen and check.

> Bruce ¹*was / has been* my teacher for about two years now. ²*I started / I've started* coming here during a bad period at work. Bruce's classes are great – ³*I never had / I've never had* so much fun! ⁴*I met / I've met* all kinds of people here. Some of them ⁵*became / have become* really good friends. At first, I ⁶*didn't know / haven't known* how to dance. But I soon ⁷*realized / have realized* that you can't get embarrassed – you just have to dance! Everyone here ⁸*felt / has felt* the same way at some point.

11 Pronunciation weak forms

a ▶ 14 Listen to four sentences from Exercise 10 again. Notice how the verb *have* is not stressed in present perfect statements.

b Work in pairs. Practise saying the four sentences.

12 Match the pairs of verbs with the sentences. Use the present perfect simple and the past simple form of the verbs to complete the sentences.

come out / be	not book / not enjoy
never try / go	see / go
not be / break	start / not watch

1. *Dancing on Ice* _____ on TV last month, but I _____ it yet.
2. I first _____ *River Dance* in April and I _____ three times since then!
3. I _____ Zumba, but I _____ to an aerobics class a few months ago.
4. Jack _____ in the show since he _____ his ankle.
5. We _____ tickets for Enrique Iglesias this time. We _____ his last concert.
6. When _____ the film *Strictly Ballroom* _____ ? It _____ on TV several times.

Speaking my life

13 Work in pairs. Ask questions with *Have you ever ... ?*, *Did you (ever) ... when ... ?* and *When was the last time you ... ?* Ask follow-up questions using the past simple and *where, what, who, why* or *when*.

act in a play	play an instrument
give a speech	sing in front of an audience
perform in public	tell a joke

A: **Have you ever acted** in a play?
B: Yes, **I acted** in Macbeth *in my final year at school.*
A: What part **did you play**?
B: Actually, **I was** Lady Macbeth.

reading performance art • word focus *kind* • critical thinking balance • speaking a survey on the arts

2c Living statues

Reading

1 Look at the photo and write three sentences to describe it.

2 Work in pairs. Compare your sentences and discuss what you think it feels like to be a living statue.

3 Read the newspaper article. Underline the parts of the article that tell you:
   1 what a living statue is
   2 where you can see living statues
   3 what similar art forms in history there have been
   4 what it feels like to be a living statue

4 Work in pairs. Read the article again and discuss these questions.
   1 Who is the main audience for this kind of performance?
   2 What are the main differences between living statues and *tableaux vivants*?
   3 What makes a living statue successful?

5 Find these words in the article. Look at how the words are used and try to guess their meaning. Then replace the words in bold in the sentences (1–6) with these words.

illustrate (line 15)	begging (line 31)
resident (line 28)	costume (line 35)
pavement (line 30)	react (line 47)

   1 An actor usually wears **a set of special clothes** on stage.
   2 Don't walk in the road – get on the **path**.
   3 Sadly, we see a lot of people who are **asking people for money** in the street nowadays.
   4 The audience was shouting at him, but he didn't **say or do anything in response**!
   5 The pictures in the book **show** what the story is about really well.
   6 We spoke to a **person who lives in this area** about the traffic problems.

6 Work in pairs. Cover the article and tell your partner what you can remember about the answers in Exercise 3.

7 Would you like to be a street entertainer? Why? / Why not? What kind would you be? Tell the class.

| living statue | busker | magician |
| pavement artist | sand sculptor |

Word focus *kind*

8 Read the two examples from the article. Say if *kind* is an adjective or a noun.
   1 … you'll see a special kind of display …
   2 … not everyone is so kind and generous …

9 Complete the sentences with these expressions.

a kind of	really kind of
How kind	that kind of thing
kind and thoughtful	

   1 Flowers! _____ !
   2 Grunge is _____ rock music that started in the 1980s in the USA.
   3 I love going to exhibitions and _____ .
   4 It's _____ you to lend me the money.
   5 My aunt always gives me the perfect present. She's such a _____ person.

Critical thinking balance

10 Work in pairs. Discuss the questions.
   1 What kind of reader is the article for?
   2 Does the article change your opinion of living statues? How?
   3 Is there anything you want to know about living statues that the article doesn't tell you?

11 According to the article, this type of street performance is not popular with everyone. Discuss the questions.
   1 Who feels negative about living statues? What three points does he make?
   2 What does the performer from London say about one of these points?
   3 Do you think the author gives equal importance to both views?

Speaking my life

12 Work in pairs. Prepare six questions for a survey on prices and art events in your country or the country where you are now. Use these ideas. Then ask and answer your questions in groups.

| street entertainers / art exhibitions / museums / concerts |
| free of charge / tickets / entry price / donation |
| too expensive / about right / not enough |

Do you ever give money to street entertainers? How much is about right?

13 Share the results of your survey with the class. What was the majority opinion about paying for art?

Living statues

Entertainment on the street

▶ 15

Go sightseeing in many cities today and among the famous buildings, street markets and other attractions, sooner or later you'll see a special kind of display – living statues. These street performers, who are usually dressed as famous characters from history or from popular culture, have become a common sight in tourist areas of Paris, London, Barcelona and other cities. The performance involves standing completely still for long periods of time. The performers are like statues, but they are human.

This kind of performance has a long history and it has existed in various forms since the sixteenth century. The French used the term *tableaux vivants*, which means 'living pictures'. A group of actors stood in positions to illustrate a scene, but they didn't speak or move during the display.

The subject of the displays was often religious or from mythology. In some places, they were part of royal occasions. In the Catalan region of Spain, *tableaux vivants* has been a popular tradition since the early eighteenth century. The performances are called *Els Pastorets* (shepherds). They take place at Christmas and show the nativity scene. Nowadays, Catalonia is also famous for its modern living statues. In fact, there are so many of them on the streets of Barcelona that the city council has decided to control the number and give out only thirty licences for fifteen locations. Local resident Joan Castells explained, 'You can't move past the crowds on the pavement, and most of them are not really entertaining people, they're just begging.' Now, each licensed artist can perform either in the morning or in the afternoon.

So why do so many people want to be living statues? Joan Castells says, 'It's an easy way of earning money. All you need is some makeup and a costume.' But according to one of the living statues in London's Covent Garden, 'Preparation takes ages – and so does getting clean at the end of the day. It's also extremely difficult to stay completely still for long periods. I can't even move my eyes or show that I'm breathing.' And although it's 'understood' that if you take a photo or a selfie, you leave some money, not everyone is so kind and generous. 'Nobody gets rich doing this,' said the living statue I spoke to in London.

Perhaps they don't get rich, but every performer has some tricks to encourage people to give them money. Every time a tourist throws them a coin, they react with a quick, small movement. Perhaps they wave, or turn their head or reach to touch the person. The statue comes to life for just a moment, entertaining the crowd and rewarding the payment. And maybe giving the tired and aching performer a chance to move into a new, more comfortable position.

---

art form (n) /ˈɑːt fɔːm/ a creative, artistic activity
royal (adj) /ˈrɔɪəl/ connected to a king or queen
still (adj) /stɪl/ not moving

A living statue in São Paulo

real life choosing an event • vocabulary describing performances • pronunciation intonation with *really, absolutely,* etc.

2d What's on?

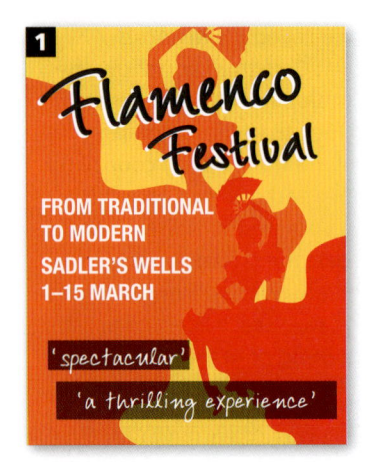

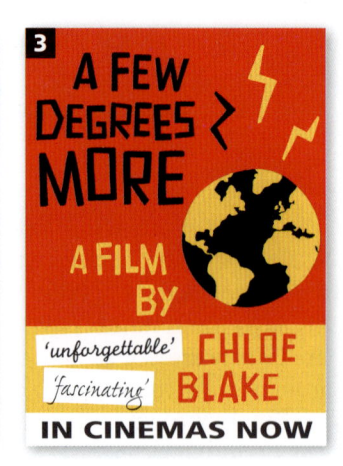

1 Flamenco Festival
FROM TRADITIONAL TO MODERN
SADLER'S WELLS
1–15 MARCH
'spectacular'
'a thrilling experience'

2 who's laughing now?
THE CITY THEATRE
BRITAIN'S TOP COMEDIANS IN AN ALL-NEW SHOW
'terrific' 'hilarious'
IN AID OF COMIC RELIEF
One night only. 9 pm 5 March

3 A FEW DEGREES MORE
A FILM BY CHLOE BLAKE
'unforgettable'
'fascinating'
IN CINEMAS NOW

Real life choosing an event

1 Work in pairs. Look at the adverts. Which event would you most like to go to? Which would you not like to go to? Tell your partner.

2 ▶ 16 Read the comments. Then listen to two people, Lesley and Richard, making plans to go out. Write the number of the advert (1–3) next to the comments. Which event do Lesley and Richard decide to go and see?

   a   It sounds really awful.
   b   That sounds really interesting.
   c   Apparently, it's absolutely brilliant.
   d   It looks pretty good.
   e   Roger Whitehead is absolutely hilarious.
   f   He's not very funny.

3 ▶ 16 Look at the expressions for choosing an event. Listen again and tick the expressions Richard and Lesley use.

▶ CHOOSING AN EVENT

Suggestions and responses
Do you feel like / fancy going out tonight?
Do you want to go the theatre?
Would you like to see a movie?
Do you like the sound of that?

Yeah, why not?
Yes, sure.
I like the sound of that.
I'm not keen on him.
I'm not in the mood for anything depressing.
It doesn't really appeal to me.
It sounds great.

Details of the event
What's on?
Who's in it?
What else is on?
Who's it by?
Where / When / What time is it on?
What's it about?

Vocabulary describing performances

4 Look at the sentences in Exercise 2. Write the adverbs used before these adjectives. Which adjectives have stronger meanings?

   1 .... : awful, brilliant, hilarious
   2 .... , ... , ... : interesting, good, funny

5 Which adverbs do you use with these groups of adjectives?

A fascinating   marvellous   spectacular
   terrible   terrific   thrilling   unforgettable

B boring   depressing   disappointing   dull
   entertaining

6 Pronunciation intonation with *really, absolutely,* etc.

a ▶ 17 Listen to the sentences from Exercise 2 again. Notice how the speaker stresses both the adverb and adjective in the affirmative statements.

b Work in pairs. Practise these exchanges. Pay attention to your intonation.

   1   A: What was the film like?
       B: It was really awful.
   2   A: Do you like flamenco?
       B: Yes, I think it's pretty interesting.
   3   A: Was it a good festival?
       B: Yes, it was absolutely brilliant.
   4   A: How was the show?
       B: Oh, very entertaining!

7 Work in pairs. Invite your partner to see the event that you would most like to go to in Exercise 1. Include words from Exercises 4 and 5. Use the expressions for choosing an event to help you.

my life   ▶ NEW RELEASES   ▶ PERFORMING   ▶ A SURVEY ON THE ARTS   ▶ ARTS EVENTS
▶ A REVIEW

writing a review • writing skill linking ideas (1)   Unit 2 Performing

2e A portrait of an artist

Writing a review

1 Who is your favourite performer or artist? Tell your partner about this person and why you like him/her.

2 Read the review of Baz Luhrmann's work. What kind of information about Luhrmann is included? Choose the correct options (a–d).

  a his influences
  b his plans for the future
  c his private life
  d his work

3 Read the review again. Underline the information which is factual and circle the opinions. Then find two direct quotes from Luhrmann.

4 Which sentence (a–d) best describes the review? Explain your choice(s).

  a It summarizes several different opinions.
  b It only talks about negative things.
  c It only talks about positive things.
  d It's a personal point of view.

Baz Luhrmann is a film director whose films include *Strictly Ballroom*, *Romeo + Juliet*, *Moulin Rouge!* and *Australia*. I have seen every one of his films and in my opinion, Luhrmann's work just gets better and better. He says that 'putting on a show' has always come naturally to him and that Bollywood is his biggest influence. Although he is best-known as a film director, Luhrmann has also directed opera. Consequently, his films are usually exciting, energetic and spectacular. They have had box office success despite being unusual: in *Romeo + Juliet* the actors speak in verse, in *Moulin Rouge!* they sing their lines. On the other hand, the epic *Australia* wasn't so popular with the critics. Nevertheless, as an ordinary film fan, I thought it was absolutely fantastic. Luhrmann says the high point of his career has been 'achieving so many of the dreams I had as a kid – from going to the Oscars to getting a letter from Marlon Brando'. To me, his films have the power of dreams. They take you into thrilling, unforgettable worlds.

5 Writing skill linking ideas (1)

a Look at the table. Which group of words can replace each highlighted word in the review? Write the words from the review in the table.

in spite of	even though while	in contrast, but however,	because of this, for that reason, so therefore

b Choose the correct option to complete the senences.

  1 *Although / Despite* his name is Mark, everyone calls him Baz.
  2 *Although / Despite* working mainly in Australia, he has had international success with his films.

c Rewrite the sentences using the words in brackets. Make any changes to verbs and punctuation as necessary.

  1 They have had box office success despite being unusual films. (even though)
  2 I enjoyed *Romeo + Juliet* in spite of not understanding all the dialogue. (but)
  3 While I love epic films, I didn't enjoy this one. (Nevertheless)
  4 Although they praised Luhrmann's earlier films, the critics did not like *Australia*. (In spite of)
  5 I've seen all of the films, but I haven't seen any of the operas. (However)
  6 His last film was absolutely brilliant. Because of this, I'm looking forward to seeing the next one. (so)

6 Write a review of an artist whose work you know and enjoy. First, look at the headings and make notes. You may need to do some research first. Then write about 150 words. Use a variety of adjectives and linkers.

  Basic biographical information
  Facts (life, work)
  Opinions (mine, others)

7 Use these questions to check your review.
  • Have you used linkers correctly?
  • Have you expressed clearly why you like this artist's work?

8 Read some reviews your classmates have written. Use these questions to check your classmates' reviews.
  • What do you learn about the subject from reading the review?
  • Do you agree with the opinions expressed in the review?

my life ▶ NEW RELEASES ▶ PERFORMING ▶ A SURVEY ON THE ARTS ▶ ARTS EVENTS
▶ A REVIEW

29

2f Taiko master

Taiko is an art form that brings together sound, body and mind.

Before you watch

1 Look at the photo and the caption. Discuss the questions.

1. What is the man doing?
2. How do you think he feels?
3. What do you think the caption means?

2 Key vocabulary

a Read the sentences. Try to guess the missing words.

1. After the meeting, my _____ was full of ideas.
2. Text messages introduced a new _____ of writing.
3. When you're driving, _____ can be very dangerous.
4. I like music that has a fast _____ .
5. Phil Collins was a popular _____ and singer in the 1980s and 1990s.
6. I'm not feeling well today. I don't have the _____ to go to class.

b Read the words in bold and their definitions. The words are used in the video. Complete the sentences in Exercise 2a with the words.

a **beat** (n) a regular sound
b **drummer** (n) a musician who plays the drums
c **energy** (n) power and force
d **mind** (n) your thoughts, feelings, memories, etc.
e **style** (n) a way of doing something
f **tiredness** (n) the feeling of being tired

While you watch

3 ▶ 2.1 Watch the first part of the video (0.00–0.54). Are the sentences true (T) or false (F)?

1. Japanese warriors used drums 2,000 years ago.
2. The sounds of drums told people where a village boundary was.
3. The sound of drums in Japan has never gone away.
4. Taiko drumming is now popular in San Francisco.

4 ▶ 2.1 Watch the second part of the video (0.55 to the end). Put the events (a–d) in the history of taiko drumming into the correct order.

a About 800 groups started in the United States and Canada.
b Japanese–American communities enjoyed traditional taiko drumming.
c People lost interest in taiko drumming.
d Seiichi Tanaka arrived in the United States.

5 ▶ 2.1 Work in pairs. Choose the correct option to complete the sentences about taiko. Then watch the whole video again and check your answers.

1. Japanese warriors used drums to make their enemies *attack / fear* them.
2. The essence of taiko is that it's not just people drumming. It's the unity of the *audience / drummers* amongst themselves.
3. In San Francisco, *the movement of the body / the human voice* has now been added to traditional taiko drumming.
4. Taiko drummers sometimes have to play *through pain and tiredness / with energy and enjoyment* while practising and performing.
5. Seiichi Tanaka is giving North America the chance to *enjoy / see* the energy and excitement of traditional taiko drumming.

After you watch

6 Vocabulary in context

a ▶ 2.2 Watch the clips from the video. Choose the correct meaning of the words and phrases.

b Complete the sentences in your own words. Then work in pairs and compare your sentences.

1. I think I've … a dozen or so times.
2. In this school, there are something like … students.
3. I didn't speak English until … . At that point, I started to learn.
4. I felt better when … went away.
5. Many people in … [place] in … [time] were just fresh off the boat.

7 Work in pairs. Discuss which art forms (including performances, music, etc.) are or have been traditional in your country or countries. How have they changed in recent decades?

---

boundary (n) /ˈbaʊndri/ the outside limit of an area or a place
essence (n) /ˈesəns/ the basic quality
hit (a point) (v) /hɪt/ reach, get to, arrive at
pioneer (n) /ˌpaɪəˈnɪə/ somebody who is the first person to do a new thing
unity (n) /ˈjuːnɪti/ a state of being whole and complete
warrior (n) /ˈwɔːriə/ soldier, fighter

UNIT 2 REVIEW AND MEMORY BOOSTER

Grammar

1 Read part of a blog by a UK visitor to Japan. Find ten places in the blog where words are missing. Complete the blog with these words.

didn't	for	for	has	just	since	since
was	went	yet				

I've lived in Japan three months now and I'm really enjoying it. I know any Japanese before I came, but I've learned a bit I got here, including the word matsuri, which means 'festival'. One of my favourite pastimes is going to matsuri. I've got home from the Nango summer jazz festival – it was great to sit around in the sunshine listening to brilliant music! Last week we to Tenjin matsuri here in Osaka. It been part of Osaka summer events about a thousand years and some performances have hardly changed then – the traditional kagura music, for example, which I loved. There also an amazing puppet theatre. Tomorrow there's a big procession of boats on the river. I haven't been on the river, so I'm really looking forward to that.

2 Answer the questions about the blog in Exercise 1.
1 When did the writer learn Japanese?
2 What time of year was it when the writer wrote the blog?
3 What did the writer see at the Tenjin festival?
4 How many times has the writer been on a boat on the river in Osaka?

3 >> MB Work in pairs. Underline the present perfect simple verbs and circle the past simple verbs in the blog in Exercise 1 and explain why each is used.

4 Work in pairs. Tell your partner about a festival you have been to.

I CAN
talk about things that have happened in a time period up to or including the present (present perfect simple)
use the correct tense when talking about things that have happened in the past (present perfect simple and past simple)

Vocabulary

5 Work in pairs. Which two people are usually involved in these performances? Then choose four types of performer and tell your partner about people you have heard about.
1 FILM: actor, director, magician
2 CONCERT: clown, conductor, musician
3 BALLET: choreographer, comedian, dancer
4 MUSICAL: audience, singer, orchestra

6 >> MB Work in groups. In two minutes, write the names of as many 'hit' art events (films, books, albums, exhibitions, etc.) as you can. Then discuss the ones you have all heard of. Each person must use all of these words. You can't use more than two words about one event. Continue until everyone has used all the words at least once.

boring	depressing	disappointing	dull
entertaining	fascinating	marvellous
spectacular	terrible	terrific	thrilling
unforgettable

7 >> MB Work in pairs. Describe what kind of music makes you do the following.

| cry | feel happy | feel sad | laugh | smile |

I CAN
talk about performers and performances
describe different types of music
give my opinion about art events

Real life

8 Work in pairs. Choose the correct option in the questions.
1 A: Do you fancy *to go / going* out tonight?
2 A: Would you like *to see / seeing* a movie?
3 A: *Do you / Would you* like the sound of that?
4 B: Who's *in / on* it?
5 B: Who's it *by / for*?
6 B: What's it *about / of*?

9 Take the roles of A and B in Exercise 8 and act out the conversation, giving answers to the questions and adding more information.

I CAN
ask for and give information about arts events

Unit 3 Water

A sailing crew battle with a storm during a yacht race.

FEATURES

34 The story behind the photo
When things go wrong in the water

36 Return to *Titanic*
The truth about a famous underwater discovery

38 Love and death in the sea
An article by marine ecologist Enric Sala

42 Four women and a wild river
A video about a trip down a dangerous river

1 Work in pairs. Look at the photo and the caption. Answer the questions.
   1 What do you think the people are thinking?
   2 Have you ever tried this activity? If not, would you like to?
   3 How many words can you think of to describe this experience?

2 ▶ 18 Listen to the introduction to a radio programme. Look at the two groups of words. Tick the activities and places you hear.

Activities
diving   jet-skiing   kayaking   rafting   rowing
snorkelling   water-skiing   windsurfing

Places
lake   ocean   pool   river   sea   stream   waterfall

3 Work in pairs. Where do you think the best place to do the activities in Exercise 2 is?

4 Can you think of other sports and leisure activities connected with water? Do you do any of these activities? Where do you do them? Tell your partner.

I go swimming in a lake near here but only in the summer.

my life   ▶ THE FIRST TIME   ▶ WHAT HAD HAPPENED   ▶ LEARNING A LESSON   ▶ IT HAPPENED TO ME
▶ A BLOG POST

33

listening what happened next? • pronunciation *d* and *t* after *-ed* endings • vocabulary describing experiences • wordbuilding adverbs with *-ly* • grammar past simple and past continuous • speaking the first time

3a The story behind the photo

A

B

Listening

1 Look at the photos (A–C). Match the captions (1–3) with the photos.

1 diving in an underground lake in Mexico
2 snorkelling with a whale shark in the Indian Ocean
3 white-water rafting on the Zambezi River

2 ▶19 Listen to the people in two of the photos talking about their photo. Are the sentences true (T) or false (F)?

1 The girl was rafting for the first time.
2 The raft was approaching some rapids.
3 She saw a hippo near the river bank.
4 The boy learned to dive because he was bored.
5 He went diving in a dangerous cenote.
6 He wasn't concentrating on what he was doing.

3 ▶20 What do you think happened next? Choose one of the options (a–c). Then listen to the whole story and check your ideas.

1 a The hippo came after them and attacked the raft.
   b A crocodile jumped into the river close to the raft.
   c The raft sank and they all swam to the river bank.

2 a His air ran out and he had to go to the surface.
   b His mother saw a sea snake just behind him.
   c He almost got lost in the underground tunnels.

4 Pronunciation *d* and *t* after *-ed* endings

a ▶21 Listen to this sentence from the second story. Notice how the speaker links the *-ed* verb ending to the *t* at the start of the next word. Do you hear one sound or two?

I actually learned to dive while I was on holiday in Mexico.

b ▶22 Listen and repeat the sentences you hear.

Vocabulary describing experiences

▶ **WORDBUILDING adverbs with *-ly***

Some adverbs are formed by adding *-ly* to adjectives. Sometimes there is a spelling change.
add *-ly*: loud → lou**dly**
drop *-e*, add *-ly*: gentle → gent**ly**
drop *-y*, add *-ily*: lucky → luck**ily**

For further practice, see Workbook page 27.

5 Look at the wordbuilding box. Underline the adverb in these sentences. What is the adjective from which the adverb is formed?

1 The hippo suddenly saw us.
2 We reached the river bank safely.
3 I found the way out of the cave easily.
4 The crocodile jumped noisily into the water.
5 Fortunately, nobody was hurt in the accident.
6 I got into the pool very carefully.
7 I cut my feet badly on the rocks.
8 I got on the surfboard and immediately fell off.

34

Unit 3 Water

9 Choose the correct option to complete the rules.
1 We often ask questions in the *past simple / past continuous* about activities at the time of the key event.
2 We often ask questions in the *past simple / past continuous* about actions after the key event.

10 Complete the text about photo A with the past simple and past continuous forms of the verbs.

> While I ¹ _____ (work) in the Maldives, I ² _____ (hear) that there were whale sharks in the area. That's why I ³ _____ (begin) snorkelling – whale sharks are the world's biggest fish and they aren't dangerous! I ⁴ _____ (buy) a snorkel and ⁵ _____ (set out) with some friends on a boat. Almost immediately, a whale shark ⁶ _____ (swim) past the boat. It ⁷ _____ (move) really quickly, but we ⁸ _____ (manage) to catch up with it. We all ⁹ _____ (get) into the water and ¹⁰ _____ (spend) about two minutes with the shark. Afterwards, I ¹¹ _____ (feel) absolutely wonderful!

11 Write sentences with the past simple and past continuous forms of the verbs. Use *because, when, while* and *so*.
1 I / take / a photo / I / drop / my camera.
2 They / not hear / you / they / not listen.
3 I / have / problems / my teacher / help me.
4 We / see / bears / we / hike.
5 He / not look / at the road / he almost / have / an accident.
6 I / fall over / I / run / for the bus.

12 Work in pairs. Ask and answer questions about the other sentences with both the past simple and the past continuous forms of the verbs.
1 I lost my wallet.
   When did you realize?
   Were you shopping at the time?
2 I met an old friend in the street.
3 A car ran into me.
4 A friend of mine got some good news.
5 My neighbour saw a robbery.

6 Work in pairs. Think of at least two activities you can do in the manner of each adverb.

angrily   calmly   bravely   happily   politely   secretly

Grammar past simple and past continuous

▶ **PAST SIMPLE and PAST CONTINUOUS**

Past simple
It **jumped** into the water about a metre away from our boat.
My mom **realized** pretty quickly that I was missing and she **came after** me.

Past continuous
We **were going** around a small island.
The sun **was shining** in through an opening in the roof.

For further information and practice, see page 160.

7 Look at the grammar box. Which verb form do we use to talk about these things?
1 an unfinished and continuing activity or background situation
2 a short completed action or a sequence of actions

8 Underline the key event in these questions (1–2) about the rafting story in Exercise 1. Then match the questions with the answers (a–b).
1 What were they doing when they saw the hippo?
2 What did they do when they saw the hippo?
a They tried to get away.
b They were coming down the river.

Speaking my life

13 Work in pairs.

Student A: Think about an interesting thing that happened the first time you tried something new. Answer your partner's questions.

Student B: Ask ten questions and decide if your partner had a good or bad experience.

What were you trying to do?
Did you have any special equipment?

reading underwater discoveries • grammar past perfect simple • speaking what had happened

3b Return to *Titanic*

Reading

1 ▶ 23 Read the interview with the man who discovered the wreck of *Titanic*. Match three of the questions (a–e) with the paragraphs (1–3). Then listen and check your answers.

a Did you know you were looking at *Titanic* when you saw the first pieces of debris?
b How did you discover *Titanic*?
c How long did it take to locate *Titanic*?
d Tell me about the experience of seeing *Titanic* again in 2004.
e When did you find out about how *Titanic* sank?

2 Read the interview again. Answer the questions.

1 What was the secret mission that Ballard was involved with?
2 How did Ballard and his team feel when they found *Titanic*?
3 How did Ballard feel when he returned to the wreck in 2004? Why?

3 Work in pairs. Do you think the remains of *Titanic* should be left on the seabed? Or should they be removed and put in a museum? Tell your partner.

RETURN to TITANIC

On 15 April 1912, the largest passenger steamship ever built hit an iceberg and sank in the North Atlantic Ocean. *Titanic* had left Southampton, England, five days earlier and was on her first voyage.

In 1985, the explorer Dr Robert Ballard found the wreck of *Titanic*. He went back to *Titanic* nineteen years later to see how it had changed.

1 It was during the Cold War. I was on a secret mission when we found *Titanic*. The US Navy had agreed to pay for our new underwater video technology. In return, we had agreed to use the technology to look for two submarines which had disappeared in the 1960s.

2 Not at first, because many ships had sunk in that area. When we realized it was *Titanic*, we jumped for joy. Then we realized we were celebrating something where people had died.

3 I saw champagne bottles with the corks still in. The box holding the bottles had disappeared long ago. Suddenly, I noticed a woman's shoe. Nearby, I saw a pair of smaller shoes – perhaps they'd belonged to a child. I felt that the people who had died here in 1912 were speaking to me again. But I knew that other people had been there since my first visit. Hollywood filmmaker James Cameron had been there. A New York couple had even got married. I was disappointed. It was exactly what I didn't want to happen. I'd asked people to treat *Titanic*'s remains with respect. The story of *Titanic* is not about the ship, it's about the people.

See the whole story on the *National Geographic* Channel.
Titanic: The Final Secret

Grammar past perfect simple

4 Put each group of events (a–c) in the order they actually took place. Which of the verbs in the sentences are in the past perfect simple in the interview? Why?

1. a Ballard found *Titanic*.
   b The US Navy agreed to pay for new video technology.
   c Ballard agreed to look for two submarines.

2. a Ballard jumped for joy.
   b Many people died.
   c Ballard realized the wreck was *Titanic*.

3. a James Cameron went to the wreck.
   b Ballard noticed a shoe.
   c The box for champagne bottles disappeared.

▶ **PAST PERFECT SIMPLE**

1 He went back to Titanic nineteen years later to see how it **had changed**.
2 I saw some shoes that **had belonged** to a child.

For further information and practice, see page 160.

5 Look at the grammar box. Underline what happened first. Then choose the correct option to complete the sentence.

We use the past perfect simple to show that an event took place *before / after* another event in the past.

6 Choose the correct option to complete the sentences.

1 When *Titanic* hit the iceberg, it *was / had been* at sea for four days.
2 When *Titanic* hit the iceberg, it *sank / had sunk*.
3 By the time they sounded the ship's alarm, it *was / had been* too late.
4 By the time a rescue boat came, many people *died / had died*.
5 When Ballard used video technology, he *found / had found* the wreck.
6 By the time Ballard returned to the site, several people *visited / had visited* it.

7 Use the past perfect simple to answer the questions with your own ideas. Then work in pairs and compare your answers.

1 Why did *Titanic* collide with an iceberg?
2 Why did so many people die when the ship sank?
3 Why was Ballard upset in 2004?
4 Why do you think a couple got married at the wreck site?
5 Why do you think James Cameron visited the wreck?

8 Complete the text with the past simple and past perfect simple forms of the verbs.

Captain Henry Morgan [1] _____ (be) one of the most famous pirates of the seventeenth century. In 2010, archaeologists [2] _____ (begin) to lift cannons from a ship they [3] _____ (discover) two years earlier, near the coast of Panama. The archaeologists [4] _____ (feel) confident that the ship was Morgan's main ship, *Satisfaction*. This ship and several others [5] _____ (sink) in 1671 when they [6] _____ (hit) rocks. Three years later, after Morgan [7] _____ (become) extremely rich from pirate attacks, he [8] _____ (retire) from pirate activities to become the governor of Jamaica.

Speaking my life

9 Work in two pairs within a group of four. Read these puzzles. Then follow the instructions.

Pair A: Turn to page 153 and follow the instructions.

Pair B: Turn to page 154 and follow the instructions.

A A ship came across a yacht in the middle of the ocean. There were no other ships or boats in the area. The bodies of several people were floating in the water nearby.

B A man was on holiday on his yacht. He fell over the edge of the yacht into deep water. He couldn't swim and he wasn't wearing any gear to help him float. The yacht carried on until his friends realized he had disappeared. They found him several hours later. Why hadn't he drowned?

10 Work in pairs. Complete this sentence in as many ways as you can. Use the past perfect simple. Take turns to begin another sentence with *By the time*.

By the time this lesson started , …

Unit 3 Water

my life ▶ THE FIRST TIME ▶ WHAT HAD HAPPENED ▶ LEARNING A LESSON ▶ IT HAPPENED TO ME
▶ A BLOG POST

reading an unforgettable experience • critical thinking drawing conclusions • word focus *get* • speaking learning a lesson

3c Love and death in the sea

Reading

1 Work in pairs. Discuss the questions.
   1 Where's the best place to go swimming? A pool, a lake, the sea, … ?
   2 What kind of problems can swimmers have in each place?

2 Enric Sala is a marine ecologist. Read the article he wrote for World Ocean Day. Answer the questions.
   1 What happened to Enric Sala?
   2 Why did this happen to him?
   3 How has the experience changed him?

3 Find the expressions in the article. What do they mean? Choose the correct option.
   1 a couple of times
     on *several / two* occasions
   2 my heart races
     I feel *afraid / angry*
   3 I decided to call it a day
     I decided to *stop / try again tomorrow*
   4 I was having a hard time
     it was difficult for me / it took a long time
   5 I decided to let myself go
     I decided to *stop swimming / try again*
   6 I have learned my lesson
     my *bad / good* experience taught me something

4 Discuss the questions with your partner.
   1 Sala talks about three decisions he took. What were the decisions and what were the consequences of each one?
   2 Sala describes how he feels about the sea. Do you think what he says is unusual? Why? / Why not?
   3 Do you think the title of the article is a good one? Why? / Why not?

Critical thinking drawing conclusions

5 We can sometimes draw conclusions from a piece of writing even if the author does not state these things specifically. Read the sentences and say which three things are conclusions and which one is stated in the text.
   1 The Costa Brava is a dangerous place for swimmers.
   2 Enric Sala has recovered from the experience now.
   3 He was lucky to be alive after the experience.
   4 The experience has made him wiser.

6 Work in pairs. Do you agree with the conclusions in Exercise 5? Give reasons for your answers.

Word focus *get*

7 Look at the verbs in bold in these sentences. Find expressions with *get* in the article which have the same meanings as the verbs. Then rewrite the sentences with *get*.
   1 I **entered** the pool.
   2 The weather **didn't improve**.
   3 I couldn't **reach** the shore.
   4 I wasn't **moving towards** the land.
   5 We **receive** so much from nature.
   6 We put the bird in a cage, but it **escaped**.

8 Write six more sentences with the expressions with *get* from the article. Write about your own experiences.

Speaking my life

9 Think about an experience you had where you 'learned a lesson'. Use these ideas to think about the details.

   what was the lesson you learned
   the place/situation
   any other people involved
   what happened
   why/how it happened
   how the experience changed your behaviour afterwards

10 Work in small groups. Tell each other about your experiences. Has anyone else had a similar experience?

   A: *I almost had an accident once when I was driving and I was really too tired.*
   B: *Where were you going?*

Unit 3 Water

Love and death in the sea

▶ 24

The sea has almost killed me a couple of times. It wasn't her fault; it was mine, for not respecting her. I still remember the last time, a stormy day off the Costa Brava of Spain, in early summer 2008. Every time I think about it, my heart races.

The place where I used to swim every day was hit by a storm with strong eastern winds. The clear blue waters of summer quickly changed into a dirty soup of sand and cold grey water. Waves were breaking in all directions. But beyond the surf zone, the sea seemed swimmable. In a moment of Catalan bravado, I put on my swimming suit, mask and fins, and got into the water. It was crazy, but I did it. I swallowed sand and salt while I was trying to swim through the surf zone. Fighting against the water, I swam – I still don't know why – for twenty minutes. The storm got worse and I decided to call it a day. I turned to swim back. Then I realized I couldn't get to the beach.

Waves were breaking all around me. I tried to bodysurf one wave to the shore, but it took me down under the water. When I came up, I turned around and a second wave hit me just as hard, taking me down again. I hit the sandy bottom. I pushed myself up, but once again, waves were coming and I couldn't rest or breathe. I was caught in the surf zone, with waves pushing me out and a current pulling me in. I wasn't getting any closer to the beach.

The sea is our mother, sister and home, and as such I love her. We get so much from the sea. She gives us life, oxygen and food. Without the ocean and all the life in it, our planet would be much poorer. We should thank the sea, the ocean, every day. But on this day, I was having a hard time feeling grateful.

After a few more attempts, I decided to let myself go and give up the fight. I took a deep breath. The next wave took me down and forward. I hit the bottom with my back. I rolled over, hit my head, and after what seemed the longest minute of my life, I found myself lying in a foot of water. I crawled out of the water and onto the beach. I'd got out, but I'd lost my mask, snorkel and one fin. My whole body was sore. I sat on the beach watching the sea and feeling lucky to be alive. I walked back home slowly, like a beaten dog.

Some days the sea wants us and some days she doesn't. Since that day, I have not been to the sea when she does not want me. I have learned my lesson. I now thank the sea every day the surface is calm, the waters are clear and diving is easy.

---

bravado (n) /brəˈvɑːdəʊ/ false bravery
crawl (v) /krɔːl/ to move slowly on your hands and knees
current (n) /ˈkʌrənt/ a strong movement of water in the sea or a river

---

my life ▶ THE FIRST TIME ▶ WHAT HAD HAPPENED ▶ LEARNING A LESSON ▶ IT HAPPENED TO ME
▶ A BLOG POST

real life telling stories • pronunciation *was* and *were*

3d No way!

Real life telling stories

1 Work in groups. Which of these statements (a–d) are true for you? Tell your group.

   a When I'm in a group, I listen more than I talk.
   b I'm always telling funny stories about things that happen to me.
   c I'm no good at telling stories, but I'm a good listener.
   d People say I exaggerate, but they always laugh at my stories.

2 Look at the photo. Which group of words (A or B) do you think are from the story of the photo? Then work in pairs. Compare your ideas and explain your reasons.

   A
   looking after it
   food and water
   empty cage
   searched everywhere
   having a bath

   B
   learned to fly
   jump in the air
   above the kitchen sink
   a lid on a tank
   there was some water in it

3 ▶ 25 Listen to two stories. Which story matches the photo? What would a photo of the other story show?

4 ▶ 25 Look at the expressions for telling stories. Listen to the stories again. Tick the expressions the speakers use.

   ▶ **TELLING STORIES**

   Beginning a story
   Did I ever tell you about … ?
   I remember once …
   A couple of years ago, …
   You'll never believe what happened once …

   Saying when things happened
   after we saw …
   after a few days
   a couple of weeks later
   one day
   all of a sudden
   suddenly
   immediately
   then
   the next thing was
   while I was …
   during the night

5 Only one of the stories is true. Which one do you think it is?

6 **Pronunciation *was* and *were***

   a ▶ 26 Listen to the sentences from the stories in Exercise 3. Notice the sound /ə/ in *was* and *were*.

   b ▶ 26 Listen again and repeat the sentences. Pay attention to how you say *was* and *were*.

7 Work in pairs. Choose one of the stories from Exercise 3. Take a role each. Look at the audioscript on page 182 and prepare your role. Then close your books and practise the conversation. Change roles and repeat with the other story.

8 Work in pairs.

   Student A: Tell your partner about three surprising or embarrassing things that happened to you or to someone you know. One of the things should be untrue. Use the expressions for telling stories to help you.

   Student B: Try to guess which of your partner's stories is untrue.

   A: *Did I ever tell you about the time I found some money?*
   B: *No, you didn't.*

my life ▶ THE FIRST TIME ▶ WHAT HAD HAPPENED ▶ LEARNING A LESSON ▶ IT HAPPENED TO ME ▶ A BLOG POST

writing a blog post • writing skill interesting language   Unit 3 Water

3e What a weekend!

Writing a blog post

1 Do you read or write any blogs? What kind of things do people write about in personal blogs? And in professional blogs?

2 Read the post and answer the questions.
   1 What is the topic of this post?
   2 What do you think *beach gear* refers to?
   3 Who do you think Ellie, Louis and Oscar are?

3 Put the main events of the story (a–g) in the correct order.
   a Ellie, Louis and Oscar **ran** to the sea.
   b The sun **started to shine**.
   c There was a storm.
   d A ship lost a cargo of trainers.
   e They **got** into the car.
   f They **picked up** things to take to the beach.
   g They **went** to the beach.

4 **Writing skill** interesting language

a Compare the post with the sentences in Exercise 3. Which verbs does James use instead of the verbs in bold? Why?

b Circle the verbs and adjectives that James uses instead of these words.

   | raining   full of people   looking   arrived |
   | holding |

c Read the sentences. Replace the words in bold with these words.

   | fell down   got   ran   really   tired   walked |

   1 The kids **raced** along the street.
   2 I felt **exhausted** after my walk.
   3 The weather was **boiling** hot.
   4 We **crawled** up the river bank with difficulty.
   5 I **wandered** along the beach, enjoying the silence.
   6 At the end of the game, we **collapsed** on the sand.

5 Think about a recent weekend or one where something unusual happened. Make notes of the main events in your weekend. Then add notes with background information.

6 Write a first draft of a blog post or other social media post about your weekend. Then look at the vocabulary you have used. Try to use interesting language in your post.

The calm after the storm

It was pouring with rain all weekend, so we spent almost the whole time indoors trying to entertain the kids. Then, unexpectedly, the sun came out late on Sunday afternoon. We grabbed our beach gear, jumped into the car and headed down to the bay. When we got there, we realized that everyone had had the same idea! The beach was packed. But everyone was staring out to sea and picking stuff up off the sand. Ellie, Louis and Oscar rushed down to the water's edge, full of excitement. It turned out that a ship had lost its cargo in Saturday's storm. Five containers of Nike trainers had washed up on the beach! Everyone was clutching odd shoes, looking for the other one to make a pair! What a strange end to the weekend!

Written by James   28 Feb 23.17

See older posts

7 Use these questions to check your post.
   • Have you used different past verb forms correctly?
   • Have you used interesting vocabulary to tell the story?

8 Work in pairs. Exchange posts. Can you suggest two more verbs or adjectives that your partner could use?

my life ▸ THE FIRST TIME ▸ WHAT HAD HAPPENED ▸ LEARNING A LESSON ▸ IT HAPPENED TO ME
▸ A BLOG POST

3f Four women and a wild river

Amber Valenti and some of her team on their trip down the Amur River

Before you watch

1 Work in pairs. Look at the photo and the caption. Then read the information. Would you like to do this kind of trip? Why? / Why not?

Amber Valenti was the leader of a kayak trip down the Amur River in Mongolia, Russia and China. The river is one of few major rivers that flow from their start to the sea without dams or reservoirs. The Amur River begins in Mongolia and part of its 2,800 kilometres marks the border between Russia and China. The trip took two months to complete.

2 Key vocabulary

a Read the sentences. The words in bold are used in the video. Guess the meaning of the words.

1 The **concept** of the new TV show is to explain how everyday objects work.
2 We've found a **sponsor** to give us most of the money we need for our expedition.
3 The most **memorable** holiday I've ever had was in China.
4 I'm **passionate** about my hobby playing drums in a band.
5 **Conservation** is a big part of the work of the World Wildlife Fund.
6 The most enjoyable **aspect** of my job is meeting new people.

b Match the words in bold in Exercise 2a with these definitions.

a difficult to forget
b having strong feelings about something
c idea
d one part of a problem or situation
e someone who supports people's activities with money, equipment, etc.
f the protection of natural places, plants and animals

While you watch

3 ▶ 3.1 Watch the whole video. Which of these words do you think describe the experience the women had? Give reasons for your answers.

dangerous   enjoyable   frightening   relaxing

4 ▶ 3.1 Watch the first part of the video (0.00–0.45) again. Complete the sentences with the information you hear.

1 Amber Valenti wanted to explore the Amur River and also to … .
2 The people she wanted to invite on the trip were … .
3 Having an all-woman trip was an advantage with … .

5 ▶ 3.1 Watch the second part of the video (0.46 to the end) again. Answer the questions.

1 Amber Valenti describes moments of the trip as 'joyful and light' and 'intense'. What scenes in the video show this?
2 What kind of things do you see when they reach the mouth of the river?
3 Why does Amber Valenti want people to fall in love with the 'human aspect' of the river?

6 After watching the video, do you feel differently about your answer to Exercise 1?

After you watch

7 Vocabulary in context

a ▶ 3.2 Watch the clips from the video. Choose the correct meaning of the words and phrases.

b Complete the sentences in your own words. Then work in pairs and compare your sentences.

1 I think … is awesome.
2 In my experience, … is really fun.
3 I can't … all on my own.
4 People today are hungry for … .
5 I think that … take themselves very seriously.

8 The trip described in the video was filmed for a documentary called *Nobody's River*. From what you have learned, why do you think the film-makers chose that title?

9 Imagine you are going to be away from home for two months. What would you take with you from home? What essential things would you take in each of these situations? Discuss your answers with the class.

1 You're going on an expedition to a place similar to the video.
2 You're going on a long holiday with your family or friends.
3 You're a professional sportsperson and you're going on a world trip.

---

free-flowing (adj) /ˌfriːˈfləʊɪŋ/ when a river or water moves naturally
intense (adj) /ɪnˈtens/ extremely strong or powerful
joyful (adj) /ˈdʒɔɪfəl/ very happy and cheerful
perspective (n) /pəˈspektɪv/ a point of view
showcase (v) /ˈʃəʊkeɪs/ to explain or show something in a positive way

UNIT 3 REVIEW AND MEMORY BOOSTER

Grammar

1 Change the verbs in this story to the past continuous or past perfect simple where appropriate.

'I ¹ *learned* to surf a few years ago when I ² *was* in my teens. My dad ³ *paid* for a course, as a present, because I ⁴ *just passed* some important exams. It ⁵ *was* a sunny weekend in June. Anyway, the whole first day ⁶ *went by* and I ⁷ *didn't manage* one successful ride. All my friends ⁸ *watched* and of course I ⁹ *wanted* to impress them. I eventually ¹⁰ *paddled out* for my last attempt of the day when the sun ¹¹ *set* over the bay. I ¹² *scrambled* onto the board and for the first time I ¹³ *didn't fall off* straightaway. I ¹⁴ *just got up* on my feet on the board when someone almost ¹⁵ *crashed* right into me! But I ¹⁶ *stayed* on!'

2 Answer the questions about the story in Exercise 1.
  1 What was the speaker's reason for learning to surf?
  2 Why was the speaker so happy when he/she didn't fall off the board?

3 **» MB** Try to remember the main events from the story in Exercise 1. Make notes using single words. Then work in pairs. Exchange your notes with your partner. Retell the story using your partner's notes.

I CAN
talk about a sequence of events in the past (past simple, past perfect)
describe the background to past events (past continuous)

Vocabulary

4 Match the adverbs (1–6) with the phrases (a–f). Then write six sentences.

  1 badly   a check exam answers
  2 calmly   b drive a car
  3 carefully   c sit in a dentist's chair
  4 politely   d have a brilliant idea
  5 secretly   e talk to a stranger
  6 suddenly   f organize a party

5 **» MB** Work in pairs. What are these places? Can you think of two more places with water? How many examples of each place can you name?

6 **» MB** Work on your own. Choose the two activities you think best match each category (1–4). Then work in pairs. Explain your reasons.

| diving | jet-skiing | kayaking | rafting | rowing |
| snorkelling | water-skiing | windsurfing |

  1 people find this relaxing
  2 people do this to get a thrill
  3 it's best to do this with other people
  4 people do this at weekends

I CAN
use adverbs to describe experiences
talk about water sports activities

Real life

7 Work in groups. Tell a story starting with this sentence. Take turns to add a sentence to the story, using one of these expressions.

'Did I ever tell you about the time my cat ate my homework?'

a couple of … later	one day
after a few …	suddenly
all of a sudden	the next thing was
during the …	then
immediately	while I was …

8 **» MB** Use one of these first sentences and tell another story.

'I remember once, I was waiting at the bus stop.'
'A couple of years ago, I went for a job interview.'
'You'll never believe what happened once when I was doing an exam.'

I CAN
tell a story
say when things happened in a sequence of events

44

Unit 4 Opportunities

Children play in the back of an old *jeepney*, the popular public transport vehicle in the Philippines.

FEATURES

46 Will a robot take your job?

The future of work

48 What's next?

We hear from people facing life-changing decisions

50 A better life?

One reporter's view of the economic boom in China

54 Everest tourism changed Sherpa lives

A video about the people who live near Everest

1 Work in pairs. Look at the photo and the caption. What kind of game do you think the children are playing?

2 Did you want to do any of these jobs when you were a child?

ballerina   film star   firefighter   footballer   pilot
police officer   rock star   scientist   train driver   vet

3 Look at the words that can describe jobs. Are they positive or negative? Which words can describe the jobs in Exercise 2?

badly paid   boring   challenging   dangerous   dirty
enjoyable   exciting   responsible   stressful   well-paid

4 ▶ 27 Listen to three people talking about their childhood ambitions. Answer the questions for each person.

 1 Which job did they want to do when they were young?
 2 Which job do they do now or do they plan to do?
 3 How do they describe the jobs?

5 Work in pairs. Ask and answer the questions in Exercise 4 about your own ambitions.

my life   ▶ PREDICTIONS   ▶ PLANNING YOUR WORK   ▶ THE PERFECT JOB   ▶ REQUESTS
▶ A COVERING LETTER

45

word focus *job* and *work* • reading the future of work • grammar predictions • speaking predictions

4a Will a robot take your job?

Word focus *job* and *work*

1 Look at the sentences. How do we use *job* and *work*?

1 A lot of **jobs** are quite boring, but my **job** has lots of variety.
2 I've **worked** as a firefighter for ten years – it can be hard **work**.

2 Complete the sentences with the correct form of *job* or *work*.

1 Where do you _____?
2 Do you have an interesting _____?
3 Do you usually take _____ home in the evenings?
4 Is your company good to _____ for?
5 'Where's your boss?' 'She's off _____ today.'
6 My sister _____ in the same company as me.
7 I'll be late home tonight. There are a few _____ to finish here.
8 'Is your brother around?' 'No, he's at _____.'

3 Work in pairs. Take turns to ask and answer questions 1–4 from Exercise 2.

Reading

4 Work in pairs. Look at the jobs. Is your job, or a job you'd like to do, here? Do you think a robot could do these jobs? Why? / Why not?

| electrician | engineer | nurse | office worker |
| taxi driver | teacher | telephone salesperson |

5 Read the article and check your ideas from Exercise 4.

6 Read the article again and say:

1 which jobs are already done by robots
2 what the Oxford University study looked at
3 two types of work that are described

7 Work in pairs. Find predictions for the future in the article about these things. Do the predictions surprise you? Why? / Why not?

1 factory work
2 changes to UK employment
3 engineers
4 taxi drivers

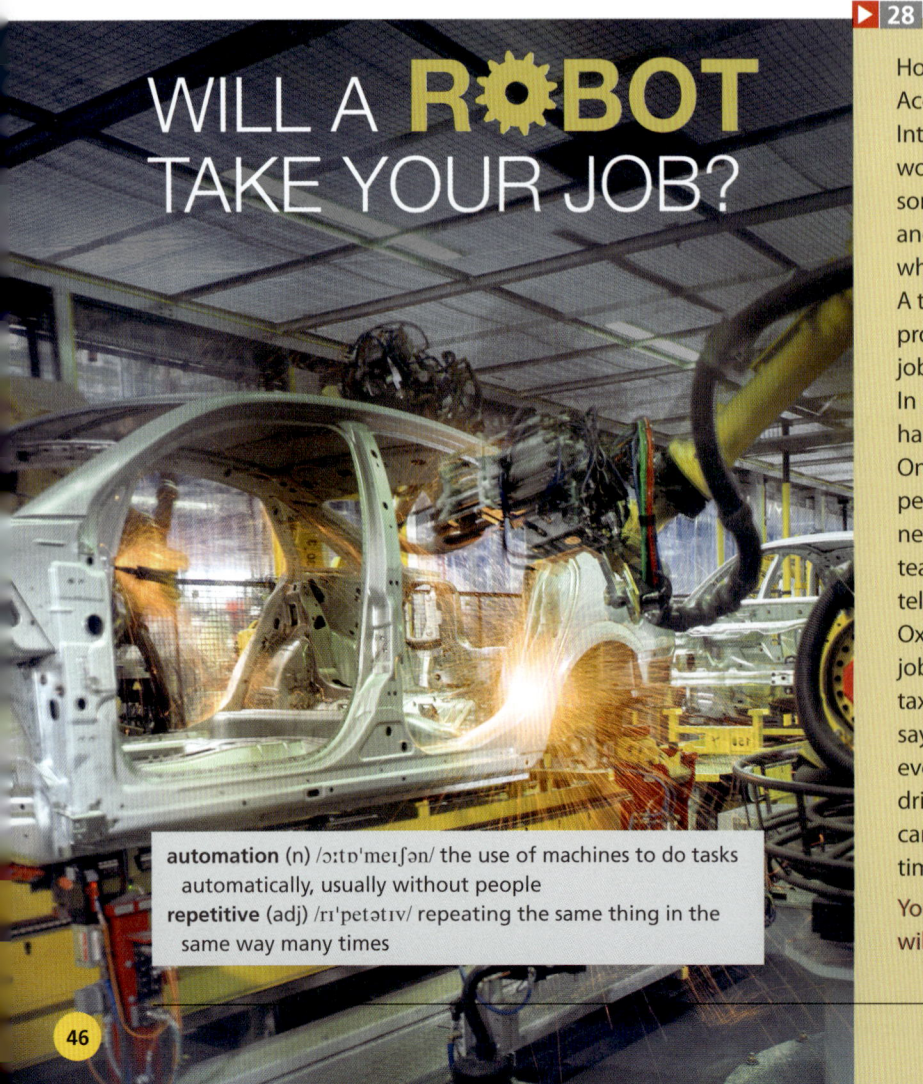

▶ 28

WILL A ROBOT TAKE YOUR JOB?

How likely is it that you'll lose your job to a robot? According to Toby Walsh, a professor in Artificial Intelligence, it's hard to think of a job that a computer won't be able to do. It's true that there are already some factories where all the work is done by robots, and there will certainly be more in the future. But what about teachers, engineers and electricians? A team at Oxford University studied 350 different professions and suggested that 35 per cent of UK jobs might go to robots in the next twenty years. In particular, work that is repetitive or involves handling small objects will be at risk of automation. On the other hand, jobs that involve helping other people or having original ideas will probably always need people. So journalists, nurses, engineers and teachers won't be at risk, but office workers and telephone salespeople may not be so lucky. The Oxford study gives the probability for each of the 350 jobs. Electricians (65 per cent) are more at risk than taxi drivers (57 per cent). One global taxi company says driverless taxis will be on every street corner eventually. However, a spokesperson for London taxi drivers isn't convinced. 'It won't happen. Driverless cars will never be able to work on roads at the same time as normal vehicles.'

You can find out what the future of your profession will be by clicking *here*.

automation (n) /ɔːtəˈmeɪʃən/ the use of machines to do tasks automatically, usually without people
repetitive (adj) /rɪˈpetətɪv/ repeating the same thing in the same way many times

Grammar predictions

> **PREDICTIONS WITH WILL, MAY and MIGHT**
>
> | Robots | will
won't
will certainly/definitely
certainly/definitely won't
may (not), might (not)
will probably
probably won't | do these jobs. |
>
> For further information and practice, see page 162.

8 Look at the grammar box. Underline the future forms (verb + infinitive) in the article.

9 Look at the sentences you have underlined in the article. Which two predictions does the writer think are much less certain than the others?

10 Choose the appropriate option to complete the text about household robots.

The robots are coming, according to robot manufacturers. They say that in five or ten years, we ¹ *will / won't* all have robots in our homes. Very soon, robots that can cook and fold clothes ² *mightn't / will* be available. In the future, there ³ *may / won't* even be robots to babysit our children. Or they ⁴ *may not / might* look after our elderly parents and we ⁵ *will / won't* be able to watch them from a computer wherever we are. One thing is certain, we ⁶ *mightn't / won't* be able to live without the help of robots in several aspects of our lives.

11 Cross out the option which is not logical, as in the example, to complete the sentences.

1. Hyundai is building a new factory. They *may / will / won't* need more workers.
2. Ravi isn't very good at his job. He *might / mightn't / won't* get a promotion.
3. I'm bored with my job. I think I *may / mightn't / will* look for a new one.
4. The office changes are not important. They *mightn't / will / won't* affect our work.
5. I've just bought a car, so I *might / will / won't* need to learn to drive soon!
6. Don't worry about your exam! You *may / might / won't* do better than you expect.

12 Write predictions as in the example. Use a form from the grammar box. Then compare your predictions with your partner. Do you agree?

1. My English exam results / good (probably / definitely)
   My English exam results will probably be good because I've worked hard.
2. Finding a good job / not easy (certainly / probably)
3. People's salaries / go down (definitely / might)
4. Unemployment / get better (definitely / probably)
5. Environmental problems / get worse (definitely / may)
6. The amount of free time we have / go up (certainly / might)

Speaking my life

13 Work in groups. How likely are you to do the following in the next two years? Give reasons. Use future forms from the grammar box in your conversations. Add ideas of your own.

1. buy a motorbike
2. do a degree
3. get a cat
4. get married
5. look for a job
6. make new friends
7. move house
8. travel to a foreign country

A: Are you likely to buy a motorbike in the next two years?
B: Actually, I **might buy** one this summer. I'd love to do a big road trip across Europe.

vocabulary education • wordbuilding prefix *re-* • listening decisions • grammar future forms • speaking planning your work

4b What's next?

Vocabulary education

1 What is your path in education? Look at the expressions and tell your partner what you have done or what you think you will do.

> apply to college/university
> become an apprentice
> do a (training) course
> do/get a degree
> get good/poor results
> go to college/university
> graduate
> retake an exam

A: When I left school, I applied to college. Then I …
B: I got good exam results, so I think I'll graduate with a good degree. Then I'll …

▶ **WORDBUILDING prefix *re-***
Adding *re-* to the start of a verb means 'to do something again'.
retake, reapply, redo, retrain, reread, rewrite

For further practice, see Workbook page 35.

2 Work in pairs. Ask and answer the questions. Ask follow-up questions.
1 Have you ever had to retake an exam?
2 Do you often rewrite your English homework?
3 How many times have you reread your favourite book?
4 Do you know anyone who has retrained for a different job?

Listening

3 Have you made any important decisions recently? Work in pairs. Tell your partner about one of your decisions.

I've decided to change my job. I don't want to work in an office any more.

4 Work in pairs. Look at the women in the photos. Discuss where you think they are from and what they do.

48

Unit 4 Opportunities

5 ▶29 Listen to an extract from a radio programme celebrating International Women's Day. Choose the correct option to complete the sentences about the three women featured in the programme.

1 Devi *works / studies*.
2 Devi wants to be *a boss / a nurse*.
3 Elisabeth *has a job / doesn't have a job*.
4 Elisabeth intends to *leave her job / retire*.
5 Sahera has just *started university / graduated from university*.
6 Sahera plans to *stay in Kabul / leave Kabul*.

6 ▶29 Listen to the extract again and correct the factual mistakes.

1 Devi isn't going to stay at home forever.
2 Devi is taking an exam tomorrow.
3 Elisabeth is going to start a new job.
4 Elisabeth is meeting her new boss on Wednesday.
5 Sahera's friend is going to work in the United States.
6 Sahera's friend is leaving Kabul next month.

7 Which of the three women has decided what she is going to do? Who doesn't know yet?

Grammar future forms

8 Look at the sentences in bold in the audioscript on page 182. Find the following.

1 something that is scheduled in a timetable
2 something Devi decides to do as she is speaking
3 something Devi has arranged to do
4 something Devi has already planned to do

9 Read what Elisabeth and Sahera say in the audioscript. Underline at least six other sentences like those in Exercise 8.

▶ **FUTURE FORMS**

1 present continuous
I'm taking the exam next month.

2 will
Just a moment, *I'll get* you some.

3 going to
I'm going to start my own business.

4 present simple
The course *starts* in January.

For further information and practice, see page 162.

---

10 Look at the grammar box. Match the future forms (1–4) with the uses (a–d).

a a plan or intention decided before the moment of speaking
b a decision made at the moment of speaking
c an event that follows a regular schedule or timetable
d a fixed arrangement to do something at a specified (or understood) time in the future

11 Choose the correct option.

I left school last month. ¹ *I take / I'm going to take* the summer off, but in September ² *I'll start / I'm starting* as an apprentice in a garage. ³ *I do / I'm doing* an evening course as well. That ⁴ *starts / is going to start* in October. I'm lucky – some of my friends don't know what ⁵ *they do / they are going to do*. ⁶ *We'll meet / We're meeting* next week for the first time since our exams. Actually, I think ⁷ *I'll send / I'm sending* them a message about that right now.

12 Complete the responses with the most appropriate future form. Then work in pairs. Compare and discuss your answers.

1 A: Have you got any plans for when you leave college?
   B: Yes, I _____ (take) a year off.
2 A: I can't decide what to do.
   B: It's OK, I _____ (help) you.
3 A: Is it true that Samira is leaving?
   B: Yeah, she _____ (get) married next month.
4 A: My company has offered me redundancy.
   B: _____ (you / take) it?
5 A: Did you enrol for evening classes?
   B: Yes, _____ (go) to my first class tonight.
6 A: Look, my exam results are here!
   B: Give me the envelope. I _____ (open) it.

Speaking   my life

13 Draw a calendar for the next four weeks. Write in these things.

plans you have made (shopping trips, etc.)
arrangements (hair appointments, etc.)
things you are still unsure about (weekend activities, etc.)

NOVEMBER		
2–8	9–15	16–22
6th–7th Weekend away?	10th – dentist's 3 pm	

14 Work in pairs. You need to meet several times for a project for your English course. Find dates when you can get together.

A: *What are you up to next week? Maybe we can get together early in the week.*
B: *OK. But I'm going to the dentist's on Monday, so what about Tuesday?*

my life ▶ PREDICTIONS ▶ PLANNING YOUR WORK ▶ THE PERFECT JOB ▶ REQUESTS
▶ A COVERING LETTER

reading **the economic boom in China** • critical thinking **the author's view** • vocabulary **pay and conditions** • speaking **the perfect job**

4c A better life?

Reading

1 How can these things improve your opportunities in life? Make notes and then compare with your partner.

> the place you go to school
> the place you live
> the career you choose
> your family

2 Read the article quickly. Which paragraph(s) talk(s) about these topics?

　a　training and education
　b　the movement of people
　c　the development of new towns

3 Read the first two paragraphs of the article. Put these things in the order in which they appear in a new town in China.

　a　street stalls
　b　cellphone companies
　c　clothes shops
　d　construction work *1*
　e　entrepreneurs
　f　shops
　g　female factory workers

4 Read the rest of the article. Are the sentences true (T) or false (F)?

　1　Most of the population in China is school age.
　2　About ten million people a year move from their villages.
　3　Few school leavers in China are interested in higher education.
　4　It's difficult to find training courses in factory towns.
　5　So far, China has focused on making products for foreign markets.

5 Work in pairs. Do you think that the people in the new towns have a better life than they did in their villages? Why? / Why not?

Critical thinking the author's view

6 Authors can show things in a positive, negative or neutral way. Read these extracts from the article and say which one expresses a positive view and which two are neutral. Which words help you decide?

　1　When the town starts to grow, the cellphone companies arrive.
　2　The human energy in one of these towns is amazing: the brave entrepreneurs, the quick-moving builders, the young workers a long way from home.
　3　Another young man I met is learning Arabic and is going to work as a translator for Middle Eastern buyers.

7 Find at least two more sentences in the article in which the author shows his view. What is his view?

8 Work as a class. How do the changes described in the article compare to a place or country you are familiar with?

Vocabulary pay and conditions

9 Read the sentences. Which jobs can they describe?

　1　In this job, people work **long hours**.
　2　Employees get four weeks' **paid holiday** a year.
　3　Workers get regular **pay rises**.
　4　The **salary** is excellent.
　5　Employees can choose to work **flexi-time** if they need to.
　6　There are lots of opportunities for **promotion**.
　7　Staff often have to work **overtime**.
　8　All employees are covered by a generous **pension scheme**.

10 Put the words in bold in Exercise 9 into three groups: *money* (M), *hours* (H) and *benefits* (B). Then add these words to the groups.

> clocking on and off　　　　bonuses
> discounts on company products　company car
> free language classes　　　part-time
> health insurance　　　　　wages

Speaking 　my life

11 Work in pairs. What four things in Exercises 9 and 10 does the perfect job have? Put them in order, 1 to 4. Then compare with a new pair. If you have different things in your lists, discuss them and try to agree on only four.

Unit 4 Opportunities

A better life?

▶ 30
We spoke to Peter Hessler about his experience of fast-changing life in China.

People at Guangzhou Railway Station in Guangdong

How does a factory town begin?

The beginning of a Chinese factory town is always the same: in the beginning nearly everybody is a construction worker. They are men who have come from country villages and they are quickly joined by entrepreneurs. These businessmen sell meat, fruit and vegetables on street stalls. Later, the first real shops appear and the same businessmen give up their stalls and start to sell construction materials.

What comes next?

When the town starts to grow, the cellphone companies arrive. They sell prepaid phonecards to the workers so that they can phone the families they left behind in their villages. When the factories built by the men from the villages start production, you begin to see women. The factory managers prefer to give jobs to young women because they think they are more hard-working. After the arrival of the women, clothes shops and shoe shops appear. And eventually, you see public services, like buses, and so on.

What does it feel like to be there?

The human energy in one of these towns is amazing: the brave entrepreneurs, the quick-moving builders, the young workers a long way from home. A combination of past problems and present-day opportunities has created an extremely motivated population. There are 1.3 billion people in China and 72 per cent of them are between the ages of 16 and 64. And a huge number now live in towns rather than villages. Every year about ten million people move to the cities. Social scientists predict that the urban population will be 60 per cent by 2030.

What kind of life do people want?

Most people in China have seen their standard of living go up in recent years. Chinese schools have been very successful and the literacy rate is over 90 per cent. So the next step is to develop higher education because many people are looking for better training. There's a huge number of private courses in a Chinese factory town: English classes, typing classes, technical classes. One young man I know couldn't read or write when he left his village. He now works in a factory and spends a quarter of his wages on training. Another young man I met is learning Arabic and is going to work as a translator for Middle Eastern buyers. People also have dreams of a more materialistic life just as people do in the West. The new factory towns of China have grown in order to make products for the rest of the world. And now, the workers want to be able to have these products for themselves as well.

entrepreneur (n) /ˌɒntrəprəˈnɜː/ someone who starts new companies
literacy rate (n) /ˈlɪtərəsi reɪt/ the number of people who can read and write
materialistic (adj) /məˌtɪəriəˈlɪstɪk/ interested in possessions and consumer goods

Individual portraits in Beijing on Chinese National Day

my life ▶ PREDICTIONS ▶ PLANNING YOUR WORK ▶ THE PERFECT JOB ▶ REQUESTS ▶ A COVERING LETTER

vocabulary job requirements • **real life** making and responding to requests • **pronunciation** weak and strong auxiliary verbs

4d Would you mind … ?

Vocabulary job requirements

Assistant Researcher
NaturalHistoryNet TV

Full-time position + benefits. Initial 12-month contract.

You will be responsible for
- assisting the Research Coordinator on a variety of film projects.
- managing film production materials.
- dealing with queries related to current and past projects.

You will have
- a degree in a relevant subject.
- preferably 1–2 years' experience in film production.
- excellent database and research skills.

You will be
- organized and independent.
- able to meet strict deadlines.
- good at working under pressure.

Send CV and covering letter to:
Anila.Jones@NHNTV.com
Closing date 15 June

1 Read the job advert and find the following.
1. duties
2. deadline for applications
3. skills and qualifications required
4. personal qualities required

2 Which of these qualities would be useful for the job in the advert?

| conscientious | creative | energetic |
| hard-working | methodical | self-confident |

3 Work in pairs. Choose three jobs you know something about. What are the most important requirements of those jobs? Compare your ideas.

Real life making and responding to requests

4 ▶ 31 Listen to two friends, Rudi and Mark, discussing the position in the advert. Answer the questions.
1. Does Mark meet all the requirements?
2. Is his CV ready?
3. What will he need for the interview?

5 ▶ 31 Look at the expressions for making and responding to requests. Listen again and tick the expressions Rudi and Mark use.

▶ **REQUESTS**

Making requests
Is it all right if I give you as my referee?
Would it be OK to borrow your suit?
Is it OK to take your car?
Would it be all right if I used your phone?

Would you mind checking my application form?
Do you mind helping me with my CV?

Could you give me a lift to the interview?
Can you have a look at my covering letter?
Will you be able to do it today?

Responding to requests
Of course (not).
I'm not sure about that.
Yes, I will.
Sure, no problem.

6 Would you like to do a job like the one in the advert? Why? / Why not?

7 Pronunciation weak and strong auxiliary verbs

a ▶ 32 Listen and repeat the exchange. Notice how the auxiliary verb *will* is not stressed in the full question and is stressed in the response.

A: Will you be able to do it today?
B: Yes, I will.

b ▶ 33 Match the questions (1–6) with the responses (a–f). Then listen and check. Work in pairs. Practise the exchanges.

1. Are you going to apply for the job?
2. Will he help you with your CV?
3. Are they still advertising that job?
4. Does she meet our requirements?
5. Will it be an all-day interview?
6. Is it OK to phone you at work?

a. I don't think she does.
b. I think it might.
c. No, they aren't.
d. Of course he will.
e. Yes, I think I will.
f. Yes, of course it is.

8 Work in pairs. You are going to act out short conversations in different situations. Turn to page 155.

---

52 | **my life** ▶ PREDICTIONS ▶ PLANNING YOUR WORK ▶ THE PERFECT JOB ▶ **REQUESTS** ▶ A COVERING LETTER

4e I enclose my CV

Writing a covering letter

1 Work in pairs. Which do you think is the most common way to apply for a job? Tell your partner.

   a CV
   a letter
   a personal contact
   a phone call
   an application form

2 Read the covering letter in reply to the advert on page 52. Match the information (a–j) with the parts of the letter. What (if any) information can you leave out if you send the letter as an email?

   a   a reference to your CV
   b   the date
   c   the name and address of the person you are writing to
   d   the reason for your letter
   e   your address
   f   your interest in the position
   g   your phone number
   h   your qualifications
   i   your relevant experience
   j   your skills

3 Compare the letter to the style you use in your country. Answer the questions.

   1   Is the layout different? How?
   2   Does it include the same information?
   3   Is the information in the main part of the letter sequenced in the same way?

4 Writing skill formal style

a A formal letter in English uses these features. Underline examples of each one in the letter.

   1   concise sentences
   2   formal phrases to begin sentences
   3   no contractions
   4   standard phrases to open and close the letter

b Rewrite the sentences in a more formal style.

   1   I'll finish my degree soon.
   2   Give me a call.
   3   I was looking through the paper and I saw your ad, and I thought it looked really interesting.
   4   My phone number is on my CV, which I've sent you as well.
   5   I'll be free from August.

---

27 Harbour Road
Manchester
M21 7PF
7 July 2017

NHN TV
Burton House
Bristol
BS9 2HL

Dear Ms Jones,

I am writing in reply to your advertisement in the *Daily Herald* for the position of Assistant Researcher. I will graduate in Digital Media this month from Manchester University. I have experience in film production and post-production as I have worked part-time in my university television station for the last year.

I consider myself to be hard-working and organized in my work. As part of my job with the university television station, I was responsible for planning schedules and programme archiving.

I am available for interview at any time and available to start work after July. I am willing to relocate if necessary.

I enclose my CV which gives full details of my qualifications, work experience and skills as well as my contact details.

I look forward to hearing from you.

Yours sincerely,

Mark Nolan

---

5 Write a covering letter to go with an application for a job you would like. Follow the layout and style of the letter from Mark.

6 Exchange letters with your partner. Use these questions to check your partner's letter.

   • Is it clear how to contact this person?
   • Is the style appropriate?
   • Does the person sound like a good candidate?

7 On the basis of the letter your partner has written, would you give him/her an interview? Explain your reasons to your partner.

4f Everest tourism changed Sherpa lives

> Without Sherpas, it is impossible for people to climb Everest.

Before you watch

1 Look at the photo and read the caption. Where do Sherpa people live? What is the area famous for?

2 Work in pairs. Do you think Everest tourism is a good thing or a bad thing for Sherpas? Give your reasons.

3 Key vocabulary

a Read the sentences. Try to guess the missing words.

1 Some people do two jobs to increase their _____ .
2 My _____ is very different to my parents' generation. They live quite simply.
3 One per cent of the world's population owns forty per cent of the world's _____ .
4 There are _____ differences between my first job and my current job – it was a big shock at first.
5 I'm training to go on the next international _____ across Antarctica.
6 We live in an _____ society, and mainly keep sheep and cows.

b Read the words in bold and their definitions. The words are used in the video. Complete the sentences in Exercise 3a with the words.

a **agrarian** (adj) based on farming
b **expedition** (n) an organized exploration or journey
c **income** (n) the money that you earn from a job
d **lifestyle** (n) the way a person lives, the typical things they do and own
e **substantial** (adj) large and important (quantity)
f **wealth** (n) the money a person has

While you watch

4 ▶ 4.1 Watch the video. Check your ideas from Exercise 2.

5 ▶ 4.1 Watch the first part of the video (0.00–1.33) again. Match the beginnings of the sentences (1–4) with the endings (a–d).

1 The Sherpa
2 The name Sherpa
3 The Sherpa culture
4 Sherpa society now

a changed in 1953.
b has mobile phones and the internet.
c means 'Easterner'.
d are one of seventy ethnic groups in Nepal.

6 ▶ 4.1 Work in pairs. Look at the list of things Sherpas have gained and lost. Write G or L. Then watch the second part of the video (1.34 to the end) again and check your answers.

1 education
2 healthcare
3 clothing
4 wealth
5 a simple life
6 happiness

After you watch

7 What can you remember? Try to answer the questions. Then compare with the class.

1 How did Sherpas learn to tell the time?
2 What was the only thing Kancha Sherpa worried about?
3 What did Max Lowe say people are losing?

8 Vocabulary in context

a ▶ 4.2 Watch the clips from the video. Choose the correct meaning of the words and phrases.

b Answer the questions in your own words. Then work in pairs and compare your answers.

1 Can you remember a time something happened to you just by chance?
2 Do you think some people in your country take things for granted? What kind of thing?
3 If life feels rushed, what can you do to feel more relaxed?
4 Where do new people usually settle in your country?
5 Can you name any communities who've had little contact with the outside world?

9 Work in pairs. Tourism changed the Sherpa way of life. What are the effects of these things on people's ways of life?

the internet
industrialization
large-scale road or rail systems
cheaper air travel

---

advancement (n) /əd'vɑːnsmənt/ an improvement in a person's life
ethnic group (n) /eθnɪk 'gruːp/ a group of people belonging to the same culture
healthcare (n) /'helθkeə/ medical services
idyllic (adj) /ɪ'dɪlɪk/ peaceful and calm
self-gain (n) /self'geɪn/ getting more money or things for yourself

UNIT 4 REVIEW AND MEMORY BOOSTER

Grammar

1 Complete each comment from student chefs with one word or contraction.

1 'I'm sure nobody _____ be able to eat this!'
2 'I'm _____ to change jobs soon.'
3 'I' _____ having a drink on my next break.'
4 'This _____ definitely impress the diners.'
5 'I'm going _____ be the best chef in the country one day.'
6 'My parents _____ be so proud of me.'
7 'This may _____ turn out as I expected.'
8 'Wow, my hat _____ catch fire in this kitchen.'
9 'My friends _____ believe me when I tell them about my day.'
10 'I'm _____ a take-away for dinner tonight.'

2 Which comments in Exercise 1 do you think the students in the photo above might make? Why? Work in pairs and compare your ideas.

3 >> MB Work in pairs. Find two plans and two predictions in Exercise 1. Explain the use of the verbs in each comment.

4 >> MB Work in pairs. Ask your partner about plans and arrangements they have for when your English course finishes.

I CAN
make predictions about future events (predictions with *will*)
show different degrees of certainty about predictions (*may, might, could*)
ask and answer questions about future plans and arrangements (*going to*, present continuous)

Vocabulary

5 Match the verbs (1–5) with the nouns (a–e) to make expressions about education.

1 apply   a an apprentice
2 become   b an exam
3 get   c from university
4 graduate   d good results
5 retake   e to college

6 >> MB Work in pairs. For each of these jobs, discuss the qualities and qualifications you need, and the pay and conditions. Then say which job would be best for your partner and give reasons.

I CAN
talk about stages in education and getting qualifications
describe different jobs, job requirements and conditions
talk about water sports activities

Real life

7 Work in pairs. Match the beginnings of the sentences (1–4) with the endings (a–d). Then act out a conversation which includes the requests and appropriate replies.

1 Could you
2 Is it all right if I
3 Would you mind
4 Would it be all right if I

a borrow your phone?
b help me with this application?
c lending me some money?
d took off my jacket?

8 >> MB With your partner, act out similar conversations for two of these situations.

a problem at work
an important exam ahead
a meeting with a new boss
your first day at college

I CAN
make and respond to requests

56

Unit 5 Wellbeing

Some fruit and vegetables are thrown away because they are 'too ugly' to sell.

FEATURES

58 Pizza with a pedigree
Traditional dishes get special status

60 Imaginary eating
Discover the power of your mind!

62 A caffeine-fuelled world
An in-depth look at the role of caffeine in modern life

66 Dangerous dining
A video about an unusual Japanese delicacy

1 Find these foods in the photo. Which ones do you eat? How often do you eat them?

apple   carrot   green pepper   onion   red pepper
squash   sweet potato

2 Work in pairs. Discuss the questions.

1. How much do you know about the recommended amount of different food groups you should eat each day?
2. How do you decide what is the right size of a portion of food?
3. Does everyone need to eat the same amounts?

3 ▶ 34 Work in pairs. What do you think the portion sizes of these types of food are? Listen to an extract from a radio programme about food. Complete the table.

Type of food	Size of portion
cereal/rice/pasta/potato	.... clenched fist
meat/poultry/fish	the palm of .... hand
snacks: popcorn/crisps	.... handfuls
cakes: brownies/flapjacks	.... fingers

4 Discuss the questions with your partner.

1. Does any of the information in Exercise 3 surprise you?
2. How much attention do you pay to your diet?
3. In what ways can food and diet influence your health?

my life   ▶ RULES AND REGULATIONS   ▶ CONSEQUENCES   ▶ MODERN LIFE   ▶ RESTAURANT DISHES
▶ A FORMAL LETTER/EMAIL

57

reading traditional dishes • grammar modal verbs (1) • pronunciation weak forms • speaking rules and regulations

5a Pizza with a pedigree

Reading

1 Work in pairs. Discuss the questions.
   1 What are the traditional dishes of your country or region?
   2 How often do you eat or make these dishes?
   3 How often do you eat or make dishes from other countries? Which ones?
   4 What's your favourite pizza? What's on it?

2 Read the news item *Pizza with a pedigree*. Answer the questions.
   1 Why is Pizza Napoletana in the news?
   2 What are some of the other foods in the same group as Pizza Napoletana?
   3 What are the rules for an 'authentic' Pizza Napoletana?

Grammar modal verbs (1)

> **MODAL VERBS**

Obligation	No obligation
have/has to, must	don't/doesn't have to
	Prohibition
	mustn't
Permission	**No permission**
can, is/are allowed to	can't, is/are not allowed to
Recommendation	
should	should (not)

For further information and practice, see page 164.

3 Look at the grammar box. Answer these questions.
   1 Which verb forms from the box are in the news item? Underline the verb forms in both the box and in the news item.
   2 What form do we use to talk about obligation in the past? Circle this form in the news item.
   3 Two of the modal verbs in the news item do not express rules. Which verbs?

F O O D

▶ 35

Pizza with a pedigree

There is pizza – and there is Pizza Napoletana. The two, experts say, have as much in common as virgin olive oil has with ordinary cooking oil. Now, authentic Pizza Napoletana is one of the elite group of European Union-certified food and drink products – like Scottish Farmed Salmon, Spanish Melon from La Mancha and English Blue Stilton cheese. In order to qualify for this list, these food products had to pass strict tests.

Once a product achieves Guaranteed Traditional Speciality status, other similar products are not allowed to use the same name. For example, if your sparkling wine doesn't come from the Champagne region of France, you can't call it 'Champagne'. But be warned: the EU specifications for 'real' Pizza Napoletana are very complicated – it takes almost as long to read them as it does to make the pizza. To be labelled 'Guaranteed Traditional Speciality', the pizza mustn't be over 35 centimetres in diameter and the crust mustn't be more than two centimetres thick. The ingredients must include type 00 flour and up to 100 grams of San Marzano tomatoes applied in a spiral. And the cheese has to be fresh 'Mozzarella di Bufala'.

Of course, pizza has a long history in Italy. The word 'pizza' first appeared in an AD 997 manuscript from Gaeta, a southern Italian town. A millennium later, in 1997, political groups in northern Italy tried to ban pizza because it was a symbol of their rivals in the south. You don't have to know anything about pizza's history to enjoy eating it, of course. But you should try an authentic Pizza Napoletana at least once, and see if you can taste the difference!

elite (adj) (n) /ɪˈliːt/ a small group of the best
pedigree (n) (adj) /ˈpedɪɡriː/ a documented history
strict (adj) /strɪkt/ precise and rigorous

4 Read the labels from food packaging. Look at the example. Write sentences using one of the modal verbs in brackets.

1 *Not suitable for vegetarians*
(shouldn't / don't have to)
Vegetarians shouldn't eat this product.

2 **NOT SUITABLE FOR PEOPLE WITH NUT ALLERGIES**
(don't have to / mustn't)

3 **DO NOT EAT MORE THAN THE RECOMMENDED DAILY INTAKE OF SALT**
(can / shouldn't)

4 **MULTIPACK OF FOUR – NOT FOR SALE SEPARATELY**
(don't have to / not allowed to)

5 *Heat before serving*
(can / have to)

6 **NOT RECOMMENDED FOR DIABETICS**
(allowed to / shouldn't)

5 Work in pairs. Look at these food items. Discuss the questions.

| durian | eggs | fugu | hakarl | oysters |
| potatoes | red beans | steak | | |

1 Have you eaten any of these food items?
2 Do you know of any special treatment these things need before you can eat them?

6 ▶ 36 Listen to eight short conversations about the food items in Exercise 5. Complete the notes for each item.

1 durian: you aren't allowed to _____
2 fugu: _____ are allowed to _____
3 hakarl: you have to _____
4 potatoes: you don't have to _____
5 oysters: you mustn't _____
6 eggs: you should _____
7 red beans: _____ must _____
8 steak: you can _____

ferment (v) /fəˈment/ to leave food or drink to a natural chemical reaction
peel (v) /piːl/ to remove the skin from fruit or a vegetable

7 Pronunciation weak forms

a ▶ 37 Listen to the sentences from conversations 1–4 in Exercise 6. Notice how *to* is not stressed. Repeat the sentences.

b Work in pairs. Decide if you (don't) have to do these things. Discuss with your partner.

keep eggs in the fridge
wash rice before you cook it
eat fish on the day you buy it
cook meat until it isn't pink

Speaking my life

8 Work in pairs. Write down at least two ideas for each topic.

1 rules you had to follow when you were in primary school
2 information that should be on food labels
3 places where you're not allowed to eat hot food
4 table manners
5 things you're only allowed to do when you're eighteen
6 questions you shouldn't ask someone you don't know well

9 Work with a new partner. Compare your ideas from Exercise 8. Do you both agree?

A: When we were at primary school, we **had to line up** outside the classroom.
B: Oh, yes! So did we!

fugu (puffer fish) | a durian | hakarl (shark meat) | oysters

reading and listening **the power of the mind** • grammar **first conditional** • vocabulary **a healthy lifestyle** • speaking **consequences**

5b Imaginary eating

Reading and listening

1 Work in pairs. Discuss the statements. Do you agree with them? Give examples to support your arguments.

1 Self-belief: the difference between a winner and a runner-up is in attitude, not skill.
2 Willpower: you can achieve anything if you think you can do it.
3 Train your mind: people who consider themselves to be lucky have more 'lucky' moments.

2 Read the news item *Imaginary eating*. What does the imaginary eating technique involve?

3 ▶ 39 Listen to two people discussing the news item. Are these sentences true (T) or false (F)?

1 Jack doesn't believe the claims in the news item.
2 Lin is open-minded about the idea of imaginary eating.
3 Both of them agree that willpower is important.
4 Lin thinks Jack should try out the technique.
5 Lin eats too many crisps and snacks.
6 Jack is going to buy some chocolate.

4 ▶ 39 Listen to the conversation again. Match the beginnings of the sentences (1–6) with the endings (a–f).

1 I'll believe it
2 If you don't train your mind,
3 I won't find out
4 When I want to eat a snack,
5 I'll never need to buy chocolate again
6 As soon it starts working,

a if this technique works.
b I'll let you know.
c I'll try just imagining it.
d unless I try.
e when I see it.
f you won't be able to lose weight.

5 Read the comment at the end of the news item again. Do you agree with the comment? With your partner, write a comment to add to the comments section.

▶ 38

Imaginary eating

Christine Dell'Amore
National Geographic News

Obesity rates are climbing fast and we need to find new techniques to help people control overeating. According to new research, 'imaginary eating' could be one such technique. It's based on the idea that if you are less interested in a certain food, you will eat less of it. But how do you reduce your interest? A psychologist in the United States reports that if you just imagine eating a specific food, your interest in it will drop. Often people try not to think about food when they need to lose weight. But avoiding these thoughts might not be a good strategy. With imaginary eating, if you force yourself to think about chewing and swallowing food, you'll actually reduce your desire to eat.

Comments

👤 **Rpineapple23**

This study is just another proof of how powerful our brain is. The better we are at using that power when making decisions and controlling certain behaviours, the healthier we will become.

REPLY   RECOMMEND

Grammar first conditional

▶ **FIRST CONDITIONAL**

1 If you **don't train** your mind, you **won't be able to lose** weight.
2 I'**ll never need** to buy chocolate again **if** this technique **works**.

For further information and practice, see page 164.

6 Look at the grammar box. Answer the questions.

a Which verb forms are used to make the first conditional?
b Where can *if* go in conditional sentences?
c Look at the position of *if* in the sentences. When do we use a comma (,)?
d Which of the sentences refers to future possibility and which refers to something which is generally true?
e Find three sentences with the first conditional pattern in the news item. Do the sentences refer to future possibility or to something which is generally true?

7 Complete the sentences with the present simple and *will* + infinitive. Which sentences refer to future possibility and which refer to something which is generally true?

1 If you _____ (believe) in yourself, you _____ (be) more successful.
2 I _____ (need) a lot of willpower if I _____ (want) to give up chocolate.
3 If you _____ (not buy) snacks, you _____ (not be able) to eat them.
4 If you _____ (find) any more information, _____ (you / let) me know?
5 If you _____ (reduce) the amount of food on your plate, you _____ (lose) weight.
6 I _____ (give up) junk food if you _____ (do) too.
7 If I _____ (not try) it, I _____ (never know).
8 _____ we _____ (eat) less if we _____ (use) smaller plates?

▶ **WHEN, AS SOON AS, UNLESS, UNTIL, BEFORE**

When
As soon as
Unless   + present simple, *will* + infinitive
Until
Before

For further information and practice, see page 164.

8 Jack and Lin are discussing Lin's efforts to eat more healthily. Cross out any options which are not possible.

1 You won't change *as soon as / unless* you make an effort.
2 *As soon as / When* you make up your mind, you'll be able to act.
3 I'll weigh myself *before / when* I start my diet.
4 I'll keep trying *before / until* I see a change.
5 You won't see any results *unless / when* you try hard.
6 *If / Unless* you give up easily, you won't achieve your target.
7 *If / When* you go shopping, don't buy sweets.
8 I'll follow the diet *unless / until* I lose ten kilos.

Vocabulary a healthy lifestyle

9 Work in pairs. Match the verbs with the nouns to make strategies for a healthy lifestyle. You can match some verbs with more than one noun and some nouns with more than one verb. Add ideas of your own.

Verbs	Nouns
avoid	a new sport
change	an outdoor activity
cut down on	bad habits
cut out	computer and TV time
give up	fatty food
learn	heavy meals at night
reduce	junk food
take up	relaxation techniques
	smoking
	snacks between meals
	stress

10 Think of a specific result for each strategy from Exercise 9. Write sentences with the first conditional.

If you avoid heavy meals at night, you'll sleep better.

Speaking ⌐ my life

11 Work in pairs. Make a list of all the possible consequences you would face in these situations.

1 giving up junk food
2 changing your job / studies
3 sharing a flat with friends
4 taking up extreme sports

12 Work in groups of four. The aim of this game is to keep answering questions as long as you can. Student A is going to do one of the things in Exercise 11. The rest of the group asks the questions. If Student A can't answer, Student B takes a turn, and so on.

A: I'm going to give up junk food.
B: What **will you eat when you want** a snack?
A: Don't worry. **If I want** a snack, **I'll eat** nuts or some fruit.
C: And what **if you find out** you're allergic to nuts?

reading **modern lifestyles** • critical thinking **writer's pupose** • word focus **so** • speaking **modern life**

5c A caffeine-fuelled world

Reading

1 Work in groups. Discuss the questions.

1. Is your lifestyle very different to that of your parents' generation? In what way(s)?
2. Do you often hear comments about modern life? What kind of comments?
3. How much tea/coffee or other drinks do you have in a normal day?

2 Read the article on page 63 quickly. Choose the correct option to complete the sentence.

The article is about caffeine and *children / daily life / sugar*.

3 What are the effects of caffeine? Complete the table.

Harmful effects	Beneficial effects
changes your mood	makes you less tired
1 _____ blood pressure	relieves 3 _____
increases the 2 _____ of heart disease	reduces 4 _____ symptoms

4 Complete these sentences with words from the article.

1. Caffeine is an _____ of tea, coffee, soft drinks, energy drinks and chocolate.
2. Caffeine is a drug which changes your _____.
3. Several countries put health _____ on energy drinks.
4. People have changed to a less natural work _____.
5. Caffeine is popular with people who need to stay _____.

5 Work in pairs. Do you think anything the writer says is true about your own lifestyle? What?

Critical thinking writer's purpose

6 What is the writer's main purpose in this article? Give reasons for your answer.

to entertain / to inform / to persuade the reader

7 Look at the list of features which are typical of informative texts. Find examples in the article.

1. the present simple
2. the third person
3. questions and answers
4. facts
5. specific examples
6. quotes, often from experts
7. linkers to show how ideas are connected

8 Work in pairs. Discuss the questions.

1. Do you think the writer is successful in his/her purpose?
2. Did you change your ideas about caffeine after reading the article?
3. In what way has the article influenced your opinion of caffeine?

Word focus so

9 Look at how *so* is used in the article. In which sentence can we replace *so* with *as a result*? What can replace *so* in the other sentence?

1. Why are these drinks so popular?
2. It raises blood pressure and so increases the risk of heart disease.

10 Work in pairs. Complete the sentences. Then write two-line exchanges using some of the sentences. Act out your exchanges.

1. I've had five cups of _____ so far today.
2. Thank you so much for _____ you've done.
3. I'm so happy I could _____.
4. _____ me so I know when to expect you.
5. I think I'm right. I _____ so.
6. No, I don't _____ so.
7. Don't be so hard on yourself – it's not easy to give up _____.
8. Oh, that's _____ ! So did I!

Speaking my life

11 Complete the slogans about modern life with these words. Where do you think the slogans are from?

| all | close | day | night | on | today |

1. We never _____ .
2. See the films of tomorrow _____ .
3. Open _____ hours.
4. 'Always _____ ' broadband.
5. Late _____ shopping every Thursday.
6. All _____ breakfasts served here.

12 Work in small groups. These things are typical of a 24-hour society. Discuss the questions.

1. Are the things positive or negative?
2. Which ones affect you? In what way?
3. What are some of the consequences for you or for other people?

24-hour shopping	shift work
difficulty sleeping	smartphone addiction
eating takeaway food	tiredness

Unit 6 Wellbeing

A caffeine-fuelled world

▶ 40

by T.R. Reid

Over the centuries, people have created many traditions around preparing and drinking their favourite drinks, tea and coffee. Just think of the Japanese tea ceremony, British afternoon tea or the morning coffee custom in many societies. Why are these drinks so popular? The answer is their secret ingredient – caffeine. In the modern world, the new caffeine 'delivery systems' are canned 'energy' drinks. And the more modern our world gets, the more we seem to need caffeine.

Caffeinated drinks make you less tired and more alert. This double power of caffeine to reduce physical tiredness and increase alertness is part of the reason why it is the world's most popular mood-changing drug. It is the only habit-forming drug we routinely serve to our children (in all those soft drinks and chocolate bars). In fact, most babies in the developed world are born with tiny amounts of caffeine in their bodies.

Most people don't think twice about their caffeine intake being harmful. However, it raises blood pressure and so increases the risk of heart disease. That's why the use of caffeine is considered to be a problem by scientists and public health authorities. In the United States, for example, many canned energy drinks carry warnings. In most European countries, manufacturers have to label cans with warnings. But in France and Denmark you are not even allowed to sell energy drinks.

On the other hand, there's also research which suggests that caffeine may have benefits for human health. It helps relieve pain, reduces asthma symptoms and increases reaction speed.

And it seems we need coffee – or Diet Coke® or Red Bull – to get us out of bed and back to work. Charles Czeisler, a neuroscientist at Harvard Medical School, explains that traditionally people went to sleep and woke up following sunset and sunrise. Then the way we worked changed and people did more indoor jobs. Consequently, we had to adapt. Electric light, and caffeinated food and drink allowed people to follow a less natural work pattern. Therefore, without caffeine, the 24-hour society of the developed world simply couldn't exist.

Czeisler says, 'Caffeine helps people try to ignore the natural human rhythms.' He warns us that 'there is a heavy, heavy price to pay' for all this extra alertness. Without enough sleep – the traditional eight hours out of each 24 is about right – the human body will not function at its best, either physically, mentally, or emotionally, the doctor says.

According to Czeisler, the modern desire for caffeine is a 'Catch 22 situation'. 'The main reason that people want caffeine is to stay awake,' he says. 'But the main reason that people can't stay awake is they don't get enough regular sleep – because they use caffeine.'

alert (adj) /əˈlɜːt/ awake and paying attention

The Shibuya Crossing in Tokyo, Japan is always busy.

my life ▶ RULES AND REGULATIONS ▶ CONSEQUENCES ▶ MODERN LIFE ▶ RESTAURANT DISHES
▶ A FORMAL LETTER/EMAIL

vocabulary restaurants • real life describing dishes • pronunciation disappearing sounds

5d Eating out

Vocabulary restaurants

1 Work in pairs. What are the most important things to consider when eating out? Does it depend on what sort of occasion it is?

> the atmosphere in the restaurant
> the food choice and/or quality
> the prices and/or value for money
> the service

2 Put these stages in eating out (a–h) into a logical order (1–8).

- a book the table 1
- b have a starter
- c have dessert
- d have the main course
- e leave a tip
- f look at the menu
- g order a drink
- h pay the bill

3 Are these comments usually said by a customer (C) or a waiter (W)?

1 Are you ready to order?
2 Would you like something to drink while you decide?
3 What's that made from?
4 What do they taste like?
5 I think I'll try that.
6 Can I take your order now?
7 And I'll have the same.
8 And for your main course?
9 Does it come with vegetables?
10 And what about you, sir?
11 Certainly.

Real life describing dishes

4 ▶ 41 Listen to the conversation in a Jamaican restaurant. Check your answers from Exercise 3.

5 ▶ 41 Look at the expressions for describing dishes. Listen to the conversation again. How are the dishes in the photos described?

▶ DESCRIBING DISHES

It's / They're a sort / type / kind of:
baked / boiled / fried dish
fruit / meat / fish / vegetable
It's / They're made from:
a kind of bean / meat / vegetables
It tastes / They taste:
bland / hot / salty / spicy /sweet
It's / They're a bit like:
fresh cod / potatoes / lamb

6 Which of the four dishes do the customers order? Would you order the same?

7 Pronunciation disappearing sounds

a ▶ 42 Listen to the sentences with these words. Cross out the part of the word which is not pronounced – the disappearing sound – in each word. Listen again and repeat the sentences.

1 interesting
2 savoury
3 traditionally
4 vegetables

b Cross out the disappearing sounds in these words. Then work in pairs. Write sentences with the words for your partner to read out.

> chocolate   natural   restaurant   separately
> technique

8 Write a list of six food dishes, vegetables, fruit or other food which are either from your country or which you have eaten abroad. Make notes which describe each item. Use the expressions for describing dishes to help you.

9 Work in groups of three. Take turns to describe your mystery foods. Who can guess each one the quickest?

plantain fritters

akkra

ackee and saltfish

goat curry

my life ▶ RULES AND REGULATIONS ▶ CONSEQUENCES ▶ MODERN LIFE ▶ RESTAURANT DISHES
         ▶ A FORMAL LETTER/EMAIL

writing a formal letter/email • writing skill explaining consequences   Unit 5 Wellbeing

5e We look forward to your reply

Writing a formal letter/email

1 A group of students has written to the manager of a local supermarket. Read the letter quickly. What is its purpose? Choose the correct option (a–c).

a to ask about prices in the supermarket
b to complain about the supermarket's actions
c to invite the supermarket to stock new products

Dear Sir

We are writing to express our shock at the news that your supermarket is throwing out huge amounts of fresh food every day. Not only that, but you put bleach on the food and as a result it becomes inedible.

In our view, this will have serious consequences for people in need. As you may know, many people can't afford to buy enough food every week. If you stop putting bleach on the food that you throw out, this will mean people can make use of it.

There are several local organizations that could use this unsold food. Will your supermarket consider working with them to pass on unwanted food to people who need it? Most food is still of good quality for some time after its sell-by date and therefore it should not be thrown out.

In addition, a lot of the unsold food that you throw out has reached its sell-by date. If your supermarket reduces the price of this food (as some of your competitors do), more people will be able to buy it. This will lead to less waste and more profit for you.

We look forward to your reply.

Yours faithfully
Year 11
Broadchurch High School

bleach (n) /bliːtʃ/ a chemical for cleaning kitchens, bathrooms, etc.

---

2 Read the letter again. Answer the questions about each paragraph.

Paragraph 1   What two actions are the students writing about?
Paragraph 2   Who is affected by the supermarket's actions?
Paragraph 3   What question do the writers have?
Paragraph 4   What alternatives do the writers suggest?

3 Writing skill explaining consequences

a Find these words in the letter. They link causes and consequences. For each word, underline the cause and circle the consequence.

1 as a result (paragraph 1)
2 mean (paragraph 2)
3 lead to (paragraph 3)

b Complete the sentences with these words. Sometimes, more than one option is possible.

| as a result   consequently   lead to   mean |
| result in   therefore |

1 We object strongly to this plan. _____, we will not be able to support it.
2 We welcome the new community kitchen. This will _____ more people eating a hot meal.
3 The prices have gone up. _____, fewer people will shop here.
4 New price policies _____ we'll be able to buy more.
5 We suggest lowering prices as this could _____ more customers coming in.
6 We reduced our prices and _____ increased the number of customers.

4 Prepare a letter with your reaction to one of these situations. Make notes before you start. Use the questions in Exercise 2 to guide you.

- Your college is going to close the student cafeteria.
- Your favourite TV show is being scrapped.
- Your employer/school has banned junk food and drink machines.
- Your local swimming pool is being closed.

5 Write your letter. Follow the structure of the paragraphs in Exercise 2. Use these questions to check your letter.

- Is the style correct for a formal letter?
- Is the purpose of the letter clear?
- Is it clear what action the person who the letter is addressed to needs to take?

6 Exchange letters with your partner. Read your partner's letter. Take the role of the person it is addressed to. Are you going to take any action as a result of the letter? Write a short reply to the letter.

my life ▸ RULES AND REGULATIONS ▸ CONSEQUENCES ▸ MODERN LIFE ▸ RESTAURANT DISHES
▸ A FORMAL LETTER/EMAIL

5f Dangerous dining

A fugu restaurant in Osaka, Japan

Unit 5 Wellbeing

Before you watch

1 Look at the photo and write six words connected to it. Then work in pairs. Compare your list with your partner.

2 Key vocabulary

a Read the sentences. The words in bold are used in the video. Guess the meaning of the words.

1 Sugar is a **major** cause of people's problems with their teeth.
2 Some snakes have **poison** in their teeth.
3 Check the **regulations** before you enter the competition.
4 Lots of people go to the dentist **annually**.
5 If you feel nervous, **breathe** in and out slowly.

b Match the words in bold in Exercise 2a with these definitions.

a something that can kill you if you eat or drink it
b every year
c take air into your lungs
d official rules
e important, big

While you watch

3 ▶ 5.1 Watch the first part of the video (0.00–0.42) with the sound OFF. Discuss the questions.

1 Which country are the people in?
2 What kind of food can you see?
3 What do you think could be dangerous about this food?

4 ▶ 5.1 Watch the first part of the video again with the sound ON. Check your ideas from Exercise 1 and find out the name of the food.

5 ▶ 5.1 Watch the second part of the video (0.43–1.43) with the sound OFF. What do you think the diners (Tom and Aki) and the chef are saying to each other? Then watch with the sound ON and check your ideas.

6 ▶ 5.1 Watch the whole video. Choose the correct option to complete the sentences.

1 A lot of people died from eating fugu *after / during* World War II.
2 At this time, licences for *catching and selling / preparing and serving* fugu were introduced.
3 There were *2,500 / 10,500* deaths from fugu from 1945 to 1975.
4 Nowadays only about three people die every year, mostly from poisoning *at home / in restaurants*.
5 One tiger fugu has enough toxin to kill *3 / 30* people.
6 The fugu toxin attacks a person's *heart / lungs*.

After you watch

7 Vocabulary in context

a ▶ 5.2 Watch the clips from the video. Choose the correct meaning of the words and phrases.

b Complete the sentences in your own words. Then work in pairs and compare your sentences.

1 I saw an advert for a holiday with a complete … experience.
2 One thing that concerns me is … .
3 The last time I got sick was … .
4 Have you ever fooled anyone?
5 Do people in your country eat mainly in restaurants or in private homes?

8 What, in your opinion, is the best ending (a–c) for this sentence? Compare with your partner.

The best way to avoid getting sick from fugu is:

a by going to a well-known restaurant.
b not to eat it.
c to take anti-toxin medicine.

9 Work in pairs to prepare a survey on risk-taking. Look at the sentence in Exercise 8 and write three similar sentences for activities that include risks. Then ask your classmates their opinions. Which are the most popular responses?

---

anti-toxin (n) /ˌæntɪˈtɒksɪn/ a substance/medicine which can treat a problem caused by a toxin
cyanide (n) /ˈsaɪənaɪd/ an extremely poisonous chemical/substance
milligram (n) /ˈmɪlɪɡræm/ a quantity: there are one thousand milligrams in a gram
paralyse (v) /ˈpærəlaɪz/ to affect something so that it can't move
toxin (n) /ˈtɒksɪn/ a kind of poison

67

UNIT 5 REVIEW AND MEMORY BOOSTER

Grammar

1 Read the conversation between two friends who are cooking. Cross out any incorrect options.

A: Do you know how to make risotto?
B: Oh yes. ¹*I show / I'll show* you if you want.
A: OK, great. ²*Can / Must* I use this pan?
B: Yes, sure. You ³*have to / don't have to* ask.
A: When the onion ⁴*is / will be* ready, I add the rice.
B: Yes, then the liquid. But you ⁵*must / have to* add it slowly. Don't add more until the rice ⁶*absorbs / will absorb* it.
A: OK, that's all the liquid in. ⁷*Am I allowed to / Should I* stir it all the time now?
B: Yes, because you ⁸*must / mustn't* let it stick to the pan. If it ⁹*sticks / will stick*, it will burn.
A: ¹⁰*Should I / Do I have to* add salt?
B: You can if you want to, but you ¹¹*mustn't / don't have to*. And the risotto ¹²*can't / has to* rest for a while before ¹³*you eat / you'll eat* it.
A: ¹⁴*Am I allowed to / Do I have to* taste it?
B: Of course you are. You made it!

2 Answer the questions about the conversation in Exercise 1.

1 Are the friends making a hot or a cold dish?
2 Why is it important to add the liquid slowly?
3 Why is it important to stir all the time?

3 **» MB** Work in pairs. Think of other modal verbs you can use in Exercise 1 items 2, 5, 7, 8, 10, 12 and 14. How does the meaning of the sentences change?

4 **» MB** Work with a new partner. Take turns to state an intention and start a 'chain'.

buy a bike	give up smoking
cut down on snacks	join a gym
give up / start eating meat	take a holiday

A: I think I'll buy a bike.
B: If you buy a bike, you'll get more exercise.
A: Yes. And if I get more exercise, …

I CAN
ask and answer questions about obligation, prohibition, permission and recommendation (modal verbs)
talk about the future results of present and future actions (first conditional)

Vocabulary

5 Match the verbs about change with phrasal verbs that mean the same. One of the verbs matches two phrasal verbs. Then write four sentences describing a change that leads to a healthy lifestyle.

| reduce   start | cut down on   cut out |
| stop | give up   take up |

6 **» MB** Find four things you can eat in Unit 5. Think of two ways to describe each one. Then work in pairs. Try and guess your partner's things.

7 **» MB** Work in pairs. Tell your partner if you never, always or sometimes do these things when you eat out. Explain your reasons.

book the table	leave a tip
have a starter	look at the menu
have dessert	order a drink
have the main course	pay the bill

I CAN
talk about feelings and personal states
talk about food and dishes
order food in a restaurant

Real life

8 Complete the description of a seafood dish with these words. There is one extra word.

| fruit   kind   made   raw   tastes |

Ceviche is a Latin American dish. It's a ¹_____ of seafood dish. It's ²_____ by using the juice of citrus ³_____, in this case limes, to 'cook' a mix of ⁴_____ fish and seafood.

9 **» MB** Work in groups. Prepare descriptions of as many dishes from the list as you can. Then compare your descriptions with other groups. Are there any dishes nobody is familiar with? Look at page 155 to find out what they are.

| baklava   borscht   coq au vin   couscous |
| fondue   goulash   gravlax   kebab   lasagne |
| paella   pizza   risotto   sauerkraut   tortilla |

I CAN
ask about and describe different dishes

68

Unit 6 Mysteries

Sunbathing cows in Andalusia, Spain

FEATURES

70 Flexible thinking

How good are you at puzzles and mysteries?

72 Desert art

The mysterious Nasca lines in Peru

74 Lost and found?

Current theories about Amelia Earhart's disappearance

78 Encounters with a sea monster

A video about strange creatures in the water

1 Work in pairs. Look at the image. Discuss the questions.
   1 Does it look like a painting or a photo?
   2 What is happening?
   3 What does it make you think about?
   4 Do you think the image has a message? What?

2 ▶ 43 Listen to a conversation about the image. Check your ideas from Exercise 1.

3 ▶ 43 Listen to the conversation again. What do the words in bold refer to?
   1 Do you think the photographer Photoshopped **it**?
   2 I'm surprised he didn't frighten **them**.
   3 I can't make **it** out.
   4 **They**'re parasailing.
   5 It's a really popular sport **there**.

4 The woman isn't sure if the photo is genuine. Why do people sometimes make 'false' photos? What about these things?

   bags   clothes   eyelashes   money   paintings   passports   watches

my life ▶ WHAT'S IT FOR? ▶ SPECULATING ▶ COMPARING IDEAS ▶ SURPRISING NEWS ▶ A NEWS STORY

listening and reading **flexible thinking** • word focus *long* • grammar purpose: *to ...* , *for ...* and *so that ...* • speaking **what's it for?**

6a Flexible thinking

Listening and reading

1 Work in pairs. Do you like doing puzzles? Read the puzzle and try to find the answer.

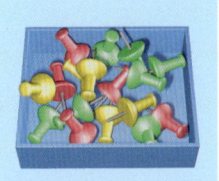

THE **CANDLE** TRICK

Your task is to attach the candle to the wall so that the wax doesn't drip on the floor below. You only have the candle, a box of drawing pins and some matches. How do you do it?

2 Compare your ideas for the candle puzzle with another pair. Then turn to page 155 to find out the answer to the puzzle. Was it easy or difficult to work out?

3 ▶ 44 Listen to a speaker at a conference. She asks her audience to do the puzzle in Exercise 1. What is the mystery she also talks about?

4 ▶ 44 Listen again and complete the sentences.
   1 How good are you at flexible and .... thinking?
   2 Does the promise of a reward make you work .... ?
   3 Imagine I offer half of you some money to do this task more ....
   4 I'm going to see how long it takes you so that we can find out the average ....
   5 The people with the reward of .... will be quicker, right?
   6 The people in the first group need more time to find the ....

5 Read the article and find the answer to the mystery the speaker mentioned. When is a reward useful? When is it not useful?

FLEXIBLE THINKING and REWARDS

▶ 45

People often think that a reward can make people work harder. However, that's not always true. Basically, it depends on the type of task or work. Rewards are great for making people concentrate and concentration helps with tasks that have a clear set of rules – the kind of thing where you follow the rules to complete the task – for example, doing maths problems or working in computer programming. But concentration doesn't help with creative and flexible thinking. When the task doesn't have a clear answer, concentration doesn't help. In fact, your brain needs to be relaxed and open so that it can look at the problem in different ways. In the workplace, the reward is usually money. So businesses need to think carefully about the relationship between work and pay – because it's true that people work harder for a reward, but only in some kinds of work.

Word focus *long*

6 Read the sentences and say if the expression with *long* refers to time (T), distance (D) or something else (S).

1. How long did it take you to do the puzzle?
2. Is it a long way from here to your house?
3. How long does the essay need to be in the exam?
4. I'm just going for a coffee. I won't be long.
5. We'll stay here as long as it takes to finish the job.
6. I love sunbathing. I could do it all day long.
7. I can't finish this book. It's just too long.
8. You can stay at my house as long as you don't mind sleeping on the sofa.

7 Work in pairs. Tell your partner about these things. Add follow-up comments.

1. something it took you a long time to do
2. a place a long way away you have visited
3. something you could do all day long
4. something you found too long

A: *When I first started learning English, it took me ages to learn how to pronounce 'daughter'.*
B: *Oh, I had the same problem with 'vegetable'!*

Grammar purpose: *to …* , *for …* and *so that …*

▶ **PURPOSE: TO … , FOR … and SO THAT …**

Imagine I offer half of you some money **to do this** more quickly.
We all work **for money**, don't we?
Drawing pins are **for attaching** things to other things.
I'm going to see how long it takes you **so that we can find out** the average time.

For further information and practice, see page 166.

8 Look at the grammar box. Answer the questions.

1. Which verb form follows *to*?
2. What can follow *for*?
3. What follows *so that*?
4. Do the sentences answer the question *how* or *why* / *what for*?

9 Look at the article *Flexible thinking and rewards*. Underline the patterns like those in the grammar box.

10 Choose the correct option to complete the sentences.

1. We worked together *for* / *to* solve the problem faster.
2. The box was useful *for* / *to* holding the candle.
3. We looked at the key *for* / *to* the answers.
4. I went to the conference *so that* / *to* find out more about the brain.
5. I sit near the front *so that* / *to* I can hear better.
6. The speaker used pictures *for* / *to* make the explanation clearer.
7. Lots of people do Sudoku *so that* / *to* keep their brain active.
8. I'm learning Chinese *for* / *so that* I can work in China.

11 Match the beginnings of the sentences (1–6) with the endings (a–f). Then complete the sentences with *to*, *for* or *so that*.

1. I want to learn another language
2. My friend called me
3. I write everything down
4. We download the homework to our phones
5. Are you going to London
6. This notebook is
7. Would you like to meet
8. Did you get much chance

a. a coffee after class?
b. ask my advice about his course.
c. help me remember it.
d. I can enjoy travelling more.
e. keep my passwords in.
f. speak Italian on your trip?
g. we can study on the bus.
h. work or on holiday?

Speaking ⌐my life⌐

12 Work in small groups. Take turns to choose one of the items from the list (without saying which one) and say why we need it. The other students in your group have to try and guess the item, and also add another reason why we need it.

A: *We need this* **to find our way around a strange place**.
B: *We need it* **so that we don't get lost**? *A map?*
A: *Yes!*

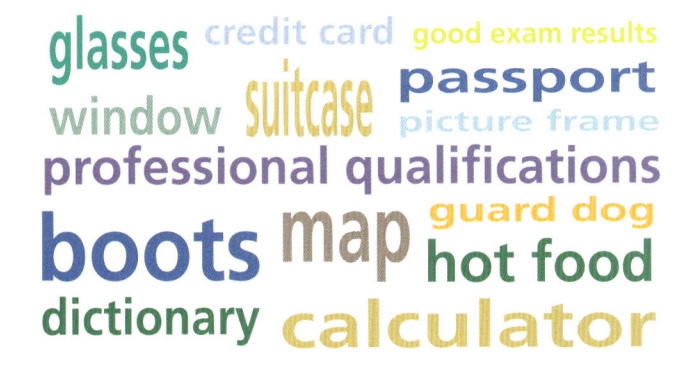

glasses   credit card   good exam results
window   suitcase   passport   picture frame
professional qualifications
boots   map   guard dog   hot food
dictionary   calculator

my life ▶ WHAT'S IT FOR? ▶ SPECULATING ▶ COMPARING IDEAS ▶ SURPRISING NEWS
▶ A NEWS STORY

vocabulary art • listening Nasca lines • grammar certainty and possibility • pronunciation weak form of *have* • speaking speculating

6b Desert art

Vocabulary art

1 Complete the sentences with these words.

> diagram   drawing   figure   line   pattern   shape

1 This looks like a child's _____ of a horse.
2 Look at that cloud. It's in the _____ of a heart.
3 Can you draw a ten-centimetre straight _____ without a ruler?
4 I can see a _____ at the door, but I don't know who it is.
5 I prefer plain shirts to ones with a colourful _____.
6 This _____ of how to cut up a pineapple isn't very clear.

Listening

2 Look at the photo and read the caption. Match the questions (1–3) with the exchanges (a–c).

1 What are they?
2 Where are they?
3 How big are they?

a 'They must be in a desert because there aren't any plants or anything there.'
  'Yes, it looks really dry.'
b 'They might be roads.'
  'No, they can't all be roads. That's clearly a spider.'
c 'There's a plane above it.'
  'Yeah, so they must be pretty big.'

3 ▶ 46 Work in pairs. What do you think the answers to the questions in Exercise 2 are? Listen to an extract from a radio programme and check your ideas.

4 ▶ 47 What do you think the purpose of the lines was? Listen to another extract from the radio programme. Complete the sentences.

1 The Nasca people couldn't have seen the _____ from above.
2 Maria Reiche was convinced that the lines must have been a type of _____.
3 Other people thought the lines may have been ancient Inca _____.
4 The strangest idea was the lines could have guided creatures from _____.
5 The Nasca people can't have known the lines would still be visible _____ later.

5 Which theory do you think is most likely? Compare your ideas with your class.

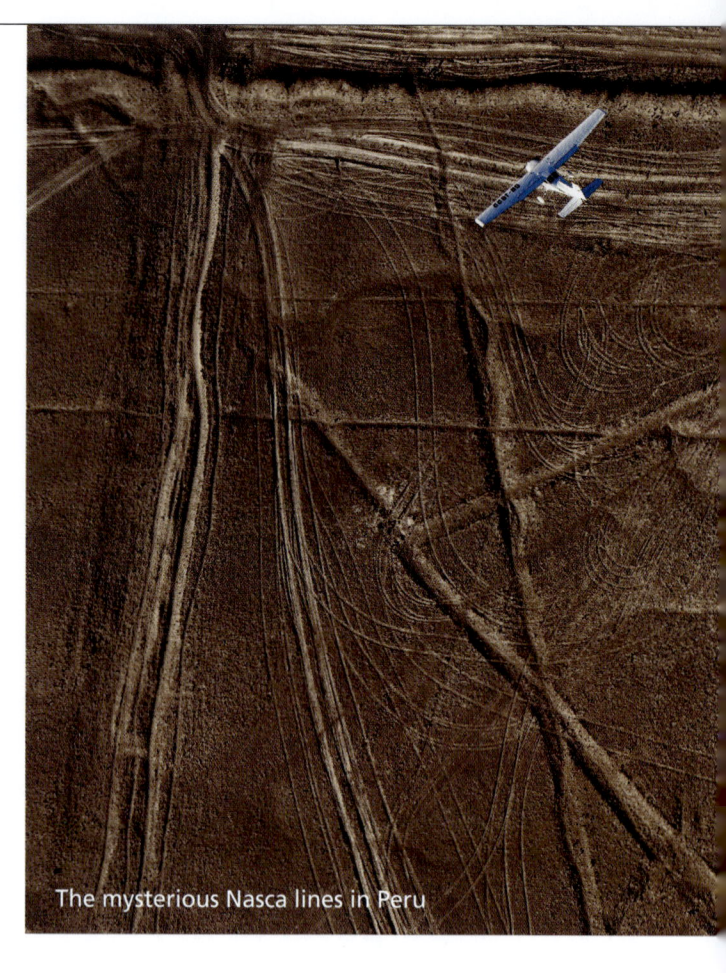

The mysterious Nasca lines in Peru

Grammar certainty and possibility

▶ **CERTAINTY AND POSSIBILITY**

In the present
must
might (not) / may (not) / could   + infinitive
can't   + be + -ing

In the past
must
may (not) / might (not) / could   have   + past participle
can't / couldn't

For further information and practice, see page 166.

6 Look at the grammar box. Underline the patterns in the sentences in Exercises 2 and 4.

7 Look at the grammar box again. Choose the correct option to complete the rules.

1 We use *must* to say if something is or was *possible / probable*.
2 We use *might*, *may* and *could* to say if something is or was *possible / probable*.
3 We use *can't* and *couldn't* to say if something is or was *impossible / improbable*.

72

Unit 6 Mysteries

8 Complete the sentences with present modal forms.

1 This drawing has eight legs. Insects have six legs. So it _____ an insect.
2 'What are the straight lines?' 'I'm not sure. They _____ paths.'
3 'What's the plane doing?' 'It _____ photographing the lines, but I can't see a camera.'
4 It's summer in Europe now, so it _____ winter in Peru.
5 I'd like to walk along the lines, but they _____ let people do that.
6 The figures are so big a plane _____ the only way to see them properly.

9 Complete the sentences about the Nasca lines with the past modal form.

1 The lines _____ something very special to the Nasca people. (must / mean)
2 We know water _____ easy to find. (can't / be)
3 The water in the area _____ . (might / disappear)
4 People _____ the drawings for fun. (might / make)
5 The animal drawings _____ roads. (couldn't / be)
6 The animals _____ in the region. (must / live)
7 The Nasca people _____ simple tools. (could / use)
8 People _____ the lines carefully. (must / look after)

10 Complete the conversations using the correct option and the verb in brackets. Use a present or past modal form.

1 A: Why hasn't my sister returned my phone call?
  B: Well, she can't / ~~may~~ _have forgotten_ (forget). She never forgets things.
2 A: Is Sandra here? I haven't seen her today.
  B: Yes, she's here. She can't / might _____ (get) a coffee.
3 A: Who's Tom talking to?
  B: It may / must _____ (be) his father. He said, 'Hi, Dad.'
4 A: Why did the plane arrive late?
  B: I don't know. It could / mightn't _____ (take off) late.
5 A: Is Joe around? We've got a meeting.
  B: Well, his computer is still on, so he can't / must _____ (go out).
6 A: Why is Phil wearing odd socks?
  B: He can't / might _____ (get dressed) in a hurry this morning.

11 Pronunciation weak form of *have*

a ▶ 48 Listen to the conversations from Exercise 10 and check your answers. Is *have* in past modals pronounced /hæv/ or /həv/? Is the *h* pronounced?

b Work in pairs. Read the conversations aloud. Pay attention to your pronunciation of *have*.

Speaking my life

12 Work in pairs. Look at the comments and think of situations when you might say these things.

1 You must have forgotten to plug it in.
2 They may have lost your application.
3 They must be at home.
4 You might have dropped it on the way here.
5 He must have forgotten to pick it up.
6 She can't have finished so quickly.
7 They might be stuck in traffic.
8 You must have spent it on something.

13 Imagine you are in the situations in Exercise 12. Have conversations that include the comments. Take turns to begin.

A: *Oh no! The battery's flat on my phone*
B: *You **must have forgotten** to plug it in. Do you want to use mine?*
A: *Thanks, but the number I need is in my contacts – I can't remember it.*

my life ▶ WHAT'S IT FOR? ▶ SPECULATING ▶ COMPARING IDEAS ▶ SURPRISING NEWS ▶ A NEWS STORY

reading testing a theory • wordbuilding nouns and verbs • critical thinking speculation or fact? • speaking comparing ideas

6c Lost and found?

Reading

1 Look at the photo and the caption. Which of these statements could be true?

1. Amelia Earhart was a famous pilot.
2. She flew across the Atlantic Ocean.
3. In the photo, she's just landed her plane.
4. She lived until she was one hundred years old.

2 Read the first article quickly. Check your ideas from Exercise 1.

3 Read the second article. Answer the questions.

1. What is the theory talked about in the article?
2. Which modern scientific technique might give an answer to the Earhart mystery?
3. If the new project is successful, what will it prove?
4. What is the biggest problem for the researchers on the new project?

4 Find these words in the articles. Look at how the words are used and try to guess their meaning. Then replace the words in bold in the sentences (1–6) with these words.

attempting (line 2)	financing (line 31)
captured (line 17)	distinguish (line 67)
samples (line 24)	identical (line 70)

1. My grandparents are **paying for** my studies.
2. It's easy to **see the difference** between a leg bone and an arm bone.
3. The doctor took **small amounts** of my blood to do tests.
4. The soldier was **caught and put in prison** by the enemy.
5. The cyclist is **trying** to break the world record.
6. The two brothers look **exactly the same** to me.

5 Work in groups. Discuss the questions.

1. The piece of bone 'might have been from one of Earhart's fingers'. Are there any other possibilities?
2. Is it certain that any saliva on the envelopes is Earhart's? Why? / Why not?
3. Do you think the project will be successful?

6 Work in pairs. Complete the summary.

The new project aims to provide a way of testing ¹ _____ . The success of the project depends on several things. Firstly, that the bone is from a ² _____ , not a turtle. Secondly, that Earhart's saliva still exists on ³ _____ . And thirdly, that there is enough saliva to ⁴ _____ .

Wordbuilding nouns and verbs

▶ **WORDBUILDING nouns and verbs**

Some nouns and verbs have the same form. They can have similar or unconnected meanings.
land – similar; *book* – unconnected

For further practice, see Workbook page 51.

7 Look at the wordbuilding box. Find these words in the two articles. Are they used as nouns or verbs?

1. fly (line 1)
2. land (line 3)
3. books (line 8)
4. records (line 11)
5. contact (line 13)
6. plan (line 23)
7. test (line 26)
8. remains (line 35)

8 Look at the same words in these sentences. Is the meaning similar to the meaning of the word in Exercise 7?

1. Have you got any plans for the weekend?
2. We always book our hotel rooms in advance.
3. I tried to contact them yesterday without success.
4. Did Amelia Earhart hold any flying records?
5. Everyone did badly in yesterday's English test.

Critical thinking speculation or fact?

9 Read the definitions. Then decide if the sentences from the articles report speculation (S) or fact (F).

Speculation is having a theory or guessing about something.
Facts are items of information that we can check, or show to be true or not true.

1. Amelia Earhart […] was attempting a round-the-world flight in 1937.
2. Earhart could have landed on a different island.
3. The problem is that the envelopes probably don't contain much DNA.
4. About 99 per cent of the genome is identical among all humans.

10 Find one more fact and one more speculation in the articles. Then work in pairs. Do you agree with your partner's choices?

Speaking my life

11 Work in groups. Think of at least three news stories you have heard about recently. Suggest as many reasons as you can for what has happened.

A: *Did you see that … isn't going to make any more films?*
B: *I know! Do you think he/she could be ill?*

74

Unit 6 **Mysteries**

Where Is Amelia Earhart?

Three Theories

▶ 49   *by John Roach*

Amelia Earhart, the first woman to fly solo across the Atlantic Ocean, was attempting a round-the-world flight in 1937. She planned to land on the tiny Pacific Ocean island of Howland just north of the equator. She never arrived. Exactly what happened to her and her navigator, Fred Noonan, is still one of aviation's greatest mysteries. Researchers have spent millions of dollars investigating the case and several books have been published that look at the different theories.

The official US opinion is that Earhart ran out of fuel and crashed in the Pacific Ocean. The radio records from a US Coast Guard ship suggest that she must have been near Howland when contact was lost.

Another theory says that Earhart could have landed and later died on a different island, called Nikumaroro. Nobody lived there.

And another theory says she was captured while on a secret mission to the Japanese-controlled Marshall Islands in the North Pacific and eventually returned to the USA with a new identity.

Lost and found? The missing pilot

▶ 50

by Ker Than

Amelia Earhart's dried saliva could help solve the mystery of the aviator's 1937 disappearance. Scientists plan to take samples of her DNA from letters she wrote and create a genetic profile. This could be used to test recent suggestions that a bone found on the South Pacific island of Nikumaroro is Earhart's.

Justin Long is a Canadian whose family is financing part of the DNA project. He makes the point that at the moment, anyone who finds pieces of bones can say that they are Amelia Earhart's remains. According to Long, Earhart's letters are the only existing items that are definitely hers and that might contain her DNA. The remains of Earhart, her navigator Noonan and their twin-engine plane were never found. But in 2009, researchers with the International Group for Historic Aircraft Recovery discovered a piece of bone on Nikumaroro, which they believed might have been from one of Earhart's fingers. However, some scientists have suggested the Nikumaroro bone isn't human at all but may be from a turtle.

The new Earhart DNA project will be organized by Dongya Yang, a genetic archaeologist at Simon Fraser University in Canada. Yang will work on four letters Earhart wrote to her family. More than 400 of Earhart's letters still exist today. Much of Earhart's correspondence was dealt with by her secretary. However, with the four personal letters, it is believed that Earhart must have sealed the envelopes herself.

Meanwhile, geneticist Brenna Henn of Stanford University, USA said she knows of no other case where DNA has been collected from old letters. The problem is that the envelopes probably don't contain much DNA. The project needs a big sample to distinguish between Earhart's DNA and that of other living people because about 99 per cent of the genome is identical among all humans. To make sure that the DNA from the letters belonged to Earhart, the team will compare it to DNA from Earhart's relatives who are still alive and also DNA extracted from another letter, written by Earhart's sister.

---

genome (n) /ˈdʒiːnəʊm/ the genetic information of each living thing
navigator (n) /ˈnævɪˌɡeɪtə/ the person who plans the direction of a plane or ship
saliva (n) /səˈlaɪvə/ the liquid normally in your mouth
sealed (adj) /siːld/ closed safely so that it's hard to open

---

my life ▶ WHAT'S IT FOR? ▶ SPECULATING ▶ COMPARING IDEAS ▶ SURPRISING NEWS
▶ A NEWS STORY

real life **reacting to surprising news** • pronunciation **showing interest and disbelief**

6d You must be joking!

Real life reacting to surprising news

1 ▶51 Listen to three conversations about news items. Choose the best headline (a–b) in each case.

1. a ESCAPED SHEEP TAKE OVER LONDON PARK
   b SHEEP IN GLOBAL WARMING SHOCK
2. a FALSE BANK NOTES ALERT
   b USA TO JOIN THE EURO ZONE
3. a FUEL PRICES TO DOUBLE NEXT WEEK
   b PETROL PRICES HALVED

2 Can you remember? Answer the questions for each story.

1. What is the problem?
2. Does the second speaker believe the first speaker?
3. What is the date?

3 ▶51 Look at the expressions for reacting to surprising news. Listen to the conversations again. Put the expressions in order (1–9).

▶ REACTING TO SURPRISING NEWS

Are you serious?
Are you sure?
Come off it!
Come on!
Oh yeah?
Really?
That can't be right!
They must have made a mistake.
You must be joking!
You're having me on!

4 April Fools' Day (1 April) is a day when people try to trick each other in many countries. Do you do anything similar in your country?

5 Pronunciation showing interest and disbelief

a ▶52 Listen to these expressions for reacting to surprising news. Notice how the speaker's intonation rises to show interest and falls to show disbelief.

1. Oh yeah?
2. Come off it!

b ▶53 Listen to the other expressions for reacting to surprising news. Repeat the expressions.

c Work in pairs. Take turns to respond to these statements.

1. I'm setting off on a round-the-world trip on Monday.
2. A meteorite has crashed to Earth in the middle of Berlin.
3. I found a wallet full of money in the street this morning.
4. Biologists have discovered a parrot that can speak three languages.
5. I'm starting a new job tomorrow.

6 Work in pairs. Choose one of the other April Fools' Day headlines from Exercise 1. Decide what the hoax – the trick – is. Make notes about the main points of the story. Invent as many details as you wish. Practise telling the story with your partner.

7 Work with a new partner. Take turns to listen and react to your stories. Use the expressions for reacting to surprising news to help you. Don't forget to show interest or disbelief with your intonation.

my life ▶ WHAT'S IT FOR? ▶ SPECULATING ▶ COMPARING IDEAS ▶ SURPRISING NEWS ▶ A NEWS STORY

6e In the news

Writing a news story

1 Work in pairs. Read the news story. Do you think it is true or not? Work in pairs. Explain your reasons to your partner.

2 Writing skill structuring a news story

a Read the introductory sentence in the news story again. Answer the questions.

1. What happened?
2. Who was involved?
3. Where did it happen?

b Read the main paragraph and find:

1. how the woman cut the cable.
2. four things that happened after she cut the cable.
3. two pieces of background information.

c Read the main paragraph again. How are the events and background details organized?

3 Vocabulary *-ly* adverbs in stories

a Find these adverbs (1–5) in the story. Then match the adverbs with their meanings (a–e).

1 accidentally	a at once
2 unfortunately	b by mistake
3 temporarily	c for a short time
4 immediately	d it seems
5 apparently	e we are sorry to say

b Cross out any options which are not possible.

1. *Apparently,* / *Quickly,* this type of incident is increasing in Georgia.
2. *Fortunately,* / *Incredibly,* nobody was hurt.
3. Internet services were *amazingly* / *gradually* restored across the region.
4. *Coincidentally,* / *Rapidly,* internet services also failed in other regions last week.
5. Software providers say hackers *deliberately* / *sadly* damaged the service.
6. *Hopefully,* / *Slowly,* the police will release the woman because of her age.

c Work in pairs. Decide which of the sentences in Exercise 3b fit into the story and where they fit.

4 You are going to write an April Fools' story or a news story that is not true. This can be invented or it can be a story you have heard. First, make notes about the main events and the background details of the story. Think about *what? who? where?* and also *why?* and *how?*

GEORGIAN WOMAN CUTS OFF WEB ACCESS TO WHOLE OF ARMENIA

An elderly Georgian woman has accidentally cut through an underground cable and cut off internet services to a whole country, Armenia.

The woman, 75, was digging for metal near the Georgian capital Tbilisi and her spade damaged the cable. Unfortunately, Georgia provides 90 per cent of Armenia's internet. Web users in the nation of 3.2 million people were left with no internet for up to five hours. Large parts of Georgia and some areas of Azerbaijan were also temporarily affected. The damage was discovered by an automatic system and a security team immediately went to the place where the cable was cut. The cable is protected, but apparently landslides or heavy rain may have left it exposed on the surface. The woman, called 'the spade-hacker' by local newspapers, was arrested for damaging property. She may have to spend up to three years in prison.

5 Write an introductory sentence to summarize the story. Then number your notes in the order you will write about them. Include at least three adverbs where appropriate.

6 Work on your own. Write your story in about 150–200 words. Write an interesting headline.

7 Work with a new partner. Exchange stories. Use these questions to check your partner's story.

- Did the headline make you interested in reading the story?
- Are the facts of the story clear?
- Do you think the story is true?

6f Encounters with a sea monster

What could that be?

Before you watch

1 How much do you know about these monsters? Compare your ideas with the class.

> Frankenstein   The Loch Ness monster   Godzilla
> Shrek   Bigfoot

2 Key vocabulary

a Read the sentences. Try to guess the missing words.

1 Don't take the boat out past the red ....
2 Police talked to several .... who saw the accident.
3 Do camels have one .... or two?
4 Can you switch off the boat's ...., please? It's very noisy.
5 It's surprising how quickly submarines can .... into the water and disappear.
6 There were lots of seabirds following the .... of the ferry.

b Read the words in bold and their definitions. The words are used in the video. Complete the sentences in Exercise 3a with the words.

a **motor** (n) an engine
b **buoy** (n) a coloured object that floats in water to indicate danger for boats
c **eyewitnesses** (n) people who see something happen, especially an accident, a crime, etc.
d **hump** (n) something that has a round shape and that sticks out
e **wake** (n) the waves behind something that moves through water
f **submerge** (v) to go under the surface of water

While you watch

3 🎥 **6.1** Work in pairs. Watch the first part of the video (0.00–0.51) with the sound OFF. You will see Bob Iverson explaining something he saw as an eyewitness. What do you think he's saying to the reporter?

4 🎥 **6.1** Watch the video with the sound ON. You will hear three eyewitness reports in total from Bob Iverson, Marjory Neal and Richard Smith. Correct the factual mistakes in the sentences.

All three eyewitnesses …

1 saw the monster on the same day.
2 saw three or more humps.
3 were in exactly the same place.
4 were alone at the time.

5 🎥 **6.1** Work on your own. Watch the video again. Make notes to answer the questions for each speaker.

1 Where was the eyewitness?
2 What were the weather or water conditions like?
3 How far away from the eyewitness was the monster?
4 What did the monster do?

6 Work in groups of three. Compare your notes. Is there any information still missing? If you need to, watch the video again and check.

After you watch

7 Work in groups of three. Read what the reporter says at the end of the video. Discuss your ideas for possible explanations.

> '… three remarkable stories, but are there more plausible explanations before we cry "sea monster"?'

8 Vocabulary in context

a 🎥 **6.2** Watch the clips from the video. Choose the correct meaning of the words and phrases.

b Complete the sentences in your own words. Then work in pairs and compare your sentences.

1 I was on my way to class once when all of a sudden …
2 Sometimes when I watch TV, I wonder …
3 I spend anywhere between … hours studying English each week.
4 A news story about … caught my attention last week.

9 Would you believe a friend if they told you a story like the ones in the video? Why? / Why not?

---

plausible (adj) /ˈplɔːzəbl/ believable, likely
remarkable (adj) /rɪˈmɑːkəbl/ unusual, extraordinary
sun deck (n) /ˈsʌndek/ a flat wooden area in a garden
tractor (n) /ˈtræktə/ a large farm vehicle

UNIT 6 REVIEW AND MEMORY BOOSTER

Grammar

1 Choose the correct options in the text about Stonehenge.

Stonehenge dates from 3–4,000 years ago. Although there ¹ *are / might be* no written records from that period, some people think Stonehenge ² *can't have / might have* been part of King Arthur's court. Others say invaders from Denmark ³ *couldn't have / could have* built it or it ⁴ *can / could* be the ruins of a Roman building. The larger stones weigh 25 tons and they come from about 30 kilometres away from the site. The smaller stones originate from Wales, 230 kilometres away.

Stonehenge ⁵ *is / may be* in the shape of a circle and the stones are placed ⁶ *so that / to* they match the sun's highest and lowest points in the sky. This has led people to suggest that it ⁷ *can't have / could have* been a scientific observatory or it was designed ⁸ *for / to* help aliens land. On the other hand, others believe it ⁹ *can / may* be a kind of cemetery – a place ¹⁰ *for / so that* burying people. Every year brings new theories about the true purpose of Stonehenge.

2 Answer the questions about the text in Exercise 1.

1. What are three theories about the origins of Stonehenge?
2. What is known about the stones?
3. What are three theories about the purpose of Stonehenge?

3 » **MB** Work in pairs. Which theory about Stonehenge do you think is the most likely? Give reasons.

I CAN	
use expressions of purpose correctly	☐
talk about events in the present and past that are certain or possible (modal verbs)	☐

Vocabulary

4 Complete the sentences with an adverb ending in *-ly*. The first letter is given.

1. I'd love to come for lunch, but u_____ I'm busy that day.
2. You need to reply to this letter i_____ . It's urgent.
3. Oh dear, I've a_____ deleted the email. How did that happen?
4. I'm working t_____ as the manager while my boss is away.
5. We checked our records and a_____ the package was posted on 2 May.
6. I think the boys arrived late d_____ to miss the test.

5 » **MB** Work in pairs. Answer as many questions as you can. The words in bold are in Unit 6.

1. What are **false** eyelashes?
2. What do you understand by the expression '**flexible thinker**'?
3. When might you get a **reward**?
4. Name two activities you could do **all day long**.
5. How many **shapes** can you name?
6. Are **lines** always straight?
7. Give examples of how to use **record** as a noun and as a verb.
8. Is a **hoax** a person?
9. What's the difference between a **trick** and a **puzzle**?
10. What do you use a **spade** for?

I CAN	
use adverbs ending in -ly in stories	☐
talk about different types of drawings	☐
talk about mysteries and puzzles	☐

Real life

6 Complete the expressions for reacting to news.

1. _____ joking!
2. _____ off _____!
3. _____ on!
4. _____ right!
5. _____ serious?
6. _____ sure?

7 Work in groups. Write surprising sentences about yourself (true and false). Take turns to read out your sentences. Use appropriate expressions to react to the sentences about the other people and try to find out which sentences are true.

I CAN	
talk about feelings and personal states	☐

80

Unit 7 Living space

Off the Izu peninsular, Honshu, Japan, a yellow goby looks at the camera.

FEATURES

82 Before New York

What came before the city?

84 Homes around the world

An architect talks about homes

86 Sweet songs and strong coffee

Visit a community in Puerto Rico

90 The town with no wi-fi

A video about an unusual town

1 Work in pairs. Look at the photo. Discuss the questions.

1 What can you see in the photo?
2 Where do you think this photo was taken?
3 Do you think this is the fish's natural habitat, a temporary shelter or a permanent home?

2 ▶ 54 Listen to three people talking about different living arrangements. Write the number of the speaker (1–3) next to the statements that summarize their comments.

a I can't wait to leave my parents' house and get some independence.
b My family's lovely, but I'd like to have my own home and some privacy.
c My flatmates aren't here much, so it's just like having my own place really.
d It's cramped and noisy, but at least you're never lonely.
e Sharing a flat with friends is not as easy as I thought it would be.
f I love living with my mum and dad and brothers. I won't leave until I get married.

3 Work in groups. Discuss the questions.

1 Which room do you spend most time in at home?
2 How do different family members use different rooms?
3 Do you consider your home a private place, just for family? Or do you often have friends round?

my life ▶ PLACES ▶ ADVICE ▶ A TOURIST DESTINATION ▶ CHOICES
▶ A DESCRIPTION OF A PLACE

vocabulary in the city • reading from farms to skyscrapers • grammar used to, would and past simple • speaking places

7a Before New York

Vocabulary in the city

1 Work in pairs. What kind of a place is New York? Try to describe New York in three words.

2 Complete the sentences with these words. Which sentences do you think are true of New York?

> atmosphere   blocks   built-up   financial   neighbourhoods
> public transport   residents   skyscrapers

1 There's an excellent _____ _____ system to get you around the city.
2 It's got an important business and _____ district.
3 It's one of the most _____ places you can live, with few open spaces.
4 The views from the _____ are spectacular, especially at night.
5 There's lots to do, both for tourists and _____ .
6 Some _____ are more dangerous than others.
7 The _____ is exciting and lively.
8 The streets divide the city into _____ .

3 Write sentences about places you know with the words from Exercise 2.

Reading

4 Work in pairs. Discuss the questions. Then read the article *Before New York* and check your ideas.

1 What do you think the area that is now New York was like before the city was built?
2 What kind of people do you think lived there?
3 What kind of landscapes do you think there were?

5 Read the article again. Answer the questions in your own words.

1 What's the connection between Eric Sanderson and the image with the article?
2 What did Sanderson aim to do with his project?
3 Why do you think the appearance of the beaver in 2007 was important for Sanderson?

Before New York

By Peter Miller

▶ 55

Of all the visitors to New York City in recent years, one of the most surprising was a beaver which appeared one morning in 2007. Although beavers used to be common in the area in the seventeenth century, and people used to hunt them for their skins, there haven't been any for more than two hundred years.

For ecologist Eric Sanderson, the beaver's appearance was especially interesting. For ten years, Sanderson has been in charge of a project to show what the area used to look like before the city changed it completely. As Sanderson says, 'There are views in this city where you cannot see, except for a person, another living thing. Not a tree or a plant. How did a place become like that?'

In fact, long before the skyscrapers came to dominate the view, this place was a pristine wilderness where animals like beavers, bears and turkeys would move freely through forests, marshes and grassland. There used to be sandy beaches along the coasts and ninety kilometres of fresh-water streams.

At the end of Sanderson's project, he built a 3D computer model of the area. (See the top photo on the right.) You can pick any spot in modern New York and see what used to be there. Take Fifth Avenue, for example. A family called Murray used to have a farm here and in 1782 (during the American War of Independence) the British soldiers landed near here. 'I'd like every New Yorker to know that they live in a place with amazing natural potential – even if you have to look a little harder to see it,' says Sanderson.

> **pristine** (adj) /ˈprɪstiːn/ pure, as new
> **wilderness** (n) /ˈwɪldənəs/ an area in a completely natural state

Unit 7 Living space

Grammar *used to*, *would* and past simple

▶ **USED TO**

1 *People **used to hunt** beavers for their skins.*
2 *The Murray family **used to have** a farm here.*
3 *There **didn't use to be** any skyscrapers.*
4 *What **did** New York **use to look** like?*

▶ **WOULD**

*Beavers, bears and turkeys **would move** freely.*

For further information and practice, see page 168.

6 Look at the grammar box and the article. Underline the sentences in the article with *used to* and *would*. Do they refer to past habits and states or to single actions in the past?

7 Look at the article again. Find three examples of single actions in the past. What is the verb form?

8 Look at the grammar box. Match the sentences with *used to* (1–4) with the uses (a–b). Then match the sentence with *would* with its use.

a past state
b past habit (repeated action)

Computer Generated Image (top) by Markley Boyer

9 Rewrite the sentences using *used to* + infinitive where possible.

1 New York was a lot greener than it is now.
2 The early residents didn't live in a large city.
3 People farmed the land.
4 Farmers hunted wild animals for food.
5 Soldiers fought an important battle on the island.
6 What was in the area where Fifth Avenue is now?

10 Complete the text with the past simple, *used to* or *would* form of the verbs. In some cases, you can use more than one form.

I remember when I first ¹ _____ (move) to New York from California with my parents. Every day for the first month, I ² _____ (stand) in the street and stare up at the skyscrapers. They ³ _____ (be) taller than anything I'd ever seen. The streets ⁴ _____ (be) much busier than in California and I ⁵ _____ (run) from one side to the other holding my mother's hand. For the first few months, we ⁶ _____ (not / go) further than four blocks from home. My parents ⁷ _____ (not / own) a car, so on Sunday mornings we ⁸ _____ (take) the subway to Central Park. We ⁹ _____ (have) breakfast at a lovely deli and then we ¹⁰ _____ (go) skating. The city ¹¹ _____ (be) a lot more dangerous and scary then.

11 Complete the sentences with the past simple, *used to* or *would* so that they are true for you. Then work in pairs. Compare your sentences and ask follow-up questions about three of the sentences.

1 Before I worked/studied here, I … .
2 When I was in primary school, I … .
3 Before we moved here, my family … .
4 I remember my first holiday. I … .
5 Whenever I had exams at school, I … .
6 In my family, at weekends we … .
7 The first time I went to school alone, … .
8 As a child, I … .

Speaking my life

12 Choose two places from the list. How have the places changed? Make notes for then and now.

- my street
- my home
- my classroom
- my school
- my village / my town

my street: then – lots of cars; now – residents only

13 Work in pairs. Tell each other about the places you chose in Exercise 12. Use *used to* and *would*. Decide which places have changed the most and whether they are better now than they were in the past.

A: *There **used to be** a lot of cars in my street, but now only residents can park on it.*
B: *What do visitors do? Can they drive up to your house?*

my life ▶ PLACES ▶ ADVICE ▶ A TOURIST DESTINATION ▶ CHOICES ▶ A DESCRIPTION OF A PLACE

83

listening house design • grammar comparison: adverbs • grammar comparison: patterns • speaking advice

7b Homes around the world

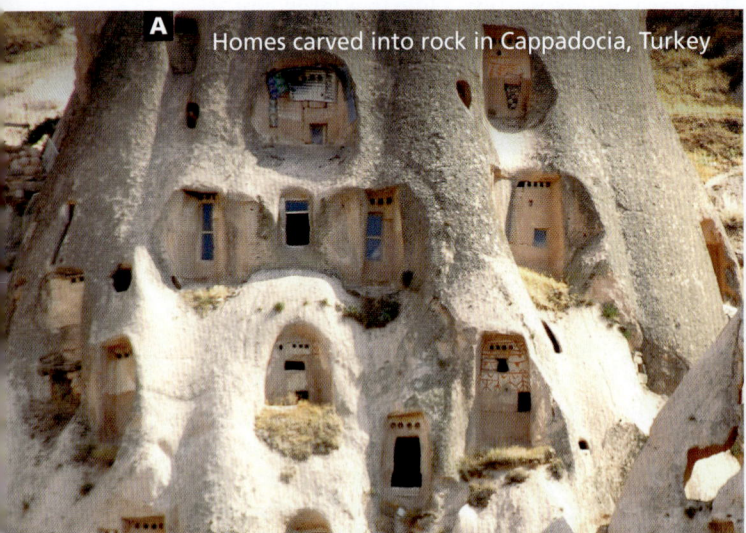

A Homes carved into rock in Cappadocia, Turkey

B A ger belonging to Tuvan nomads in Western Mongolia

C A wooden house on stilts after floods in the Mekong River in southern Cambodia

D Modern terraced houses in Sabah, Borneo

Listening

1 Look at the photos of four homes. What are they made of?

bricks   cloth   rock   wood

2 Think of a question you'd like to ask each home owner. Then work in pairs. Tell your partner.

3 ▶56 Marta Fereira presents the TV series *Home Planet*. Read the questions (a–e) that viewers have sent in to the programme's website. Then listen and match Marta's podcast replies (1–5) with the questions.

a Why are you so interested in traditional house design?   *1*
b We live in a new house that my dad calls a 'box'. What do you think of the design of modern houses?
c Why are some types of house more common in some areas of the world than in others?
d You mentioned shelters in your last programme. What's the difference between a shelter and a home?
e I'd like to stay in a ger, but they look a bit basic. What are they really like?

4 ▶56 Listen again and complete the sentences.

1 Traditional houses usually survive bad _____ conditions better than modern ones.
2 Rock homes heat up less quickly than _____ .
3 You can put up a ger much faster than a _____ .
4 You can live much more safely above the _____ .
5 Modern houses are getting smaller and _____ .
6 Unfortunately, sometimes _____ are also built badly.
7 Modern houses don't work as efficiently as _____ .

5 Which of the homes in the photos would you like to spend time in? Why?

84

Grammar comparison: adverbs

▶ **COMPARATIVE ADVERBS**

Adverb	Comparative forms
quickly/easily	more quickly/easily (than)
	less quickly/easily (than)
	not as quickly/easily as
	as quickly/easily as

Note: well → better, badly → worse, fast → faster

For further information and practice, see page 168.

6 Look at the grammar box. Underline the comparative adverbs in the sentences in Exercise 4.

7 Read the three sentences. Do they mean the same thing? Do you agree with the sentences?
1 A brick house heats up more quickly than a rock house.
2 A rock house heats up less quickly than a brick house.
3 A rock house doesn't heat up as quickly as a brick house.

8 Complete the text about house sales and rentals in the UK with the comparative form of the adverbs.

Home | Properties | About | Contact

Last year, terraced houses sold ¹_____ (quickly) than flats, but one-bedroom flats did ²_____ (well) with young buyers. The number of large houses for rent rose ³_____ (fast) than other types of home. Sales of large flats did ⁴_____ (badly) than in previous years. So what does this mean for you? You can now rent a large house ⁵_____ (cheaply) than ever before, but if you're trying to sell yours, you probably won't find a buyer ⁶_____ (easily) as in previous years. Renting it out is a good alternative, so come and talk to us today.

9 Write sentences comparing the pairs of things. Then look at your partner's sentences. Do you agree?
1 young people / older people (drive carefully)
   Older people drive more carefully than young people.
2 girls / boys (do well in exams)
3 children / adults (learn quickly)
4 women / men (work hard)
5 Americans / British people (speak slowly)
6 I / my friends (sing badly)

Grammar comparison: patterns

▶ **COMPARATIVE PATTERNS**

Modern houses are getting smaller and smaller.
House prices are going up more and more quickly.
And the higher the stilts, the safer you are.

For further information and practice, see page 168.

10 Look at the grammar box. Which sentences describe change? Which sentence describes two related things?

11 Read what two people say about where they live. Underline comparative patterns similar to the ones in the grammar box.

Josef: As this building gets older, things go wrong more and more often. But living in a block of flats is really good because I don't have to worry about repairs and things. Everyone pays an amount each month, so the greater the number of residents, the lower the monthly payment is.

Sandra: We're all students. So for us, the cheaper the place, the better. We don't have as much money as people who are working. Rents are getting higher and higher, but you can still rent more cheaply than buy.

12 Complete what two more people say. Use comparative patterns.

Marcus: Neighbours! The ¹_____ (few / good), I say. In my old flat, I used to have noisy people living right above me and I got ²_____ (angry) as the months went by. So I moved into my own house and life is much quieter now.

Frances: I love having a garden, but it's a lot of work – so the ³_____ (small / good), I think. As time passes, the garden gets untidy ⁴_____ (quickly), until in the end I have to do something about it.

Speaking my life

13 Work in groups of four. Discuss ways of doing these things. What advice would you give someone who wanted to do each one?
1 learn English more quickly
2 do better in exams
3 live more cheaply
4 eat more healthily
5 spend more wisely
6 shop more sensibly

A: I think you can **learn English more quickly** if you go to live in an English-speaking country.
B: I agree. You won't learn **as quickly** if you stay at home. You won't meet native English speakers **as easily**, for example.

▶ PLACES ▶ **ADVICE** ▶ A TOURIST DESITINATION ▶ CHOICES
▶ A DESCRIPTION A PLACE

reading a little town in Puerto Rico • wordbuilding noun → adjective • critical thinking descriptions • speaking a tourist destination

7c Sweet songs and strong coffee

Reading

1 Think of one word to describe your home town. Tell the class.

2 Read the article about a town in Puerto Rico. What is the article mainly about? Choose the correct option (a–c).
   a daily life and work
   b festivals and holidays
   c people and traditions

3 Which paragraph gives information about:
   a what life used to be like in Adjuntas?
   b a traditional activity that people still do?
   c a new activity that people have learned to do?
   d what the town looks like?

4 Work in pairs. What can you remember about these things in Adjuntas?
   1 the horses   3 Lala Echevarria
   2 the town square   4 Tato Ramos

5 What do you think of Adjuntas as a place to live? Or a place to go on holiday? Tell your partner and give reasons using information from the article.

Wordbuilding noun → adjective

▶ WORDBUILDING noun → adjective

We can make adjectives from nouns by adding a suffix such as -al or -ic. Spelling changes are sometimes needed.
nature → natural, person → personal, artist → artistic

For further practice, see Workbook page 59.

6 Look at the wordbuilding box. Find the adjectives in the article that are formed from these nouns.
   1 romance (line 10)   2 nation (line 16)

7 Complete the sentences with adjectives formed by adding -al or -ic to the nouns.

| benefit | centre | coast | economy | energy |
| fact | history | nature | origin | person |

   1 The farmer never stops working. He's _____ and enthusiastic.
   2 The _____ part of the island is quite flat and the _____ part is mountainous.
   3 Opening the forest park was _____ for the villagers and the wildlife.
   4 We saw lots of birds in their _____ habitat.
   5 The _____ crisis hasn't affected business.
   6 The _____ area of the city around the old market is worth visiting.

Critical thinking descriptions

8 The writer aims to 'paint' a picture of Adjuntas in the reader's mind. Which descriptions in the article helped you to build a mental picture of Adjuntas? Underline words and phrases in the article.

9 Work in pairs. Compare the words you have underlined with your partner. Do you think the writer has been successful in her aims?

10 Add descriptions to each sentence to help the reader build a mental image. Then exchange sentences with your partner.
   1 The village is in the forest.
      The tiny village is in the heart of the dense forest.
   2 The houses are small.
   3 You can walk through the streets.
   4 The village centre is full of people.
   5 People are working everywhere you look.
   6 From one building, you can hear music.

Speaking my life

11 Work in pairs. Choose a place that you both know well and that is attractive to tourists. Plan and practise a short presentation to persuade people to visit the destination. Use descriptions that help people to imagine the place. Talk about:
   • the best things to see
   • the best things to do
   • the best places to eat

12 Work in small groups. Give your presentation. Ask and answer follow-up questions.
   A: *… and finally, don't leave the area without trying the food at the Golden Lion. It's delicious and not expensive.*
   B: *Can you tell me what kind of restaurant the Golden Lion is?*

86

Unit 7 Living space

SWEET SONGS AND STRONG COFFEE
By Linda Gómez

▶ 57

There's a dreamy atmosphere to Adjuntas, a coffee town in the Valley of the Sleeping Giant high in the mountains of Puerto Rico. And there's love, the love of the people for their land and its customs. People here say their families have lived here 'since forever'. You feel this love in the streets, with the smell of food cooked at roadside barbecues. You see it in the beautiful horses that parade through town on holidays. And you feel it as you sit in the large, elegant square, with its romantic fountains and stone benches.

Several decades ago, this love of the land also led the local people to prevent a mining development in the surrounding mountains. They used money from the area's successful coffee production to provide the money for a national park, El Bosque del Pueblo. The park opened in 1998 and runs a reforestation programme allowing young and old to plant trees. 'Learning to manage the forest has been a kind of new life for us,' said Tinti Deya, a local resident. 'It's another world where we're like children doing everything for the first time, except in our case we're grandmothers.'

Grandmothers are everywhere in Adjuntas and they're all respectfully addressed as Doña. Lala Echevarria, an 85-year-old great-great-grandmother, was born on the oldest street in town, where she still lives in a small, neat and tidy home. Doña Lala grew up before electricity and running water, and remembers when the first car arrived in Adjuntas. 'As a child, I used to spend all my time carrying water, finding firewood, looking after the chickens and the cows,' she said. 'There were sixteen of us. We would wash our clothes in the river and we used to cook on an open fire. At meal times, we kids would sit on the floor to eat.' Doña Lala was working as a maid when she met and married the love of her life, Mariano the mechanic. They had thirteen children and shared 44 years before he died in 1983. She shows me the dozens of photographs of four generations of her family that now fill her tiny home.

People in Adjuntas play old traditional songs in little shops like Lauro Yepez's place, where men meet to swap stories and have a drink. When I was there, Tato Ramos, a local singer, appeared and began to sing in a flamenco style that hasn't changed for centuries. The shop quickly filled with working-class men clapping, tapping and nodding to the music. Ramos improvised songs on topics requested by shop customers. 'This is a forgotten art,' said Yepez. 'People give him a topic and he composes a song, in proper rhyme.'

Later, I played the recording I'd made for my 88-year-old Spanish father, who has Alzheimer's disease. His dark brown eyes shone with recognition. He nodded his head, smiled, and said, 'Oh yes, this I remember, this I remember …'

firewood (n) /ˈfɪəˌwʊd/ wood that is used as fuel

my life ▶ PLACES ▶ ADVICE ▶ A TOURIST DESTINATION ▶ CHOICES
A DESCRIPTION OF A PLACE

real life stating preferences and giving reasons • pronunciation rising and falling intonation

7d To rent or to buy?

Real life stating preferences and giving reasons

1 Work in pairs. Write a checklist of things you should think about when you are looking for somewhere to live.

2 ▶ 58 Listen to a conversation at an estate agent's. Does the woman mention the things on your checklist? What four things does she specify?

3 ▶ 58 Look at the expressions for stating preferences. Listen to the conversation again. Complete the expressions.

▶ **STATING PREFERENCES**

I think I'd rather _____ than _____ , for now anyway.
I'd prefer _____ , but not too _____ .
So, two bedrooms, and preferably with _____ .
Would you rather _____ places or _____ ones?
To be honest, I prefer _____ to _____ .
I must say I prefer living _____ .
I haven't got a car. I prefer to _____ or _____ .

4 Work in pairs. Can you remember the reasons for the speakers' preferences? Compare your ideas. Then check in the audioscript on page 185.

5 Pronunciation rising and falling intonation

a ▶ 59 Listen to this question. Notice how the intonation rises then falls.

Would you rather live in a town or a village?

b ▶ 60 Listen and repeat the questions.
1 Do you prefer playing football or basketball?
2 Would you rather have tea or coffee?
3 Do you prefer summer or winter?
4 Would you rather go by car or by bike?
5 Do you prefer maths or science?
6 Would you rather eat fish or meat?

c Work in pairs. Add at least six more pairs of items to the list in Exercise 5b. Take turns to ask and answer about your preferences.

6 Work in groups of three. Where would you rather live? Ask and answer questions using these ideas. Explain your reasons. Do you think your preferences will change in the future?
1 In a new house or an old one?
2 In a city or in a village?
3 In a town centre or in the suburbs?
4 At the coast or in the mountains?
5 In a historic area or a new development?

my life ▶ PLACES ▶ ADVICE ▶ A TOURIST DESTINATION ▶ CHOICES ▶ A DESCRIPTION OF A PLACE

writing a description of a place • writing skill organizing ideas • word focus *as* and *like*   Unit 7 Living space

7e A great place

Writing a description of a place

1 Read the text. Where do you think it's from? Choose one of the options (a–c).

    a   a personal blog
    b   an estate agent's website
    c   a tourist information website

2 How does the writer describe these things?

> streets and buildings   shops   facilities
> local residents   atmosphere

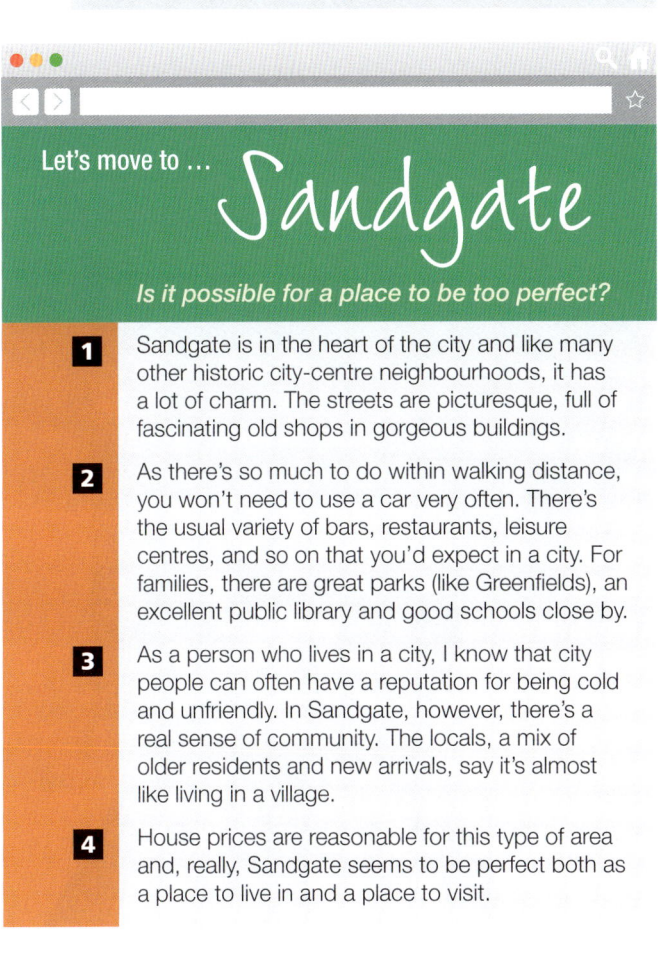

Let's move to … Sandgate
Is it possible for a place to be too perfect?

1 Sandgate is in the heart of the city and like many other historic city-centre neighbourhoods, it has a lot of charm. The streets are picturesque, full of fascinating old shops in gorgeous buildings.

2 As there's so much to do within walking distance, you won't need to use a car very often. There's the usual variety of bars, restaurants, leisure centres, and so on that you'd expect in a city. For families, there are great parks (like Greenfields), an excellent public library and good schools close by.

3 As a person who lives in a city, I know that city people can often have a reputation for being cold and unfriendly. In Sandgate, however, there's a real sense of community. The locals, a mix of older residents and new arrivals, say it's almost like living in a village.

4 House prices are reasonable for this type of area and, really, Sandgate seems to be perfect both as a place to live in and a place to visit.

3 Writing skill organizing ideas

a Read the text again. Write the number of the paragraph (1–4) next to the heading. There is one extra heading.

    a   What kind of place is Sandgate?
    b   What are the bad points?
    c   Overall opinion?
    d   What kind of people live there?
    e   What can you do there?

b Where is the best place in the text to include a paragraph with the extra heading from Exercise 3a?

Word focus *as* and *like*

4 Look at these two extracts from the text. Choose the correct option. Then find two more examples of *as* and *like* which have these meanings.

    1   … and like many other historic city-centre neighbourhoods, it has …
       It is similar to / It is many historic city-centre neighbourhoods.

    2   As a person who lives in a city, I know …
       I am similar to / I am a person who lives in a city.

5 Find two other examples of *as* and *like* in the text. Match the examples with these meanings.

    1   because
    2   for example

6 Complete the sentences with *as* and *like*.

    1   _____ a life-long resident of my town, I take pride in our community.
    2   I love modern shopping malls _____ this.
    3   It's ideal _____ a holiday destination.
    4   Our public library is _____ a palace.
    5   _____ all good cafés, the one in my village has a great atmosphere.
    6   The old buildings, _____ the town hall, are beautiful.

7 You are going to write a description of your own neighbourhood. Make notes using the headings in Exercise 3a. Use these words or your own ideas.

> a bit limited   a good range   close to …
> easy access to …   elegant   excellent   modern
> unfriendly   welcoming

8 Decide on the order of the paragraphs in your description. Then write about 150–200 words.

9 Use these questions to check your description.

    •   Are your ideas clearly organized into paragraphs?
    •   If you've included *as* or *like*, have you used them correctly?
    •   Does your description give the reader a clear picture of your neighbourhood?

10 Read a description a classmate has written about their neighbourhood. Would you like to move there or not? Give your reasons.

my life   ▶ PLACES   ▶ ADVICE   ▶ A TOURIST DESTINATION   ▶ CHOICES
               ▶ A DESCRIPTION OF A PLACE

7f The town with no wi-fi

Two satellite dishes in the USA

Unit 7 Living space

Before you watch

1 You're going to watch a video about a town in the USA that has no wi-fi or mobile phones. What would be the main change in your life if you didn't have wi-fi? Would it be good or bad?

2 The speakers in the video use American English. Match the American English terms with similar British English terms.

American English	British English
cell/cellular phone	city centre
Congress	Parliament
downtown	mobile phone
gasoline	petrol
store	shop

3 Key vocabulary

a Read the sentences. The words in bold are used in the video. Guess the meaning of the words.

1 Jack built his house to his own design – it's certainly **unique**!
2 I'd love to have a **telescope** to see the stars at night.
3 I can't call you from the beach because there's no phone **signal**.
4 The heavy traffic badly affects the city's **atmosphere**.
5 I've looked all over the house for the **cordless** phone, but I can't find it.

b Match the words in bold in Exercise 3a with these definitions.

a a piece of equipment that makes distant things seem closer
b radio waves which are sent or received
c special and different from any others
d the air in a certain place or area
e without a cable or wire attached to it

While you watch

4 ▶ 7.1 Watch the video. Complete the sentences with the names of the people you see.

Artie Barkley	Joyce Nelson
Karen O'Neil	Michael Holstine

1 .... and .... are residents of the quiet zone (QZ) in Green Bank, West Virginia.
2 .... works as the Business Manager of the National Radio Astronomy Observatory (NRAO) in Green Bank.
3 .... is the Site Director of the National Radio Astronomy Observatory (NRAO) in Green Bank.

5 Work in pairs. Discuss the questions.
1 What does *quiet zone* mean exactly?
2 What does the NRAO do in Green Bank?

6 ▶ 7.1 Watch the first part of the video (0.00–0.59) again. Check your ideas from Exercise 4. What do the people say?

1 Artie Barkley says he just listens to ....
2 Michael Holstine says that to .... the radio atmosphere, Congress created the National Radio Quiet zone.
3 Karen O'Neil says if you have a radio .... in an area of lots of radio noise, the signal you're looking for is destroyed.

7 ▶ 7.1 Watch the second part of the video (1.00 to the end) again. Answer the questions.

1 Which ONE of these modern conveniences is it OK to use in Green Bank?

gasoline engines	cellular phones
diesel engines	automatic door
wi-fi modems	openers
cordless phones	digital cameras

2 Why would it be difficult to create a new radio quiet zone?

After you watch

8 Vocabulary in context

a ▶ 7.2 Watch the clips from the video. Choose the correct meaning of the words and phrases.

b Answer the questions in your own words. Then work in pairs and compare your answers.

1 How many world-class sportspeople can you name?
2 Have you ever met anyone who is just like someone you know?
3 What's life like in your community?

9 Work in pairs. Discuss the questions.
1 Do the residents of Green Bank seem happy to live there? Give your reasons.
2 How would you feel about living in a quiet zone like Green Bank?

diesel (n) /ˈdiːzəl/ a type of fuel used in lorries and some cars
Milky Way (n) /ˌmɪlki ˈweɪ/ the galaxy that contains our solar system
modern conveniences (n) /ˌmɒdən kənˈviːniənsəz/ objects that make our lives much easier
obliterated (adj) /əˈblɪtəreɪtəd/ completely destroyed or removed
optical (adj) /ˈɒptɪkəl/ visual

UNIT 7 REVIEW AND MEMORY BOOSTER

Grammar

1 Look at the photo of rooftop golf. Then complete the text. Use comparative forms and patterns of adjectives and adverbs. Use the past simple and *used to* form of the verbs.

I've never heard of rooftop golf before. I suppose that as cities get ¹_____ (big / big), people live a long way from golf courses. When I was a kid I ²_____ (live) in a block of flats with a basement car park. During the day, the car park ³_____ (be) almost empty, so we ⁴_____ (play) football there. Obviously, we played ⁵_____ (well) on a real field and we couldn't kick the ball ⁶_____ (as / hard / as) when we played outside, but we ⁷_____ (not mind). Having the basement meant we could play ⁸_____ (often). These days in cities, gyms seem to be ⁹_____ (more / more / popular). I suppose people spend a lot of time sitting at desks or in cars. And ¹⁰_____ (less / active) they are, ¹¹_____ (healthy) they feel. Gyms have taken the place of open spaces in a lot of cities.

2 Answer the questions about the text in Exercise 1.

1 What are the advantages and disadvantages of playing football in the car park?
2 Why are gyms popular in cities?

3 Write comments about the photo with a comparative form or pattern of the adverb or adjective. Then compare your sentences with your partner.

1 hit the ball / on a normal golf course (carefully)
2 get / to the edge (close)
3 practise / want to (often)
4 play / up there (well)
5 reach the target / each day (accurately)
6 hit the ball / go (harder / further)

I CAN
talk about past states and past habits (*used to*, *would*)
compare things and describe a process of change (comparative adverbs, comparative patterns with adverbs and adjectives)

Vocabulary

4 Which is the odd one out in each group? Why?

1 bricks, igloo, wood
2 run-down, skyscrapers, traffic
3 flat, house, neighbourhood
4 built-up, polluted, residents
5 garden, town, village

5 ▶▶ MB You are an estate agent with an important house to sell – your own. Make notes on your home and the area that it's in. Decide on a price. Then try to sell your home to one of your classmates.

I CAN
talk about cities
talk about places to live

Real life

6 Choose the correct option. Then match the two parts of the exchanges.

1 A: *I'd rather / I prefer* to live on my own.
2 A: Where would you rather *go / to go*?
3 A: *I'd rather / I prefer* the country to the coast.
4 A: I prefer *living / live* near my family.
5 A: *I'd rather / I prefer* visit a few more places first.
6 A: *I'd rather / I'd prefer* a bigger kitchen.

a B: What's wrong with this flat?
b B: Are you looking for a flat-share?
c B: I can show you a fantastic beach house.
d B: This flat is nice. Are you going to take it?
e B: I don't fancy looking around the city centre.
f B: Are you going to live near your work?

7 ▶▶ MB Work in groups. Ask and answer questions about your preferences. Give reasons for your answers.

fruit or cake	rice or pasta
jazz or pop	snow or sun
mornings or evenings	spring or autumn

I CAN
ask about preferences
state preferences and give reasons

92

Unit 8 Travel

Tourists take photos of an emperor penguin on the frozen Amundsen Sea in Antarctica.

FEATURES

94 Holidays and memories

Writers return to their roots

96 Walking for wildlife

Mike Fay: a personal approach to saving wild places

98 All aboard!

A report on global tourism

102 Questions and answers

A video about National Geographic Explorers' lives

1 Work in pairs. Look at the photo. Discuss the questions.

   1 What kind of holiday do you think this is? Why?
   2 Do you think the people do this kind of trip often? Why? / Why not?
   3 Would you like to take a trip like this?

2 ▶ 61 Listen to three people talking about travel. Write the number of the speaker (1–3) next to the things they talk about.

being on planes	planning
business trips	a round-the-world trip
day trips	taking local buses and trains
delays	travelling for work
luggage	weekends away

3 ▶ 61 Listen again. Each speaker shares a travel tip. What are their tips? Discuss the tips with your partner.

4 Which countries or cities have you been to? Find people in your class who have had similar experiences to you.

   A: Have you been to Vietnam?
   B: Yes, we had a holiday there last year.
   A: Me too! Where did you go?

my life ▶ HOLIDAY COMPANIONS ▶ FAVOURITE ACTIVITIES ▶ GOING GREEN ▶ TRAVEL PROBLEMS ▶ A TEXT MESSAGE

vocabulary holiday activities • reading writers return to their roots •
grammar verb patterns: -ing form and to + infinitive • listening and speaking holiday companions

8a Holidays and memories

Vocabulary holiday activities

1 Work in pairs. Why did you choose the destination of your most recent holiday? Tell your partner.

> saw the place on TV
> followed a friend's recommendation
> wanted to visit somewhere new
> wanted to return to a place I know
> went to visit family/friends

2 Work in pairs. Match the activities (1–6) with the examples (a–f). What do you enjoy doing when you go on holiday? Give your own examples.

1 taking it easy
2 going sightseeing
3 having new experiences
4 being active
5 learning new things
6 spending time with friends or family

a hiking in the mountains
b lying on the beach
c playing board games
d riding on a camel
e taking a painting course
f visiting famous monuments

Reading

3 Look at the photo with the article. Which of these things (a–c) do you think it shows?

a a coastline
b a market
c a village

4 Read the article and answer the questions.

1 Where are the writers from and what are their destinations?
2 Which writers haven't been to these places before?
3 Which writer has problems with the language?
4 Which writer travels with his/her parents?
5 Which writer has to change his/her plans? Why?

5 Which activities in Exercise 2 did the three writers do?

Holidays and memories

Three writers return to the lands their families came from

▶ 62

1 Lucy Chang
I step off the train in Taipei and follow the crowd into Shilin, one of the city's most famous night markets. Brightly-lit red, white and yellow signs are swinging above the market stalls. I'm not very good at reading Chinese characters, in spite of being from Taiwan originally. Stall holders call out to me. It's my first visit here and I'm too embarrassed to speak. Back home in London, I learned to say a few words, but right now my mind is blank. It's not a good start to my trip.

2 Liz Mullan
Arriving at Belfast International Airport is always emotional. It feels like home. We head north to some of Europe's highest ocean cliffs. After a couple of hours, we're standing on the Giant's Causeway. The wind almost blows us off the rocks into the North Atlantic Ocean. I look west towards home and imagine sailing across this wild ocean to Canada, like my great-grandfather did in 1890. We planned to walk along the coast like last time, but it's raining hard so we decide to find a café and hot food. Maybe tomorrow will bring the sun.

3 Frank Rossellini
When I was a child, my parents always promised to take me to Sicily one day. Finally, when they are both in their eighties, we have managed to get here. In this tiny village, we sit down to a dinner with lots of aunts, uncles and cousins. Eating together is still the most important part of the day here. After enormous plates of sausage, pasta, salads and homemade bread, everyone enjoys telling us stories of the friends and family members who left for New York decades earlier. It feels great to be here and I think about coming back again in the future.

Grammar verb patterns: *-ing* form and *to* + infinitive

> **VERB PATTERNS: *-ING* FORM and *TO* + INFINITIVE**
>
> **-ing form**
> I imagine **sailing** across this wild ocean to Canada.
> **Eating** together is important.
> I'm not very good at **reading** Chinese characters.
>
> **to + infinitive**
> My parents always promised **to take** me to Sicily.
> I'm too embarrassed **to speak**.
>
> For further information and practice, see page 170.

6 Look at the grammar box. Choose the correct option to complete these sentences. Then find an example of each use in the article.

1. We use the *-ing* form of the verb after certain verbs, as the subject of a sentence and after *adjectives / prepositions*.
2. We use *to* + infinitive form of the verb after certain verbs and after *adjectives / prepositions*.

7 Each option in these sentences is grammatically possible but one option isn't true, according to the article. Which one?

1. Lucy Chang *described / finished / mentioned* going to the market.
2. Lucy Chang *needs / manages / wants* to speak Chinese.
3. Liz Mullan *adores / avoids / loves* going to Ireland.
4. Liz Mullan *expected / intended / threatened* to walk along the coast.
5. Frank Rossellini's parents *planned / refused / wanted* to travel to Sicily.
6. Frank Rossellini *fails / hopes / intends* to return to the village.

8 Choose the correct option to complete the sentences. Then work in pairs. Tell your partner which sentences you agree with.

1. *Travelling / To travel* by train is usually pleasant.
2. Good hotels are easy *finding / to find*.
3. *Cycling / To cycle* can be a good way of seeing a new city.
4. *Sleeping / To sleep* on a plane can be difficult.
5. Some hotels are too expensive *staying / to stay* in.
6. I'm interested in *trying / to try* new things on holiday.
7. *Going / To go* on holiday with friends is always fun.
8. I get fed up with *spending / to spend* every day on the beach.

9 ▶ 63 Complete the conversation about with the *-ing* form and *to* + infinitive form of the verbs. Then listen and check.

Rose: Hi there, I'm Rose.
Matt: Hi, I'm Matt.
Rose: Is this your first time in Corfu?
Matt: No, actually. We come every year. We love
¹ _____ (stay) here.
Rose: So do we. We keep ² _____ (come) back year after year. It's hard ³ _____ (find) somewhere with everything you need for a holiday – great beaches, fantastic weather and something for everyone to do.
Matt: I know. Actually, there's a paragliding class later – I fancy ⁴ _____ (try) that.
Rose: My friends want ⁵ _____ (do) that too! To be honest, ⁶ _____ (lie) by the pool is my idea of a holiday.
Matt: Oh, I get a bit bored with ⁷ _____ (do) that after the first day or two. I need ⁸ _____ (move) around and do things.
Rose: Well, why not? It's a different way of
⁹ _____ (relax), I suppose.
Matt: Yes, that's right. Well, if you decide
¹⁰ _____ (go) paragliding with your friends, we'll see you there!

Listening and speaking — my life

10 ▶ 64 Listen to people talking about holidays and complete the sentences. Do you think they would be good holiday companions for you? Which person would you prefer to go on holiday with?

1. I enjoy … .
2. I quite fancy … .
3. I don't mind … .
4. I'd like … .
5. I can't afford … .
6. I'm quite keen on … .
7. I don't like … .
8. I'm interested in … .
9. I can't stand … .
10. I'm happy … .

11 Think about how you would complete the sentences in Exercise 10. Then talk to people in your class and find someone who would make a good holiday companion.

12 Work with your holiday companion and decide what kind of holiday to have. Tell the class:

- where and when you would go
- how you'd get there
- where you'd stay
- what you'd do there and why

listening a wildlife conservationist • **grammar** present perfect simple and continuous • **grammar** *How long ... ?* • **speaking** favourite activities

8b Walking for wildlife

Mike Fay, *a conservationist whose work makes a difference*

- **trekked** 10,000 kilometres in Africa and North America
- **counted** giant redwood trees in North America, elephant populations in central Africa
- **created** 13 national parks in Gabon
- **protected** thousands of elephants from poachers
- **survived** a malaria attack, an elephant attack, a plane crash
- **flown** over the African continent for an aerial survey
- **uploaded** thousands of photos to Google Earth
- **helped** to create a marine park off the Gabon coast

poacher (n) /ˈpəʊtʃə/ someone who catches and kills animals illegally
survey (n) /ˈsɜːveɪ/ the measuring and recording of the details of an area of land
trek (v) /trek/ make a long and difficult journey

Listening

1 What kind of work does a conservationist do? What is their main aim?

2 Look at the information about Mike Fay. Do you think he's a typical conservationist? Why? / Why not?

probably not, because he's trekked 10,000 kilometres and has had some dangerous/exciting experiences

3 ▶ 65 Listen to an extract from a radio programme about Mike Fay. Complete the sentences.
 1 Mike Fay's work is about saving the last _____ on Earth.
 2 He's spent a total of more than _____ years of his life on treks.
 3 His usual luggage is a T-shirt, a pair of shorts and a _____ .
 4 He's walked in Africa, the United States and _____ .
 5 He's worried about how _____ people will affect the planet.

4 ▶ 65 Listen to the extract again and choose the correct option to complete the sentences.
 1 Recently, Fay has been *flying / walking* across Canada.
 2 Mining companies have been *looking for / producing* gold and oil.
 3 Mining companies have been *digging up / destroying* vast areas.
 4 In Gabon, people have been *asking / trying* to set up mines near parks.

5 Work in pairs. Would you like to spend a year working with Mike Fay? Why? / Why not?

Grammar present perfect simple and continuous

▶ **PRESENT PERFECT SIMPLE and CONTINUOUS**

Present perfect simple
When you**'ve walked** across half of Africa and you**'ve walked** up the west coast of North America, where do you go next?
They**'ve destroyed** hundreds of square kilometres of wilderness.

Present perfect continuous
Recently he**'s been walking** again, this time across Canada.
He **hasn't been taking** it easy!
What **has he been doing** since then?
Stative verbs like *be, have, know, like* are not usually used in the continuous form.

For further information and practice, see page 170.

6 Look at the grammar box. Answer the questions.

1 How do we form the present perfect simple? How do we form the present perfect continuous?
2 Which verb form emphasizes the duration or repetition of an activity? Which verb form emphasizes an action or an activity that is complete?

7 Complete the text with the present perfect simple and present perfect continuous form of the verbs.

This year, Mike Fay ¹ _____ (work) in Gabon. He ² _____ (check) the situation in the national parks and he ³ _____ (discover) some problems. For example, poachers ⁴ _____ (kill) elephants again. Fay ⁵ _____ (talk) about ways of controlling poaching with the Gabonese government. As a result, the Gabonese president ⁶ _____ (send) soldiers to several of the parks. So far, the poachers ⁷ _____ (not / return). Meanwhile, for the past few years, foreign ships ⁸ _____ (fish) in the marine park. The Gabonese government ⁹ _____ (try) to find ways of dealing with this problem.

8 Write questions for Mike Fay with the present perfect simple and present perfect continuous form of the verbs.

1 What / you / do / recently?
2 you / prepare for / any new trips?
3 How / you / feel / since the plane crash?
4 How many photos / you / take / in your career?
5 How long / you / travel / alone?
6 you / be / anywhere dangerous lately?

9 Match the travel preparation activities (1–6) with the results (a–f). Then write two sentences.

I've been buying holiday clothes. I've spent a fortune.

1 buy holiday clothes
2 look for cheap flights
3 talk to travel agents
4 download tourist information
5 pack my suitcase
6 practise useful phrases in Thai

a be on the phone all morning
b spend a fortune
c run out of space
d not learn many
e print a couple of pages
f not find any

Grammar How long ... ?

▶ **HOW LONG ... ?**

How long have you had this camera?
How long have you been travelling alone?
How long did it take you to get there?

For further information and practice, see page 170.

10 Look at the grammar box. Which verb form is used in each question? Why?

11 Match the questions (1–6) with the answers (a–e). Then work in pairs and continue the conversations.

1 How long have you been coming to this resort?
2 How long did the flight from London take?
3 How long have you known each other?
4 How long did you spend in Canada?
5 How long have you been waiting for the bus?
6 How long have you been here?

a About ten hours non-stop.
b For the last four or five years.
c I was there for a couple of months.
d Not long – we met on holiday this spring.
e Only a few minutes. But I think we just missed one.
f We arrived yesterday morning.

A: *How long have you been coming to this resort?*
B: *For the last four or five years.*
A: *Has it changed a lot in that time?*

Speaking my life

12 What kinds of activities are you interested in? How long have you been doing them? Work in pairs and tell your partner. Ask follow-up questions. Use some of these ideas.

*I've been ... since/for ...
I took it up when ...
I've always/never ...
In the last few ... , I've ...*

reading **tourism** • critical thinking **close reading** • speaking **going green**

8c All aboard!

Reading

1 Work in pairs. Discuss the questions.

1. Do many tourists come to your country or region? From which countries?
2. What do these tourists do? Activity holidays, backpacking, cultural sightseeing, ecotourism, or other holiday activities?
3. What are the advantages of this tourism? Are there any disadvantages?

2 Read the article quickly. What is it about? Choose the best option (a–c).

a It describes extreme activities tourists can do.
b It compares the positive and negative effects of tourism.
c It talks about the impact of lots of tourists on a destination.

3 Read the article again and complete the table.

Destination	Number of tourists	Impact
1	2 .... on a cruise ship	Falling numbers of 3 ....
Himalayas: 4	5 .... in the climbing season	6 .... each year left on the mountain
7	8	Negative effects on 9 ....

4 Answer the questions with information from the article.

1. When did the tourism industry start to be successful?
2. Why are cruises bad for the environment? Find three reasons.
3. What have groups been doing to improve the environment on Everest?
4. What action has the government of the Balearic Islands taken, and why?

5 Find these words in the article. Look at how the words are used and try to guess their meaning. Then complete the sentences (1–6).

pollution (line 11)   charge (line 37)
equipment (line 24)   challenges (line 39)
rubbish (line 26)   ecotourism (line 45)

1. Airlines usually .... you a lot of money if your luggage is over the weight limit.
2. On average, each person in the UK produces about 500 kg of .... each year.
3. I don't have much kitchen .... – just a microwave.
4. Speaking a new language can be one of the hardest .... when you travel abroad.
5. .... is a way of enjoying a holiday without damaging the environment.
6. Plastic is a major cause of .... in the oceans.

Critical thinking close reading

6 According to the article, are these statements true (T) or false (F)? Or is there not enough information (N) in the article to say if the statements are true or false?

1. The tourism industry has grown steadily and has now reached its peak.
2. There are fewer Magellanic penguins since cruises started visiting Patagonia.
3. Climbers on Everest cause problems for the local population.
4. There's not enough fresh water in the Balearic Islands in the holiday season.
5. It's better to stay at home than be an ecotourist.

7 Work in pairs. Underline the sections of the article that helped you decide about the sentences in Exercise 7. Do you agree with each other?

8 Work as a class. Discuss the questions.

1. Do you think an eco-tax on tourists is a good idea?
2. What is your answer to the final question in the article?

Speaking my life

9 Work in pairs. Look at these activities. Decide if they have a good or bad impact on the environment. Which ones does your family do?

1. flying to distant holiday destinations
2. recycling household waste (paper, glass, organic waste)
3. travelling by car
4. switching off lights and electrical appliances
5. saving water (turning off taps, not watering the garden)
6. using eco-friendly cleaning products

10 Work in groups. How easy is it for you and your family to live a green lifestyle?

A: We've been recycling paper for years. It's not hard to remember to do if you have a special box for it.
B: We do that too.

Unit 8 Travel

All ABOARD!

A plane comes in to land on the Caribbean island of Saint Martin.

▶ 66

The tourism industry started to grow rapidly in the middle of the last century and it's been growing ever since. In the last twenty years especially, more and more people have been travelling to distant places around the world. It's a wonderful thing, to be able to travel to destinations we had previously only read about or seen on television. But what kind of impact do large numbers of people have on these places?

A voyage to the end of the Earth?

A large cruise ship can carry as many as six thousand passengers at a time, with about twenty-four million people going on cruises every year. Cruise ships drop about ninety thousand tons of waste into the oceans every year and each ship produces as much air pollution as five million cars. The effects of this are made even worse by the fact that cruises visit the same places over and over again, so the damage is repeated. In Patagonia, this has been having an effect on wildlife. The numbers of Magellanic penguins have been falling for some years now, for example.

Climbing to the top of the world

Far fewer people go climbing or trekking in the Himalayas than take a cruise, but in the short climbing season each May about a thousand people try to climb Everest. At times, there are actually queues of climbers on the route to the top. The difficult conditions mean that everyone needs to take a lot of equipment with them. Unfortunately, for the last few decades, climbers have been leaving their equipment on Everest. In recent years, clean-up teams have been organizing expeditions just to pick up this rubbish. The teams are made up of local and international climbers. One group has brought over eight tons of rubbish down from the mountain!

Let's all go to the beach

What happens when a region of about a million people is visited by thirteen million tourists every year? The Balearic Islands in the Mediterranean Sea have been dealing with this situation for decades. Where has the fresh water, the food, the petrol and the electricity for thirteen million tourists come from? And how have the islands maintained the quality of the beaches, the roads and the countryside? Recently, the government of the Balearic Islands decided to charge tourists an ecotax of two euros a day. This has been tried once before, but it wasn't a success. However, the challenges have been getting harder every year. The money from the tax is used to reduce the negative effects of tourism on the local environment.

Difficult choices

So, should we travel or simply stay at home? Many destinations offer low-impact tourism such as ecotourism. It's time to ask ourselves some difficult questions. Can we really visit the world's beautiful places without destroying them?

waste (n) /weɪst/ rubbish

my life ▶ HOLIDAY COMPANIONS ▶ FAVOURITE ACTIVITIES ▶ GOING GREEN ▶ TRAVEL PROBLEMS
▶ A TEXT MESSAGE

99

vocabulary travel problems • real life dealing with problems • pronunciation strong and weak forms

8d Is something wrong?

Vocabulary travel problems

1 Work in pairs. Have you ever had any travel problems involving these things? Tell your partner. Which of these problems can a tour guide help you with?

baggage allowances	hotel rooms
boarding cards	passport control
car hire	train timetables
customs checks	travel documents
flight delays	travel sickness
food poisoning	

▶ **WORDBUILDING compound nouns (noun + noun)**
We can use two nouns together to mean one thing.
baggage allowance, car hire

For further practice, see Workbook page 67.

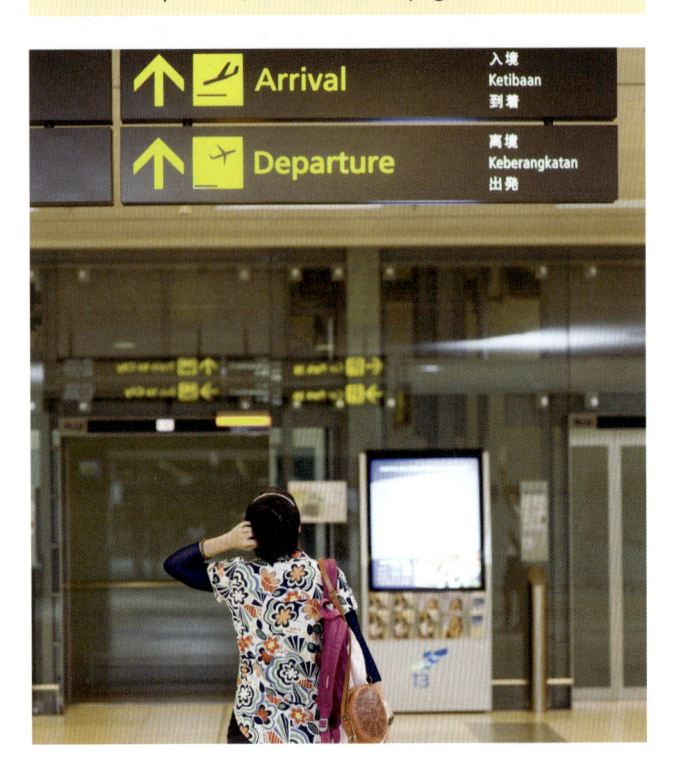

Real life dealing with problems

2 ▶ 67 Listen to two conversations between a tour guide and tourists. Write the number of the conversation (1–2) next to the problem they talk about.

a The person has missed his/her flight home.
b Someone has had an accident.
c The luggage hasn't arrived.
d The flight has been delayed.
e The person has lost his/her plane tickets.
f Someone is ill.

3 ▶ 67 Look at the expressions for dealing with problems. Can you remember who said what? Write G (guide) or T (tourist) next to the expressions. Then listen to the conversations again and check.

▶ **DEALING WITH PROBLEMS**

I wonder if you could help us?
Is anything wrong?
Can I help?

Our luggage hasn't arrived.
Which flight were you on?
How did that happen?
Do you know where our bags have gone to?
When's the next flight?
It's about my wife.
How long has she been feeling like this?
Is there anything you can do?

I'm afraid the luggage has gone to Rome.
Don't worry, we'll arrange everything.
I'll ask the hotel to send for a doctor.

4 Work as a class. Are the problems solved? How?

5 Pronunciation strong and weak forms

a ▶ 68 Look at the position of *to* in these sentences. Listen to the sentences. In which sentence is *to* strong /tuː/? In which one is it weak /tə/?

1 Do you know which airport our bags have gone to?
2 Yes, I'm afraid the luggage has gone to Rome.

b ▶ 69 Listen and repeat these questions. Use strong or weak forms of *at*, *from* and *for*. Then work in pairs. Ask the questions and give your own answers.

1 Which hotel are you staying at?
2 Are you staying at the Ocean Hotel?
3 Where have you travelled from?
4 Why haven't we heard from the airline?
5 What have we been waiting for?
6 Are you waiting for the manager?

6 Work in pairs. Choose one of the conversations from Exercise 2. Take a role each. Look at the audioscript on page 186 and prepare your role. Then close your books and practise the conversation.

7 Take the roles of a tourist and a tour guide. Choose from the problems in Exercise 2 and act out two conversations. Use the expressions for dealing with problems to help you.

my life ▶ HOLIDAY COMPANIONS ▶ FAVOURITE ACTIVITIES ▶ GOING GREEN ▶ **TRAVEL PROBLEMS** ▶ A TEXT MESSAGE writing a text message • writing skill informal style

Unit 8 Travel

8e Hello from London!

Writing a text message

1 Read the message from Lynne. Answer the questions.

1 Where has Lynne come from and where is she now?
2 Who do you think the message is for? Friends, family, or both?
3 What does Lynne say about the people and the city?
4 What has she been doing?

> Hi everyone!
> Finally made it to London after 18-hour delay in Bangkok!!! 😢 Weather here awful but people fantastic. London massive compared to Brisbane! So far have: been shopping in Oxford Street, seen the Shard (wow!), done the Harry Potter tour (awesome!), had a boat trip along the river. Then slept all day & night cos jetlagged 😟. Text from my uncle in Edinburgh – he's found me a job there for summer! Spk soon L xx 😘

2 Writing skill informal style

a Read the message again. Which of these features of informal style does Lynne use?

abbreviations	informal expressions
comments in brackets	listing items
contractions	missing out words
exclamation marks	symbols

b Look at this extract from the message. The words *I* and *an* are missing. Mark their position in the complete sentence.

> Finally made it to London after 18-hour delay in Bangkok!!!

c Mark the places in the message where Lynne has missed out words. What are the words?

d Rewrite the sentences in full.

1 city massive & noisy!
2 not got theatre tickets cos fully booked
3 been visiting Tower of London – scary!
4 took selfies (lots) on Oxford St
5 can't understand London accent (trying!)
6 text from Jo – arriving Sunday

e Rewrite the sentences. Miss out words where possible.

1 The weather is wet and it has been very cold sometimes.
2 I've been touring all the typical places – it's exhausting!
3 The people here are very kind and they have helped me a lot.
4 I took some photos of some pigeons – they're everywhere!
5 I haven't heard anything from Anton yet.
6 I'm getting a bus up to Edinburgh because flying is too expensive.

3 Choose a place you have visited or would like to visit. Make notes. Use the questions in Exercise 1 as a guide.

4 Decide who to write to. Write a message of about 75 words describing your trip. Use some of the features of informal style from Exercise 2a and miss out words which are not necessary.

5 Send your message to someone in your class. Then read the message you have received. Use these questions to check your classmate's message.

- Is everything clearly expressed?
- Are there any sections you do not understand?

6 Work in pairs. Tell your partner about the message you have received.

A: *I got a message from Daisuke the other day.*
B: *Oh! How's he getting on?*

my life ▸ HOLIDAY COMPANIONS ▸ FAVOURITE ACTIVITIES ▸ GOING GREEN ▸ TRAVEL PROBLEMS
▸ A TEXT MESSAGE

8f Questions and answers

Cory Richards on the Cordillera Blanca in Peru

Before you watch

1 You're going to watch two videos in which National Geographic Explorers give their personal answers to questions. Before you watch, discuss these questions.

1. What kind of work do explorers do? Where do they work?
2. What items might they need to take with them when they're exploring?
3. Why do you think people become explorers?

2 Key vocabulary

a Read the sentences. The words in bold are used in the video. Guess the meaning of the words.

1. If you want to watch animals in the wild, a pair of **binoculars** is very useful.
2. I'd get really burned if I didn't use **sunblock**.
3. I'm not very good with a **paintbrush** – I prefer doing pencil drawings.
4. All children are **curious** about the world around them.
5. I've been making good **progress** in Italian since I started classes.

b Match the words in bold in Exercise 2a with these definitions.

a a tool to paint with
b cream that protects your skin from the sun
c equipment with lenses for looking at things far away
d improvement and development
e interested in something and wanting to learn about it

While you watch

Video 1: What item would you not leave home without?

3 Read what four of the explorers say about why they chose the items they take with them. What do you think they are talking about?

1. Carlton Ward, photographer
'without a _____, we'd still be paddling in circles somewhere'
2. Amy Dickman, zoologist
'_____, just to have a break at the end of the day'
3. Chris Thornton, archaeologist
'_____. I'm very, very white.'
4. Cory Richards, photographer
'a _____ to record what I'm experiencing'

4 ▶ 8.1 Watch the video. Check your ideas from Exercise 3.

5 ▶ 8.1 Watch the video again. Tick the items the explorers mention.

binoculars   camera   DVDs
family photographs   GPS   hat   headlamp
knife   local person   paintbrush   pencil
sunblock   sunglasses

6 Work in pairs. Which of the items in Exercise 5 surprised you? Did the explorers mention any of the items you discussed in Exercise 1 question 2?

Video 2: Why is it important to explore?

7 ▶ 8.2 Read what the explorers in the video say. What do you think the missing word is? Then watch the video and check your ideas.

1. John Francis, ecologist
'If you have _____ and you don't pursue them, then to me it's a life unlived.'
2. Laly Lichtenfeld, big cat conservationist
'It keeps _____ exciting, I mean that's what exploring is about.'
3. Enric Sala, marine ecologist
'Without exploration, there would be no _____.'
4. Lee Berger, paleoanthropologist
'We think we _____ how things work, but we don't.'

8 ▶ 8.2 Watch the video again. Who gave the most interesting answer, in your opinion?

After you watch

9 Vocabulary in context

a ▶ 8.3 Watch the clips from the videos. Choose the correct meaning of the words and phrases.

b Answer the questions in your own words. Then work in pairs and compare your answers.

1. Does the power ever go out where you live? What do you do when that happens?
2. Do you think it's human nature to be curious? What else is human nature?
3. What kind of thing do you think drives artists and business people?

10 Work in pairs. Discuss the questions.

1. What would you not leave home without if you were travelling?
2. Why is it a good idea to travel?

---

engage (v) /ɪnˈɡeɪdʒ/ to keep your interest or hold your attention
fundamentally (adv) /ˌfʌndəˈmentəli/ basically, most importantly
paddle (v) /ˈpædəl/ to move a boat with an oar
pursue (v) /pəˈsjuː/ to follow or work at

UNIT 8 REVIEW AND MEMORY BOOSTER

Grammar

1 Complete the article about Thomas Cook with the correct verb tense or form. Use the following: past simple, present perfect simple, present perfect continuous, -ing form or infinitive with *to*.

Before 1872, people ¹ _____ (not / travel) for pleasure very much. Then a man called Thomas Cook ² _____ (change) everything when he ³ _____ (form) a travel agency, Thomas Cook & Son. Cook aimed ⁴ _____ (provide) educational and cultural tours. His son was successful in ⁵ _____ (expand) the business around the world. At first, foreign travel was expensive, but incomes ⁶ _____ (rise) since those days. Nowadays, many millions of ordinary people expect ⁷ _____ (go) on holiday at least once a year. In the twentieth century, holiday makers preferred ⁸ _____ (book) trips with travel agencies. For the last few years, travel agencies ⁹ _____ (struggle) because most people ¹⁰ _____ (make) their own plans online. Thomas Cook, however, is still one of the biggest travel companies in the world.

2 Answer the questions about the article in Exercise 1.

1 How has travel changed since the time of Thomas Cook?
2 Why do you think the travel agency *Thomas Cook & Son* was successful?

3 »MB Write four true or false sentences about yourself with these verbs. Work in pairs and say if your partner's sentences are true or false.

| have been learning | have seen |
| am interested in trying | want to go |

I CAN

use verb patterns correctly (*-ing* form and *to* + infinitive)

talk about recent activities and experiences (present prefect simple and continuous)

4 »MB Work in pairs. Have you ever been to places like these on holiday? Ask and answer questions about your experiences.

a beach resort	a safari
a cultural centre	a theme park
a natural park	a zoo

Vocabulary

5 Match nouns from A and B to make travel vocabulary. Then write questions with the expressions.

A		B	
baggage	flight	allowance	control
boarding	passport	card	delays
customs	travel	checks	sickness

6 »MB Work in pairs. Which of these activities would you do in a seaside resort, a big city, a natural park and a campsite? Give your reasons.

be active	learn new things
go sightseeing	spend time with friends
have new	or family
experiences	take it easy

I CAN

use travel vocabulary appropriately

talk about holiday activities

Real life

7 Read these sentences from a conversation at an airport. Put the sentences (a–h) in order (1–8).

a A: What? How has that happened?
b A: Well, let's have another look. Calm down.
c A: Well, have you looked through all your pockets?
d A: Is anything wrong?
e B: Yes, I have. And I've checked the suitcase.
f B: I've been worrying so much about everything, and now this!
g B: I think I've lost the boarding passes.
h B: I don't know. I thought they were in my pocket, but they aren't there now.

8 »MB Work in pairs. Act out conversations similar to Exercise 7.

Conversation 1: Student A is a tourist and Student B is a tour guide. Student A has lost his/her passport.

Conversation 2: Student A is an airline official and Student B is a customer. The flight is cancelled.

I CAN

talk about travel problems

ask for and give explanations

104

Unit 9 Shopping

Galleria Vittorio Emanuele, Milan, Italy

FEATURES

106 Shopping trends

How do you do your shopping?

108 Spend or save?

Do you buy on impulse?

110 The art of the deal

How to negotiate a price

114 Making a deal

A video about shopping in the oldest market in Morocco

1 Work in pairs. Look at the photo and the caption. Compare this place with places you usually go shopping.

2 ▶ 70 Listen to a market researcher interviewing some people who are shopping. Complete the table.

Interview	What?	Who for?
1	the latest	
2	a couple of	himself
3	some	each other

3 Discuss the questions with your partner.

books/DVDs/CDs
clothes
electronics/gadgets
jewellery

shoes
toiletries/cosmetics
other items

1 What's the best (or worst) present anyone has ever given you?
2 What kind of things do you and your family or friends buy for each other?
3 Do you buy these things for yourself?

4 Work in pairs. Prepare a survey on shopping habits. Ask at least three other people your questions. Then compare the results.

my life ▸ SHOPPING NOW AND IN THE FUTURE ▸ MY THINGS ▸ SOUVENIRS ▸ BUYING THINGS ▸ CUSTOMER FEEDBACK

reading two ways of going shopping • grammar passives • speaking shopping now and in the future

9a Shopping trends

Reading

1 Work in pairs. How do you prefer to do your shopping? Tell your partner and give reasons.

at markets (indoor or outdoor)
in department stores
in malls or shopping centres
in small local shops
online

2 Read what a farmer and a store manager say about selling their products. Answer the questions.
   1 What kind of products do they talk about?
   2 What kind of shopping do they talk about?
   3 Where do they sell their products?

3 Read the article again. Find one advantage to customers and one to sellers for each kind of shopping.

4 Work in pairs. Can you think of any disadvantages to each kind of shopping?

Shopping trends
in the UK

▶ 71

Gilly McGregor
Yorkshire farmer

'Farmers' markets are the traditional way of selling food, but they disappeared for a few years in the UK. Now they're coming back. I have a stall in the town centre four days a week. When I sell directly to the consumers, they pay less and I still get a good price. That's because the vegetables don't have to be packaged and I don't have to pay a wholesaler to distribute and sell my products. The customers are happy because the vegetables are fresher and better quality than in the supermarket, so they keep for longer. A lot of supermarket stuff has to be eaten within a couple of days.'

Mark Noble,
manager at LowCo Stores

'These days, lots of people have busy lives and we have found that online shopping is a growing area for us. It's especially popular with people who buy the same things in the same amounts every week. At first, online shopping was used mainly by our regular customers, but since we introduced our mobile phone app, more new accounts have been set up. Once the customer makes their online list, it can be used again and again or it can be changed very easily.

Food and household items are delivered to the customers' homes for a small charge, or people can collect them in the store. In that case, the order must be collected the next day. A new order tracking app is being developed at the moment, and with that we'll be able to improve our service to customers even more.'

wholesaler (n) /ˈhəʊlseɪlə/ a company that buys products in large quantities from the maker and sells them to different shops

Grammar passives

> **▶ PASSIVES**
>
> *At first, online shopping **was used** mainly **by our regular customers**.*
> *A new order tracking app **is being developed** at the moment*
> *A lot of supermarket stuff **has to be eaten** within a couple of days.*
>
> For further information and practice, see page 172.

5 Look at the grammar box. Find a simple passive, a modal passive and a continuous passive. Then answer the questions.

1. How do we form the passive? Think about the auxiliary verb and the form of the main verb.
2. What kind of information follows the word *by*?

6 Underline six more passive forms in the article *Shopping trends in the UK*. Does the use of the passive emphasize the action or the person who does the action?

7 Choose the correct options to complete the text about a company that sells coffee.

> We started direct trade about four years ago. This means that more of the final price ¹ *pays / is paid* to the growers. We have a simple system. First, the coffee beans ² *take / are taken* to a central collection point by each grower. When the loads ³ *have weighed / have been weighed*, the growers ⁴ *get / are got* the correct payment. At the moment, we ⁵ *are using / are being used* a standard shipping company to transport the coffee to Europe. But we ⁶ *are reviewing / are being reviewed* our arrangements and next year, probably, specialized firms ⁷ *will contract / will be contracted* to handle shipping. Once in Europe, the coffee ⁸ *can pack and sell / can be packed and sold* within a week.

8 Work in pairs. Write the passive form of the verbs.

1. Since its launch in 2003, 250 million *Nokia 1101 mobile phones / Apple iPods* _____ (sell).
2. With 400 shops around the world, clothing brand *Ralph Lauren / Mango* _____ (wear) by more people than any other.
3. The work of *J.K. Rowling / Agatha Christie* _____ (translate) into more languages than any other author.
4. In 1986, the film *The Color Purple / Out of Africa* _____ (nominated) for eleven Oscars but didn't win any.
5. *Solitaire / Tetris* _____ (adapt) for 65 different systems, making it the most successful computer game ever.
6. The first music video by *Justin Bieber / Lady Gaga* _____ (view) on YouTube over 500 million times.
7. Maps for the Xbox® game *Call of Duty / Grand Theft Auto* _____ (download) one million times in 24 hours when it went on sale.
8. A painting by *Picasso / Van Gogh* _____ (buy) at auction for $106 million in 2010.

9 ▶ 72 Underline the options you think are correct in Exercise 8. Then listen and check. How many answers did you get right?

Speaking my life

10 Work in pairs. Find out about shopping now and in the future.

Student A: Turn to page 153 and follow the instructions.

Student B: Turn to page 154 and follow the instructions.

11 Work in groups of four. You are the makers of a new bag for people of your own age group. Decide on the following details for your bag. Find images online or make your own.

- what it will be/look like
- where/how it will be made
- where/how it will be sold
- who it will be aimed at
- how much it will cost
- why people should buy it

12 Present your product to the class. Vote on the one you'd most like to buy.

vocabulary shopping (1) • listening impulse buying • grammar articles and quantifiers • pronunciation linking • speaking my things

9b Spend or save?

Vocabulary shopping (1)

1 Work in pairs. Have you ever bought anything on impulse? Tell your partner about it.

2 Match the beginnings of the sentences (1–8) with the endings (a–h). Check the meaning of any words in bold you are not sure about.

1 The **checkout** is where you go
2 When things are on **special offer**,
3 At some supermarkets they help you
4 Fridges, washing machines and TVs
5 You can often get good **deals**
6 Cheap and expensive items
7 It isn't a good idea to
8 A **budget** is a way of working out

a are electrical **goods**.
b buy things that you can't **afford**.
c can both be good **value for money**.
d how much money you can spend.
e on products **in the sales**.
f the price is lower.
g to pack your **purchases**.
h to pay for your shopping.

3 Work in pairs. Ask and answer questions with the words in bold in Exercise 2.

A: *How do you choose which **checkout** queue to join at the supermarket?*
B: *I usually look and see how much stuff people have in their trolleys.*

Listening

4 ▶ 73 Listen to an extract from a radio programme that discusses what's in the news. Tick the examples of impulse buying which are mentioned.

1 Buying loads of things when you only need bread or milk.
2 Buying things you can't afford to buy.
3 Buying things online.
4 Spending too much when you're hungry.

5 ▶ 73 Listen to the extract again. Correct factual errors in four of the sentences.

1 Samira has written articles on impulse buying.
2 Most of us have spent more than £500 on a purchase that wasn't necessary!
3 You never see special offers on TVs or tablets.
4 You should always have a budget when you need to buy expensive things.
5 Many women, but few men, use shopping as a way of managing their money.
6 If you make a list, you can avoid impulse buying.

6 Work in pairs. Think of three ways people can control their impulse buying.

108

Unit 9 Shopping

Grammar articles and quantifiers

▶ **ARTICLES**

1 They're based on a study by **the** BBC.
2 **The** study divided people into two groups – men and women.
3 … plan your shopping and you'll save **money**.
4 So I just need to make sure I have **a** snack before I go?

For further information and practice, see page 172.

7 Look at the words in bold in the grammar box. Which article (*a/an, the* or zero article) is used when:

a we mention something for the first time?
b we mention something which is known (because it has already been mentioned, for example)?
c there is only one of something?
d we are talking about something in general?

8 Read the ideas for saving money. Complete the sentences with the correct article (*a/an, the* or zero article).

TOP Saving Tips

1 Save your small change in _____ jar.
2 Unplug _____ electrical appliances when you're not using them.
3 Buy _____ products that are close to their sell-by date.
4 Don't get _____ credit card. If you have one, cut it up.
5 Compare _____ prices before you buy _____ expensive item.
6 Keep _____ receipts you get and add up _____ amount of money you spend every day.
7 Take _____ lunch from home instead of buying _____ sandwiches or _____ snacks.
8 Don't buy _____ books – borrow them from _____ library.

▶ **QUANTIFIERS**

1 **Several** websites have articles about impulse buying.
2 If we can save **a bit of** money, that's good.
3 … come back with **loads of** things you hadn't intended to buy.
4 … you're more likely to buy **loads of** food.

For further information and practice, see page 172.

9 Look at the grammar box. Answer the questions.

1 Look at sentences 1 and 2. Which quantifier is used with:
 a a countable noun?
 b an uncountable noun?
2 Look at sentences 3 and 4. When do we use the quantifier *loads of*?

10 Look at the audioscript on page 186. Find nine more quantifiers and say if they are used with countable nouns, uncountable nouns or both.

11 Choose the correct quantifier. Then suggest another possible quantifier for each sentence.

1 I don't think I need to go shopping. We've got *plenty of / many* food for the week.
2 I've bought *a couple of / a bit of* magazines. I can read them on the train.
3 I didn't find *much / any* shoes in my size in the sales.
4 If I've got *a little / one or two* money at the end of the month, I buy something nice.
5 I bought *a few / some* strange cheese at the shops. It's almost green!
6 You can save *several / loads of* money if you shop in the sales.

12 Pronunciation linking

a ▶ 74 Listen to these sentences from Exercise 11. Notice how the speaker links the words which start with a vowel to the final consonant of the previous word.

1 I don't think‿I need to go shopping.
2 I can read them‿on the train.

b ▶ 75 Underline the words which start with vowels in the other sentences in Exercise 11. Then listen and repeat the sentences.

Speaking *my life*

13 Work in pairs. Make true (or false) sentences with these quantifiers about things you own, have bought or have been given. Tell your partner and ask follow-up questions.

| a bit of | a couple of | a few | loads of | one or two | plenty of | several | some |

A: I've got **a bit of** wood I found on the beach.
B: Have you? Why did you decide to keep it?

my life ▶ SHOPPING NOW AND IN THE FUTURE ▶ MY THINGS ▶ SOUVENIRS ▶ BUYING THINGS ▶ CUSTOMER FEEDBACK

reading how to negotiate a price • wordbuilding compound adjectives •
critical thinking testing a conclusion • speaking souvenirs

9c The art of the deal

Reading

1 Work in pairs. Do you like bringing souvenirs back from holiday? Discuss why you think people would bring back items like these.

> brochures from galleries, museums, etc.
> decorative objects: pictures, ceramics, etc.
> duty-free goods
> locally made products
> postcards
> T-shirts with slogans
> used tickets

2 Read the article quickly. Decide what kind of shopping experience (a–c) the article describes.

   a buying crafts direct from the maker
   b choosing holiday gifts for friends and family
   c looking for bargains in local markets

3 Read the article again. Answer the questions.
   1 Who are the three main people in the article and why do they go to Morocco?
   2 What two things does Sam buy and how much does he pay for them?
   3 Which is Sam's most successful purchase?

4 Look at the words (1–8). Find the things that are described with these words in the article. Complete the phrases. Then think of more things that can be described using these words.

   1 beautiful old
   2 world-famous
   3 freshly-squeezed
   4 deadly-looking
   5 hand-dyed
   6 massive copper
   7 tall blue
   8 bright yellow, Moroccan

Wordbuilding compound adjectives

▶ **WORDBUILDING compound adjectives**

Compound adjectives are adjectives made of more than one word. The hyphen shows that the words form one adjective.
duty-free goods, two-day lemon festival

For further practice, see Workbook page 75.

5 Look at the wordbuilding box. Then work in pairs. Answer the questions.
   1 The *world-famous marketplace* is 'famous around the world'. What do the other compound adjectives in Exercise 4 mean?
   2 Can you name examples of:
      a a well-known sportsperson?
      b a best-selling singer?
      c old-fashioned clothes?
      d a hand-made item?

Critical thinking testing a conclusion

6 The writer concludes: 'Mohamed will be proud.' Look at the article again and underline the pieces of advice Mohamed gives to Sam.

7 Tick the pieces of advice that Sam follows. How effective was the advice? How do you know?

Speaking my life

8 Work in pairs. Describe typical souvenirs that people take home from your country.

9 You are a market trader. Choose four of these objects. Find or draw a picture of each object and think how you will describe it. Think about: its origin, age and material, and any interesting facts about it. Decide on a price for each object.

| boomerang | bottle | box | clock | coin | figure |
| hat | lamp | rug | stamp | sword | watch |

10 Choose objects from Exercise 9 which you want to buy. Visit different traders and find out about the objects you want. Then choose which trader you will buy from.

This rug is lovely. How much is it?

Unit 9 **Shopping**

The Art of the Deal

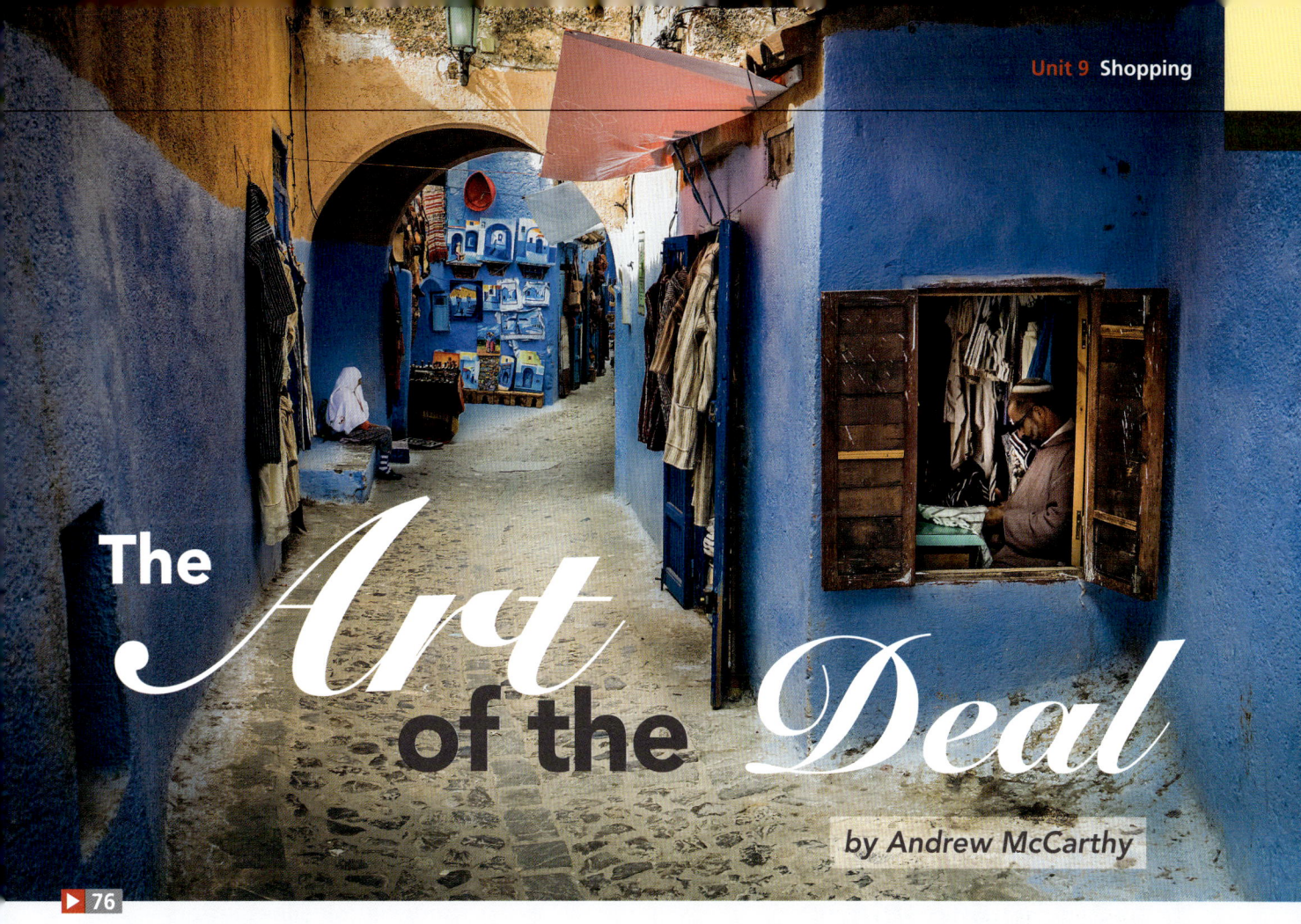

by Andrew McCarthy

▶ 76

I'M IN MARRAKECH, the bustling heart of Morocco, with my son, Sam. He's eight. We've come here with Mohamed, a friend who owns a shop in our neighbourhood in New York. Sam can often be found in Mohamed's shop, looking for a bargain. They argue about prices and chat about swords, or camels or the desert. 'You need to come to Morocco, to Marrakech,' Mohamed told me. 'I'll show you around and teach Sam how to really get a bargain!' So here we are.

We meet up with Mohamed over a cup of mint tea in the beautiful old city of Marrakech. We're sitting in an area next to the exotic stalls of the souk – Marrakech's world-famous marketplace. Market sellers with carts offer freshly-squeezed juice, others sell dates or figs. Later, as we wander around, Mohamed introduces us to olive sellers, tile makers and rug merchants. He also begins the first of his lessons in bargaining for Sam.

'The price of everything in Morocco is open to discussion, Sam. When you hear a price, the first thing you say is "Too much – bezaf" and then walk away.'

'But what if I like it?'

'When you see something you like, maybe a lamp, you ask about something else instead. Then, as you walk out, you ask, "And how much is that lamp?" as though you'd just noticed it and aren't really that interested in it.'

We turn a corner into another narrow street in the souk. 'Don't always give an offer. Make them continue to lower the price. Oh, and wear something Moroccan,' Mohamed continues as we enter a fairly large shop. Most of the stalls in Marrakech sell mainly one type of thing, but not this one. Decorative and deadly-looking swords hang beside soft hand-dyed fabrics; large camel bones covered in writing sit beside massive copper lamps. It is here that Sam spots a beautiful box. 'Look, a treasure chest!' It's made of wood, and painted red and gold. He opens the lid, then closes it. 'Cool.' Then he spots a tall blue bottle – an old perfume bottle. 'Four hundred dirham,' the shopkeeper says. Fifty dollars. Sam says nothing. I can't tell whether he's too shy or is practising what Mohamed has taught him.

He eventually agrees to pay 200 dirham, about $24. I'd say the bottle is worth $10, at most. Clearly, he needs more practice at this. 'Just to get started, Dad,' Sam tells me as he pays for the bottle.

We spend a few days sightseeing around Marrakech, but Sam is really interested in only one thing. Late one afternoon, we return to the shop where Sam saw the treasure chest. 'You have returned. Very good.' The shopkeeper opens his arms. He places the chest on the floor. Sam opens the lid. He runs his fingers over it.

The shopkeeper speaks. 'Give me 2,500.'

Sam shakes his eight-year-old head. 'Eight hundred.'

'I like your babouches,' says the man. Sam's wearing a pair of bright yellow, Moroccan slippers. He ignores the comment.

'You're very good. I'll take 1,800 dirham,' the shopkeeper announces.

'One thousand.'

Both are silent. Neither blinks. What happens next happens fast.

'Fifteen hundred, and it's yours.'

'Twelve hundred.'

'Thirteen hundred.'

'Yes!'

The man holds out his hand. Sam grabs it. The deal is done. Mohamed will be proud.

---

bargain (n) /ˈbɑːɡɪn/ something which has a low price but is good quality
blink (v) /blɪŋk/ open and close your eyes very quickly
bustling (adj) /ˈbʌslɪŋ/ energetic and busy
negotiate (v) /nəˈɡəʊʃieɪt/ to agree something by discussion
souk (n) a /suːk/ the name in some countries for a market that sells all types of products

---

my life ▶ SHOPPING NOW AND IN THE FUTURE ▶ MY THINGS ▶ **SOUVENIRS** ▶ BUYING THINGS ▶ CUSTOMER FEEDBACK

111

real life buying things • vocabulary shopping (2) • pronunciation silent letters

9d It's in the sale

Real life buying things

1 ▶77 Listen to two conversations. Answer the questions for each conversation.

 1 What kind of shop is it?
 2 What does the customer want?
 3 Does the customer buy the item?

2 ▶77 Look at the expressions for buying things. Listen to the conversations again. Underline the option the speaker uses. Identify the speakers. Write C (customer) or A (assistant) next to the expressions.

▶ BUYING THINGS

Can I have a look at / Could I see this silver chain?
It's in the sale / It's reduced actually. It's got 20 per cent off.
I wanted / I was looking for something lighter.
Can she bring it back / return it if she doesn't like it?
Excuse me, are you in / do you work in this department?
What's / Do you have the reference number or the model name?
Let me see if it's in stock / we've got any on order.
How much do you charge / does it cost for delivery?
We accept payment / You can pay by card or in cash.

Vocabulary shopping (2)

3 Work in pairs. Can you remember the question and response for each word? Check your answers in the audioscript on page 187.

return	exchange	receipt	gift-wrapping
reference number	model name	in stock	available
delivery	tills

4 **Pronunciation** silent letters

a ▶78 Listen to these words. Notice how the crossed-out letter is silent. Repeat the words.

gift-wrapping   receipt   right
though

b ▶79 Say these words and cross out the silent letters. Then listen and check.

answer   autumn   bought   design
friendly   hour   listen   weigh

5 Work in pairs. Choose one of the conversations from Exercise 1. Take a role each. Look at the audioscript on page 187 and prepare your role. Then close your books and practise the conversation.

6 Take the roles of a customer and a shop assistant. Choose two of these items and act out two conversations. Use the expressions for buying things to help you.

an item of furniture for your new home
clothes for your father on his birthday
toiletries for your sister
a DVD for a friend
a kitchen appliance for your brother
sportswear for yourself

my life ▶ SHOPPING NOW AND IN THE FUTURE ▶ MY THINGS ▶ SOUVENIRS ▶ BUYING THINGS ▶ CUSTOMER FEEDBACK writing customer feedback • writing skill clarity: pronouns   Unit 9 Shopping

9e For sale

Writing customer feedback

1 Work in pairs. Do you read customer feedback when you buy things online? Have you ever changed your mind about a purchase after reading feedback?

2 Read the customer feedback from two online shopping sites. Answer the questions.

1 Which feedback is about a product and which is about a seller?
2 What problems do the customers mention?
3 Is the feedback positive or negative?

★★★★★
I have no hesitation in recommending PetTown. I ordered two identity tags, but after two weeks **they** hadn't arrived. When I emailed the company, **they** immediately sent replacement tags via registered mail at no extra charge. **They** were courteous and efficient and I would buy from **them** again.

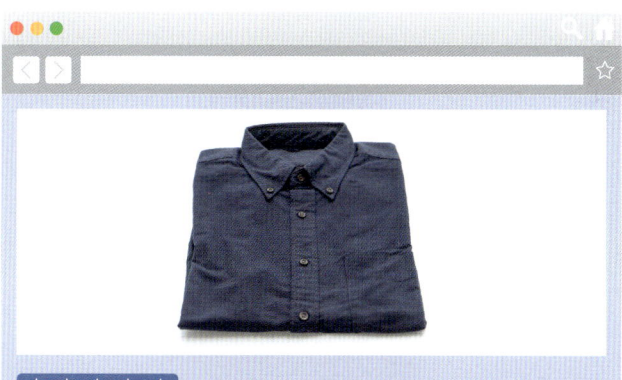

★★★★☆
Bought this lovely shirt with an even lovelier 20% off. I wasn't disappointed. Great quality material and **it**'s a perfect fit. Good for work and for social occasions. Slightly surprised when washed with other items, **they** came out pale blue! This is the first time it's happened with your products, however, and is the only reason I'm not giving **it** full marks. I do recommend the product, but care must be taken when washing.

3 **Writing skill** clarity: pronouns

a You can avoid repetition of nouns in your writing by using pronouns – as long as it is clear which noun each pronoun refers to. Look at the pronouns in bold in the customer feedback. What do they refer to?

b Read the sentences. Replace the nouns with pronouns to avoid repetition.

1 I felt that the colours of the rug in the online photo weren't accurate. The colours of the rug were much darker than I expected.
2 Two of the glasses were broken on arrival and we had to send all the glasses back.
3 My daughter received this game as a gift. My daughter loves the game.
4 This seller has always provided an excellent service and I'm happy to recommend the seller.

c Read the sentences. What do the pronouns refer to? If the sentence is not clear, replace the pronoun with a noun.

1 I bought the grey jacket and the black jumper online. When it came, I wasn't happy with the quality.
2 I ordered the books for delivery, but they missed my postcode off the address label.
3 The tracking information said the packet had been sent, but it never arrived.
4 I provided my address and a phone number. The courier said he couldn't find it.

4 Prepare customer feedback for something you have bought or about a seller. It can be an online or a shop purchase. Use these headings and make notes where relevant. Decide how many stars to give and if you recommend the product or seller.

- item
- delivery
- condition
- fit/quality
- standard of service

5 Write your recommendation. Use these questions to check your advert.

- Have you used pronouns clearly?
- Is your feedback useful to other customers?

6 Publish your feedback in the classroom. Read the other feedback comments and find out if anyone has had a similar shopping experience.

my life ▶ SHOPPING NOW AND IN THE FUTURE ▶ MY THINGS ▶ SOUVENIRS ▶ BUYING THINGS
▶ CUSTOMER FEEDBACK

9f Making a deal

In Morocco's oldest market – the souk in Fez

Before you watch

1 Look at the photo and the caption. Discuss the questions.

1. What's happening in the photo?
2. Why do you think both men are smiling?
3. What kind of things do you think you can buy in the souk?

2 Key vocabulary

a Read the sentences. Try to guess the missing words.

1. When you buy things in the sales, you can often get really good _____ on the prices.
2. I'm just going to look at the stuff in the market. I have no _____ of buying anything.
3. We'll need to take two taxis – there are eight of us and the _____ for a taxi is five passengers.
4. The hotel tried to _____ us – they charged us for four nights instead of three!
5. The price of the bus hire is _____. It's the same if we have ten people or twenty.

b Read the words in bold and their definitions. The words are used in the video. Complete the sentences in Exercise 2a with the words.

a **cheat** (v) to be dishonest
b **discounts** (n) reductions in price
c **fixed** (adj) can't be changed
d **intention** (n) plan
e **maximum** (n) top limit

3 Which is bigger, a half or an eighth? Put the amounts in order of size, starting with the smallest.

a half	a sixth	an eighth
a quarter	a third	

While you watch

4 ▶ 9.1 Watch the first part of the video (0.00–0.53) with the sound OFF. Make a note of the things that you see for sale. Make a whole-class list and compare that with your ideas from Exercise 1 question 3.

5 ▶ 9.1 Watch the first and second parts of the video (0.00–2.41) with the sound ON. Answer the questions.

1. What's the name of the small red hat described in the video?
2. Complete what these people say about bargaining in the souk with words from Exercises 2 and 3.
   a Vincent (Dutch tourist): You have to start yourself at one _____ or something,
   b Consuela (Dutch tourist): So, then you get at _____ the price they say at first.
   c Ahmed (Tour guide): We don't have really a _____ price.
3. What does Mohcine, the jewellery seller, say about some customers?

6 ▶ 9.1 Watch the third part of the video (2.42 to the end). Choose the correct option to complete the answers.

1. What happens if a customer says they don't want to buy anything?
   The seller offers *a lower price / a different item.*
2. What should all tourists make sure they don't do?
   They shouldn't *pay more than something is worth / buy too many things.*

After you watch

7 Work in pairs. How do you think the tourists felt about their experiences in the souk? Give reasons for your answers.

8 Vocabulary in context

a ▶ 9.2 Watch the clips from the video. Choose the correct meaning of the words and phrases.

b Complete the sentences in your own words. Then work in pairs and compare your sentences.

1. I like face-to-face classes because …
2. What a great present! Believe me, it's …
3. I like to go step by step when …

9 Do you prefer bargaining or fixed prices? Give your reasons.

---

craftsman (n) /ˈkrɑːftsmən/ someone who makes quality items by hand
dates (n) /deɪts/ a kind of fruit that grows on palm trees
dirham (n) /ˈdɪəˈræm/ the money used in Morocco
haggling (n) /ˈhæglɪŋ/ bargaining, discussing a price to come to an agreement
vendors (n) /ˈvendəz/ sellers

UNIT 9 REVIEW AND MEMORY BOOSTER

Grammar

1 Complete the shopping tips with verbs, articles or quantifiers where necessary. More than one option is possible in one case.

THE GREEN GUIDE

Shopping Tips: televisions

The days when ¹_____ TVs came in only a ²_____ of types – colour or black and white – have gone. Today's flat screen TVs ³_____ been developed to give ⁴_____ best possible picture quality, with ⁵_____ different viewing options that can ⁶_____ set by the user.

Many people get ⁷_____ new TV because they want ⁸_____ bigger screen. However, bigger TVs use a lot of ⁹_____ energy. A 52-inch LCD uses twice the power of a 32-inch model. Last year, new statistics ¹⁰_____ published by the United States Department of Energy. They said the amount of ¹¹_____ power that ¹²_____ used by TVs in America could supply electricity to all homes in ¹³_____ state of New York for a year. One major factor in TV power use is the picture setting. ¹⁴_____ people realize what a difference the settings can make. Electricity use ¹⁵_____ be cut by up to 50 per cent if you change to ¹⁶_____ efficient setting.

2 Read the shopping tips in Exercise 1 and find:
  1 one positive and one negative thing about modern TVs.
  2 one way of reducing the amount of energy your TV uses.

3 >> MB Work in pairs. Underline the five passive forms in the text in Exercise 1. Why are the passive forms used in the text?

4 >> MB Write sentences about some of the products and their raw materials. Use these verbs in the passive. Then work in pairs. Take turns to read your sentences without saying the subject. Try to complete your partner's sentences.

| grow | import | make | manufacture | mine |
| produce |

  1 a bar of chocolate   cocoa beans   Ghana
  2 a pair of jeans   cotton   Egypt
  3 jewellery   gold   South Africa
  4 perfume   flowers   France
  5 mobile phone batteries   lithium   Chile
  6 a loaf of bread   wheat   Canada

  ... have been grown in Ghana for many years.

I CAN
use the passive
use articles and quantifiers

Vocabulary

5 Work in pairs. What could a shop assistant or customer say using each of these words?

| delivery   exchange   gift-wrapping   in stock |
| receipt   return |

6 >> MB Work in pairs. Take turns to give a definition or example of one of these things for your partner to identify.

| budget   checkout   deals   goods   purchases |
| special offer   the sales   value for money |

7 >> MB Work in pairs. Take turns to choose one of the shops in the photos. Your partner has 30 seconds to name six things you can buy there.

A B
C D

I CAN
talk about shopping
ask for and give product and sales information in a shop
talk about everyday things we buy for ourselves and others

Real life

8 Complete the questions and statements. Then write customer (C) or shop assistant (S).
  1 We accept _____ by card or in cash.
  2 Can I bring it _____ if I don't like it when I get home?
  3 Let me see if this model is in _____.
  4 How much do you _____ for delivery?
  5 Do you have the reference _____?
  6 Can I have a _____ at this watch?
  7 It's reduced – it's got 20 per cent _____.
  8 Excuse me, are you _____ this department?

9 >> MB Work in pairs. Take turns to be the customer and the assistant in a shop. Act out conversations in which you buy a tablet, a computer, a motorbike and some perfume.

I CAN
buy and sell items in a shop

Unit 10 No limits

On the annual *Marathon des Sables* in southern Morocco, keeping the sand out of your face can be a problem.

FEATURES

118 Leaving Earth
Could we live on another planet?

120 The superhumans
Find out about the latest advances in medicine

122 Two journeys, two lives
Read about two people who have endured tough experiences

126 What does an astronaut dream about?
A video about the first British woman in space

1 Work in pairs. Look at the photo and the caption. What other problems do you think runners like this face?

2 ▶ 80 Listen to an extract from a podcast about the *Marathon des Sables*. How many of your ideas from Exercise 1 are mentioned?

3 ▶ 80 Listen to the extract again and make notes about these things. Does ultrarunning appeal to you? Why? / Why not?
   1 the age of the runners
   2 the distances
   3 anything else that interested you

4 Work in groups. Discuss the questions.
   1 Other extreme sports include bungee jumping, Base jumping, cave diving and free climbing. Have you tried any of them?
   2 Why do you think people push their bodies to the limit?
   3 Can you think of any dangers in pushing your body to extremes?

my life ▶ I'D LOVE TO LIVE IN … ▶ HEALTH EXPERIENCES ▶ INSPIRATIONAL PEOPLE ▶ TALKING ABOUT INJURIES
▶ A PERSONAL EMAIL

reading life on another planet • grammar second conditional • speaking I'd love to live in …

10a Leaving Earth

Reading

1 Work in pairs. Discuss the questions.

1 Do you think the human race will ever be able to live on another planet?
2 What kind of thing might make life on another planet difficult for humans?

2 Read the article. Answer the questions.

1 Which planets does the article mention?
2 Where are the planets?
3 Which planet do scientists already know something about?
4 Why is the colour blue important when looking at planets?

LEAVING EARTH

▶ 81

Professor Stephen Hawking has said that the human race has no future if it doesn't go into space. The planet we currently know most about is Mars. Two crewless spacecraft have already landed on the surface and have sent a lot of information to scientists on Earth.

But if we sent astronauts to Mars, would they be able to survive? How easy would it be to set up a base? We already know there would be some difficult challenges to face. Communication with Earth would have a 20-minute delay, food and water would only be provided every few months and astronauts couldn't go outside the base if they didn't wear a spacesuit. It all sounds more like science fiction than something that might actually happen.

Meanwhile, astronomers are searching for Earth-like planets outside our solar system. They hope to take images of planets in Alpha Centauri, the closest star system to Earth. According to Chris Lintott, an astrophysicist at Oxford University, it would be hugely exciting if we could get images from Alpha Centauri. If we had only a tiny image, astronomers could work out the planet's orbit and its size and colour. If the planet turned out to be blue, this might mean it had water and an atmosphere – and where there's water, there's life.

Of course, getting to such a distant planet is a different question – it makes a trip to Mars sound easy by comparison.

crewless (adj) /ˈkruːləs/ without any people – crew – working on board

3 Work in groups. Do you agree with these online comments about space exploration? Give your reasons.

1 'We can't look after Earth, so we'll never be successful on another planet.'
2 'I don't understand why we need to go into space. We should spend the money on improving life on Earth.'

Grammar second conditional

> **SECOND CONDITONAL**
>
> But **if we sent** astronauts to Mars, **would they be able to** survive?
> Astronauts **couldn't go** outside the base if they **didn't wear** a spacesuit.
> It **would be** hugely exciting **if we could get** images from Alpha Centauri.
> **If** the planet **turned out** to be blue, this **might mean** it had water.
>
> For further information and practice, see page 174.

4 Look at the grammar box. Answer the questions.

1 Which verb form follows *if* in the second conditional?
2 When is a comma used in a second conditional sentence?
3 Which three verbs are used before the infinitive without *to* in the main clause?

5 Look at how the second conditional patterns are used in the article. Answer the questions.

1 Does the second conditional refer to situations in the past or in the present and the future?
2 Does the second conditional refer to real or to unreal situations?

6 Complete the comments about space exploration with the second conditional.

1 I _____ (consider) training as an astronaut if I _____ (have) the right qualifications.
2 I _____ (pay) to be a space tourist if it _____ (not / be) so expensive.
3 Being in space _____ (be) OK if you _____ (be able) to have Skype chats with people outside.
4 If we _____ (find) Earth-like planets, we _____ (not / be able) to travel there.
5 If I _____ (be) on a long space journey, I _____ (miss) my family.
6 What _____ (happen) if you _____ (not / get on) well with the rest of the crew on a spacecraft?
7 If you _____ (be) in charge of NASA, what _____ you _____ (spend) money on?
8 If there _____ (be) life on another planet, _____ they _____ (contact) us first?

7 Work in pairs. Look again at the comments in Exercise 6. Say which statements (1–5) you agree with and answer the questions (6–8).

8 Complete the sentences with endings that are true for you. Then work in pairs and compare your sentences.

1 If I was a tourist on a space trip,
   a I'd …
   b I wouldn't …
   c I could …
   d I might …
2 If I lived on a base on Mars as part of the first exploration,
   a I'd …
   b I wouldn't …
   c I could …
   d I might …

9 Work in two pairs within a group of four. Play a guessing game.

Pair A: Turn to page 153 and follow the instructions.

Pair B: Turn to page 154 and follow the instructions.

Speaking my life

10 Work on your own. Think of a place you'd like to live in. Note down five reasons why you'd like to live there. Then work in groups. Take turns to tell your group the reasons, but don't say the place. Can they guess before you give all the reasons?

A: *I'd love to live in beep. I'd go to all the local football matches.*
B: *And if I lived in bzzz, I'd never be cold again.*

11 Think about your answers to these questions. Then tell the class.

1 If you could start a new life, what things would you change and how?
2 What would you miss about your 'old' life?

listening bionic bodies • grammar defining relative clauses • vocabulary medicine • speaking health experiences

10b The superhumans

Listening

1 Work in pairs. Look at the photo. What do you think it shows?

2 ▶ 82 Listen to a preview of a TV programme. Tick the topics you hear mentioned.

> blades
> extreme sports
> Olympic medals
> Paralympic athletes
> progress in medical science
> wheelchairs

3 ▶ 82 Match the beginnings of the sentences (1–7) with the endings (a–g). Then listen again and check.

1 The Paralympics is a sports event for people
2 The TV programme features some athletes
3 A bionic device is one
4 Amanda Boxtel uses a robotic structure
5 The structure
6 Amanda Boxtel works with an organization
7 There's no limit to the things

a whose devices are bionic.
b which supports her body.
c bionic devices will be able to do.
d that promotes bionic technology.
e that uses electronics.
f who have a disability.
g Amanda Boxtel uses is called an exo-skeleton.

4 How do you think life might be different for someone with a bionic device compared to a traditional device? Tell your partner.

Grammar defining relative clauses

▶ **DEFINING RELATIVE CLAUSES**

With relative pronouns

1 Tonight, there's **a documentary which features** some famous Paralympians.

With optional *who/that/which*

2 **The Paralympians (who/that) you mentioned** use blades and wheelchairs.
3 **The range of devices (which/that) the programme describes** is growing.

For further information and practice, see page 174.

5 Look at the grammar box. Choose the correct option.

1 In sentence 1, *a documentary* is the *subject / object* of the verb *features*.
2 In sentence 2, *the Paralympians* is the *subject / object* of the verb *mentioned*.
3 In sentence 3, *the range of devices* is the *subject / object* of the verb *describes*.
4 When *who*, *that* or *which* refers to the *subject / object*, we can miss it out.
5 We can use *that* instead of *who / which / both who and which*.

120

6 Look at the sentences in Exercise 3. Find the two types of clauses. Add a relative pronoun to the sentences that don't have them.

7 Look at the diagram of a bionic body. Complete the information for each numbered part with the words in the box. Use two words twice.

when	where	who	which	whose

1 implants in the ears _____ allow people _____ are deaf to hear
2 prosthetic arms _____ can receive signals from the brain
3 temporary artificial hearts for people _____ are waiting for transplants
4 the first replacement hips – from a time _____ bionics was an idea from science fiction
5 healthy area of bone _____ the bionic limb is attached
6 bionic limbs _____ movement mimics the body's natural steps

8 Read the comments from a hospital patient. Write *who, which* or *that* in the correct optional place.

1 The doctor I spoke to was very positive.
2 I thought the treatment I got was very good.
3 The injections the nurse gave me didn't hurt much.
4 The other patients I met had similar injuries.
5 The hospital ward I was in had only one other patient.
6 I didn't like the food they served us.

9 ▶83 Cross out any optional words in these sentences. Then listen and check your answers.

1 I know someone who has a bionic arm.
2 The hospital that we go to isn't far away.
3 Cochlear implants are devices that improve hearing.
4 I think people who do Paralympic sports are amazing.
5 Wheelchairs are often used by patients whose legs are paralyzed.
6 The doctor who we saw in the film is a pioneer in bionics.

10 Pronunciation sentence stress

a ▶83 Listen to the sentences from Exercise 9 again. Notice how the relative pronouns are not stressed.

b ▶83 Listen again and repeat the sentences.

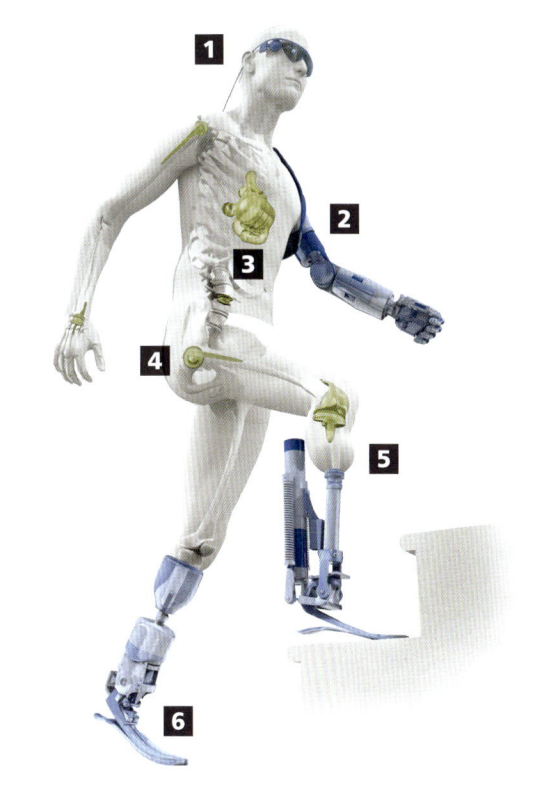

Vocabulary medicine

11 Work in pairs. Choose the best option.

1 Several people were *injured / wounded* in the accident.
2 It's just a small cut. It will *treat / heal* naturally.
3 What time is your doctor's *appointment / date*?
4 They can't *cure / heal* this yet, but they can relieve the symptoms.
5 Where does it *hurt / pain*?
6 The *healing / treatment* has some unpleasant side effects.
7 The doctor is *controlling / monitoring* the patient's condition.
8 The injection isn't *hurtful / painful*.

12 Work in groups. Take turns to choose a word and then give a definition of the word.

*Botox is something **which** celebrities use to make themselves look younger.*

surgeon injection
botox operating theatre blood test
A & E (accident and emergency)
scan ambulance stitches
donor crutches
surgery radiographer ward
X-ray paramedic first aid

Speaking — my life

13 Choose two of the words from Exercise 12 and talk about your own experience.

I've never been in an ambulance.

— my life — ▶ I'D LOVE TO LIVE IN ... ▶ HEALTH EXPERIENCES ▶ INSPIRATIONAL PEOPLE ▶ TALKING ABOUT INJURIES
▶ A PERSONAL EMAIL

reading **acts of endurance** • word focus *take* • critical thinking **reading between the lines** • speaking **inspirational people**

10c Two journeys, two lives

Reading

1 How much do you know about these people? Choose the option (a–c) you think links them.

a They broke 'unbreakable' records.
b They were successful in spite of difficulties.
c They became rich and famous in their chosen careers.

> J. K. Rowling
> Marie Curie
> Nelson Mandela
> Stephen Hawking

2 Work in pairs. You are going to read about two people who overcame obstacles in their lives.

Student A: Read about Diane Van Deren.

Student B: Read about John Dau.

Make notes to answer these questions.

1 Who?
2 Where?
3 When?
4 Distance covered?
5 Time taken?
6 Food and drink?

3 Tell your partner about the story you read. Use your notes to help you. Ask your partner at least one question about their story.

4 Now read your partner's story. Is the story what you expected to read? Did anything surprise you?

Word focus *take*

5 Look at these extracts from the stories. What do the expressions with *take* mean or refer to? Choose the correct option (a–c).

1 Diane Van Deren was […] **taking part** in the Yukon Arctic Ultra.
 a leaving b participating c winning
2 Van Deren […] had a kiwi-size piece of her brain **taken out**.
 a removed b repaired c returned
3 […] a journey which had **taken** him **more than half of his life**.
 a distance b speed c time
4 Dau […] **took care** of a group of younger children.
 a controlled b looked after c played

6 Work in pairs. What do the expressions with *take* mean in these sentences?

1 The Yukon Arctic Ultra **takes place** every two years.
2 Diane Van Deren **took up** running after an operation to cure her epilepsy.
3 Diane Van Deren couldn't **take off** her boots because they had frozen to her feet.
4 John Dau's plane to New York **took off** from Nairobi airport.
5 The fighting in Sudan **took away** John Dau's childhood.
6 John Dau **took up** a scholarship to study in the United States.

7 Using the information in the stories and your own understanding of them, discuss the questions with your partner.

1 Why did Diane Van Deren and John Dau begin their journeys?
2 Did they make their journeys through choice or necessity?
3 What have they achieved for themselves as a result of their journeys?
4 What have they achieved for others as a result of their journeys?

Critical thinking **reading between the lines**

8 Read the quotes. Who do you think said each one – Diane Van Deren or John Dau? Give your reasons.

1 'I think people refuse to try things because they fear failure.'
2 'All I have to think about is my body.'
3 'There have been many impossible situations in my life, but I keep trying.'
4 'You can't give up.'

9 Do you know of other people who have overcome obstacles to achieve something in unexpected ways?

Speaking my life

10 You are going to nominate an inspirational person for a prize. Choose someone from one of these categories. Make short biographical notes about the person and the reasons why you find them inspirational. Then give your presentation.

- art, music and fashion
- business and academia
- film and television
- local life
- science and medicine
- sport and adventure
- technology

Unit 10 No limits

Diane Van Deren
▶ 84

ON 15 FEBRUARY 2009, DIANE VAN DEREN WAS ONE OF A DOZEN RUNNERS TAKING PART IN THE YUKON ARCTIC ULTRA, A 700-KILOMETRE RACE ACROSS THE FROZEN ARCTIC IN THE MIDDLE OF WINTER. Not a single woman had ever completed it. With temperatures of 30 degrees below zero and only seven hours of daylight each day, it's probably the hardest race in the world. But then, there is no woman like Diane Van Deren.

Twelve years earlier, Van Deren, a former professional tennis player, had a kiwi-size piece of her brain taken out. It was part of the treatment for the epilepsy which she suffered from. The operation was successful, but she noticed one unexpected result: she could run without stopping for hours.

At the start of the Arctic Ultra, icy winds froze Van Deren's water supplies so she had nothing to drink for the first 160 kilometres. She kept going by sucking on frozen fruit and nut bars. On the eleventh day, the ice beneath her feet cracked open and Van Deren fell up to her shoulders into a freezing river. She managed to climb out, but it was hard to continue. Her boots had frozen to her feet.

Yet somehow through it all, Van Deren remained positive. This was perhaps helped by another curious result of her operation. 'I have a problem with short-term memory. I could be out running for two weeks, but if someone told me it was day one of a race,' she jokes, 'I'd say, "Great, let's get started!"'

On 26 February 2009 – exactly twelve years after her surgery – Van Deren crossed the finish line of the Arctic Ultra. She was one of eight people who finished – and the first and only woman.

epilepsy (n) /ˈepɪˌlepsi/ an illness affecting the brain

John Dau
▶ 85

IN 2001, JOHN DAU BOARDED A PLANE TO NEW YORK. IT WAS THE BEGINNING OF ONE TRIP BUT THE END OF A JOURNEY WHICH HAD TAKEN HIM MORE THAN HALF OF HIS LIFE. In 1987, aged thirteen, Dau had run away from his home in southern Sudan, escaping from the soldiers who came to destroy his village. He met up with a small group of boys like himself and together they walked for weeks to reach a refugee camp in Ethiopia. 'I had no shoes and no clothes; at night the desert was so cold. We thought about our parents all the time,' remembers Dau. The boys had no food and nothing to drink. 'We chewed grass and ate mud to stay alive.'

The boys walked by night and slept by day. Eventually they reached the camp, where Dau spent the next four years. As one of the older boys, Dau led and took care of a group of younger children which eventually numbered 1,200. But Dau was forced to run again when soldiers came to the camp. Along with 27,000 other boys, he set off to walk back to Sudan. To get there they had to cross Gilo River. 'Soldiers were shooting at us, so we had to dive into water full of crocodiles,' Dau recounts. Thousands of boys were killed or caught and only 18,000 of them arrived in Sudan. But the area was soon attacked again, so Dau and the other 'Lost Boys' of Sudan set off south again, this time to a camp in Kenya. By now, Dau had walked more than 1,600 kilometres.

Ten years later, Dau was one of a handful of 'Lost Boys' who were sponsored to study in the USA. A new kind of journey was about to begin.

refugee camp (n) /ˌrefjʊˈdʒiː kæmp/ a temporary home for people who have left their country of origin

my life ▶ I'D LOVE TO LIVE IN … ▶ HEALTH EXPERIENCES ▶ INSPIRATIONAL PEOPLE ▶ TALKING ABOUT INJURIES
▶ A PERSONAL EMAIL

vocabulary injuries • real life talking about injuries • pronunciation and

10d First aid

Vocabulary injuries

1 Work in pairs. Complete the table with the things that cause these injuries. Some things can cause more than one injury. Add at least one more cause of each injury.

Cuts and bruises	Sprains and breaks	Allergic reactions

blades and knives
falling off something
falling over
food poisoning
insect bites
tripping up
wasp and bee stings

2 For each injury, decide with your partner what is the best thing to do.

Real life talking about injuries

3 ▶ 86 Look at the expressions for describing injuries. Which expressions refer to the injuries in Exercise 1? Then listen to three conversations and check.

▶ **TALKING ABOUT INJURIES**

Describing injuries
I feel a bit sick.
I've been stung.
It doesn't hurt.
It hurts when I move it.
It looks a bit swollen.
It might need stitches.
it's just a sprain.
It's painful.
That looks nasty!
You might have broken something.
It's nothing.

Giving advice
If I were you, I'd go down to A and E.
I would keep an eye on it.
I wouldn't just ignore it.
You should put some antihistamine cream on it.
You'd better wash it straightaway.
Why don't you go and see Rosana?
It might be worth getting it X-rayed.
It's probably best to get it looked at.
Have you tried putting cream on it?

4 ▶ 86 Listen to the conversations again. What advice is given in each case? Check your answers in the expressions for giving advice.

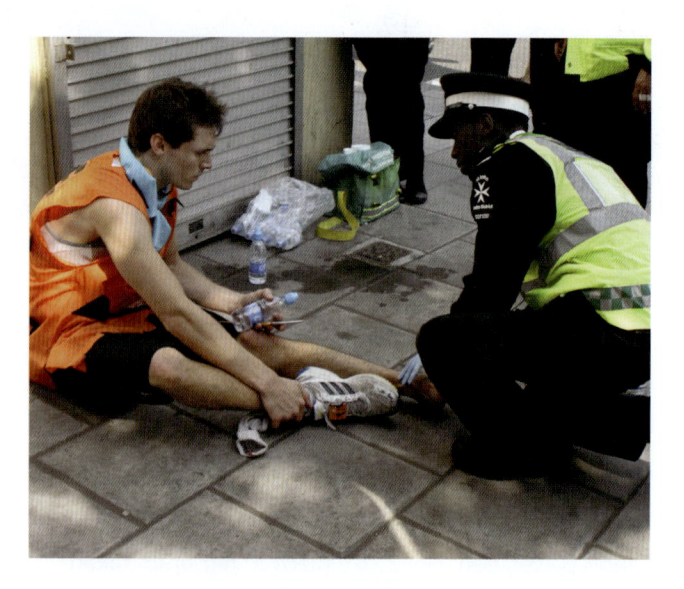

5 Pronunciation and

a ▶ 87 Listen to these expressions. Notice how *and* is not stressed.

A and E	wasp and bee stings
cuts and bruises	bites and stuff
sprains and breaks	go and see Rosana

b ▶ 87 Listen to the expressions again. Notice how *and* is linked to the word before it and how the *d* isn't pronounced. Repeat the expressions.

c Match words from A with words from B. Practise saying the pairs of words.

A day   doctors   eyes   food   fruit   hands
mind   rich

B body   drink   ears   famous   knees
night   nurses   nuts

6 Work as a class. You will be assigned a role as a patient or a doctor.

Patients: Choose one of the injuries from the list and think about how you will describe it to the doctor. Then visit each doctor and describe your problem. Who gives the best advice?

Doctors: Look at the list of injuries and think about appropriate treatment. Then listen to each patient and give advice. Which is the most difficult case to treat?

- a deep cut on your thumb from a kitchen knife
- a painful ankle after jumping off a trampoline
- feeling sick after being stung by a wasp
- multiple cuts and bruises after a mountain biking accident
- strange skin rash after a meal out
- neck and shoulder pain after a horse-riding accident

10e What do you think?

Writing a personal email

1 Who do you talk to when you need advice about these things? Work in pairs. Compare your ideas.

> car trouble
> difficulties at work/school
> health worries
> personal problems
> relationship dilemmas

2 Read the email. What is its purpose? Choose the best option (a–c).

a The writer is asking for information about a job opportunity.
b The writer is getting in touch with an old friend.
c The writer needs some help making a decision.

> Hi there,
>
> Thanks so much for the get well card! I'm feeling a lot better now, *actually*. And I've been meaning to write to you for a while – I want your advice about something.
>
> I've got the chance to spend a year away, on a project in the South Pacific. (I know, it sounds like paradise – I bet you wish you were me!) It's a job in a community health centre on Vanuatu. I'd have to do some training if I took the post, *of course*. I can do basic first aid, but I'd need to know more than that.
>
> *The thing is*, I'm not sure if I should go. It would mean giving up the job I've got now, *obviously*. But I wouldn't mind that – it's not a great job! And I've often thought about a career in nursing …
>
> *So*, what do you think?
>
> Hope all is well with you. *By the way*, did you manage to sell your car?
>
> Take care
>
> Kate

3 Is the style of the email formal, neutral or informal? Underline the words or expressions which show this.

4 What advice would you give to Kate? Tell your partner.

5 Writing skill linking ideas (2)

a Look at the table. Which group of words can replace each highlighted word in the email? Write the words from the email in the table. Add a comma where necessary.

1	clearly naturally	
2	in fact to be honest	
3	Before I forget, Incidentally,	
4	Anyway, Well,	
5	All the same, Even so, However,	

b Complete the sentences with expressions from Exercise 5a. Remember to add a comma where necessary. More than one answer is possible.

1 Your problem sounds familiar. I had to make a similar decision once, _____ .
2 It's a long way to go. You'd miss your family at first, _____ .
3 I hope I've helped you a bit! _____ how's your sister?
4 That's what I did. _____ I hope I've been of some help.
5 It could be interesting. _____ it's going to be difficult.

6 Think about a problem you need help with. Write an email to someone in your class.

7 Use these questions to check your email. Then send your email to the person you have chosen.

- Have you used a variety of linking expressions?
- Have you used linking expressions correctly?

8 Write a reply to the email you have received.

10f What does an astronaut dream about?

The Mir space station

Helen Sharman, the first British astronaut to go into space

Unit 10 No limits

Before you watch

1 Work in pairs. What do you think astronauts might dream about?

2 Key vocabulary

a Read the sentences. Try to guess the missing words.

1 In my job with an airline, it's important to have great _____ to work with.
2 Stones don't _____ on water, but pieces of wood usually do.
3 Since I left home, the thing I _____ most is my dad's cooking. He makes great pizza!
4 After six months travelling through China, we felt very _____ to the way of life there.
5 We'd read amazing reviews of the film, and when we saw it we weren't _____ . It was fantastic.

b Read the words in bold and their definitions. The words are used in the video. Complete the sentences in Exercise 2a with the words.

a **float** (v) to move slowly on the surface of water or in air
b **crewmates** (n) members of a team on a ship, plane or spacecraft
c **miss** (v) to feel sad about things or people you aren't with now
d **disappointed** (adj) to feel unhappy with something that wasn't as good as you'd hoped
e **connected** (adj) linked or associated with a thing, place or person

3 Work in pairs. In the video you hear an astronaut, Helen Sharman, talking about being on the Mir space station. Can you guess how she uses the words in Exercise 2b?

While you watch

4 ▶10.1 Watch the video. In which order (1–3) does Helen Sharman talk about these things (a–c)?

a her own feelings when she was on the Mir module
b her dream
c what astronauts feel when they look at Earth from space

5 ▶10.1 Watch the first part of the video (0.00–1.21) again. Choose the correct option.

1 She dreams about *the liftoff from Earth / being in space*.
2 She floats towards *a door / a window*.
3 She *sees / doesn't see* the stars.
4 Sergei and her other crewmates *are / aren't* in the dream.
5 She *looks out of / wants to leave through* the window.

6 ▶10.1 Watch the second part of the video (1.22–1.52). Complete the sentences with one word.

1 Everyone says the Earth looks _____ .
2 Helen Sharman felt disconnected and _____ to the Earth.
3 She knew it was her _____ .
4 She wanted to _____ .

7 Watch the third part of the video (1.53–2.27). Answer the questions.

1 Astronauts talk about different things at the start of a space trip and after a couple of days. What do they talk about?
2 What do they think about when they go over different countries?

8 ▶10.1 Work in pairs. How do you think Helen Sharman's dream ends? Watch the last part of the video (2.28 to the end) and check your ideas.

After you watch

9 Work in pairs. Compare your personal reactions to the video. Do you think the animation went well with Helen Sharman's words? Did anything surprise you? What was the overall message for you?

10 Vocabulary in context

a ▶10.2 Watch the clips from the video. Choose the correct meaning of the words and phrases.

b Complete the sentences in your own words. Then work in pairs and compare your sentences.

1 I only … on the odd occasion.
2 I never understand what … has to do with … .
3 If you asked me … , my response would be 'absolutely!'
4 On a cold night, it's nice to feel the warmth of … .
5 I was laughing and crying at once when … .
6 It's best to tell someone gently if … .

11 Work in small groups. Discuss the questions.

1 How often do you dream?
2 Do you usually have dreams or nightmares?
3 Do you remember your dreams?
4 Some people say dreams have meanings. Do you know of any common interpretations?
5 What do you think of the idea of interpreting dreams?

---

curvature (n) /ˈkɜːvətʃə/ the curve of the outline of the Earth seen from space
module (n) /ˈmɒdʒuːl/ a section of the space station
orientation (n) /ˌɔːrɪenteɪˈʃən/ the direction or way something is pointing
physical geography (n) /ˌfɪzɪkəl dʒiˈɒɡrəfi/ features such as mountains, rivers, deserts, etc.
rate (n) /reɪt/ speed
sedate (adj) /səˈdeɪt/ slow and unhurried

UNIT 10 REVIEW AND MEMORY BOOSTER

Grammar

1 Look at the photo of Base jumping. Complete the comments about the activity with the second conditional.

  1 You _____ absolutely terrified if it _____ the first time you did this. (feel / be)
  2 If I _____ to the top of the cliff, I definitely _____ off. (get / jump)
  3 If you _____ the last person left on the cliff top, _____ you _____ and go back? (be / turn around)
  4 I _____ do this if you _____ me there. (not be able to / take)
  5 You _____ yourself if something _____ wrong. (can kill / go)
  6 If I _____ over the edge, I _____ sick. (look / feel)

2 Read the comments again. Which ones do you agree with?

3 >> MB Work in pairs. For each of these things, agree on a definition and an example. Then compare with another pair.

  1 an adrenalin junkie
  2 bravery
  3 a dangerous place
  4 extreme sports
  5 a life-threatening situation

I CAN
talk about improbable situations in the present or the future (second conditional)
give descriptions or definitions of things which include essential information (defining relative clauses)

4 >> MB Work in pairs. Discuss reasons for and against making Base jumping illegal in the place in the photo. Use terms from Exercise 3. What's your conclusion?

Vocabulary

5 Complete the sentences with one word. The first letter is given.

  1 This cut on my finger is taking ages to h_____ .
  2 These machines m_____ the patient's condition.
  3 The treatment is uncomfortable, but it's not p_____ .
  4 Has she made an a_____ to see the doctor?
  5 Ow, this bright sunlight h_____ my eyes!
  6 Doctors t_____ several people for burns after the fire.

6 >> MB Work in pairs. Answer the questions in your own words.

  1 How might you sprain your ankle?
  2 What would you do if a bee stung you?
  3 What kind of things are people allergic to?
  4 Have you ever broken a bone?
  5 Do you know anyone who is afraid of injections?
  6 How serious is food poisoning?

I CAN
talk about the body and injuries
talk about medicine and emergency medical treatments

Real life

7 Choose the correct option. Then decide what injury or illness each piece of advice could refer to.

  1 You should *get / getting* an X-ray.
  2 You'd better *phone / phoning* an ambulance.
  3 It might be worth *go / going* to the doctor's.
  4 Have you tried *take / taking* antihistamines?
  5 If I were you, I'd *put / putting* some cream on it.

8 >> MB Work in pairs. Act out two conversations using advice from Exercise 7.

I CAN
describe injuries and give first-aid advice

Unit 11 Connections

The woman speaks *Koro*, a language that has just been 'discovered' by linguists.

FEATURES

130 Uncontacted tribes
How a viral video revealed a controversial story

132 Sending a message
What's the best way to get your message across?

134 Spreading the news
An article about the impact of social networks

138 Can you read my lips?
A video about what it's like to have hearing difficulties

1 Look at the photo and the caption. Which of these parts of a news website do you think this photo would appear in?

business section	homepage
celebrity news	national news
comment and analysis	politics and society
current affairs	sports section
entertainment	technology
features	world news

2 Work in pairs. Read the comments about the news. Think of at least two ways to complete each comment.

1 'I get the headlines direct to my mobile so that …'
2 'I don't usually click on headlines unless …'
3 'I don't believe everything I read because …'
4 'I sometimes send a story to friends if …'

3 ▶ 88 Listen to four people answering questions about the news. Compare their comments with your ideas from Exercise 2.

4 Work in pairs. Look at the audioscript on page 188. Add two more questions to the four questions in the audioscript. Then work on your own and ask at least three other people your questions. Compare your results.

my life ▶ NEWS STORIES ▶ PERSONAL COMMUNICATION ▶ APPS FOR MOBILE PHONES ▶ TELEPHONE MESSAGES ▶ AN OPINION ESSAY

reading **isolated tribes** • grammar **reported speech** • speaking and writing **news stories**

11a Uncontacted tribes

Reading

1 Work in groups. Look at the headline and the photo with the article. Discuss the questions.

   1 What do you think the photo shows?
   2 In which parts of the world would you expect to find uncontacted tribes?

2 Read the article. What kinds of organization are:

   1 FUNAI?
   2 *Survival*?
   3 *Science*?

3 Find this information in the article.

   1 what happened when the photos were published
   2 what *Survival* and *Science* disagree about
   3 who has had experience of contacting isolated tribes
   4 who has collected information about isolated tribes for many years
   5 what kind of life the Awá man had in the forest

4 Work in pairs. Read the Awá man's comments at the end of the article. Do you think he agrees with *Science* or with *Survival*? Give your reasons. Who do you agree with?

One of the world's last uncontacted tribes

Uncontacted TRIBES
▶ 89

Some years ago, the Brazilian department for Indian affairs (FUNAI) published photos of an uncontacted Amazonian tribe. FUNAI said that the tribe was under threat from exploitation of the Amazonian forest. Around the same time, a BBC documentary showed video of the same tribe. The photos went viral, leading to a reaction worldwide. Many online commentators asked what was being done to save the tribe. Some people also asked if contact with the outside world was actually a bad thing.

Several years after the viral video, the subject was still controversial. An article in the magazine *Science* said that it was possible to contact isolated Amazonian tribes safely. However, the NGO *Survival* disagreed. They quoted Sydney Possuelo, a former head of FUNAI who was talking about his experience with such tribes. He said that originally he had believed it would be possible to make safe contact and that he had organized one of the best prepared attempts at contact. He said at the time that he wouldn't let a single Indian die. 'But,' he said, 'when the contact came, the diseases arrived, the Indians died.'

The authors of the article in *Science* said that isolated tribes aren't viable in the long term. However, FUNAI said that populations of the tribes they had been monitoring via satellite images had increased over a 30-year period.

Speaking to *Survival*, an Awá man from Brazil's north-eastern Amazon said that when he'd lived in the forest, he'd had a good life and that if he met one of the uncontacted tribes he'd say, 'There's nothing in the outside for you.'

exploitation (n) /ˌeksplɔɪˈteɪʃn/ the unfair use of someone for another person's benefit
isolated (adj) /ˈaɪsəˌleɪtɪd/ apart from others, alone
viable (adj) /ˈvaɪəbl/ able to be successful

Grammar reported speech

> **REPORTED SPEECH**
>
> 1 FUNAI **said (that)** the tribe **was** under threat.
> 2 He **said** at the time **(that)** he **wouldn't let** a single Indian die.
> 3 FUNAI **said** the populations **had increased** over a 30-year period.
> 4 Commentators **asked what was being done** to save the tribe.
> 5 People **asked if** contact with the outside world **was** a bad thing.
>
> For further information and practice, see page 176.

5 Look at the grammar box. Choose the actual words (direct speech) the people used. What has changed in the reported speech?

1 FUNAI said, 'The tribe *is / was* under threat.'
2 He said, 'I *won't let / wouldn't let* a single Indian die.'
3 FUNAI said, 'The populations *have increased / had increased* over the last 30 years.'
4 Commentators asked, 'What *is being done / was being done* to save the tribe?'
5 People asked, '*Is / Was* contact with the outside world a bad thing?'

6 Work in pairs. Find three more examples of reported speech in the article. Write them in direct speech.

7 Look at this sentence from the article. Choose the correct option.

> The authors of the article in *Science* said that isolated tribes aren't viable in the long term.

When we report words that are still true at the time of reporting, we *need to / don't need to* change the verb form.

8 Write the direct speech as reported speech, changing the tenses correctly. Make changes to the pronouns and time expressions as necessary.

1 The BBC camerawoman said, 'I've been filming from a plane this morning.'
2 The BBC camerawoman said, 'We didn't speak to the people in the video.'
3 The FUNAI spokesman said, 'We'll publish the photos tomorrow.'
4 The FUNAI spokesman said, 'A million people have seen these photos in only three days.'
5 A viewer asked, 'How long did it take to make the film?'
6 Several viewers asked, 'Can I watch the video online?'
7 The BBC spokesman said, 'The film is being shown tonight.'
8 The interviewer asked, 'Will you go back again next year?'

9 Read about the first contact some tribes had with outsiders. Complete the text with the correct form of the verbs for reported speech.

In the *Survival* video ***Stranger in the Forest***, tribal people of Brazil spoke of their experiences of first contact. One man said that his father [1] _____ (make) friends with three white men and then he [2] _____ (fell) ill. Another man explained that they [3] _____ (never have) contact with diseases like measles or malaria before – although there [4] _____ (be) diseases in the forest, they [5] _____ (not kill) people. He said a lot of useful knowledge about forest life [6] _____ (be) lost because older tribespeople [7] _____ (die). The final speaker said that his tribe [8] _____ (be suffering) as a result of contact with outsiders and asked the filmmakers how they [9] _____ (can stop) this happening.

Speaking and writing *my life*

10 You are going to act out a news item. Work in two pairs within a group of four.

Pair A: Turn to page 153 and follow the instructions.

Pair B: Turn to page 154 and follow the instructions.

11 Work in your group again. Act out the dialogues. Then write a short news story about what happened to the other pair.

12 Compare your report with the original news item.

13 Work in pairs. Tell your partner about a viral photo or video you have seen.

vocabulary communications technology • listening talking about news headlines •
grammar reporting verbs • pronunciation contrastive stress • speaking personal communication

11b Sending a message

Young monks smile as they pose for a New Year photo.

Vocabulary communications technology

1 Which of these things do you use? Which apps or companies do you prefer for each one?

instant messaging	blogs
search engines	social media
video messaging	

2 Work in pairs. Complete the questions in your own words. Then ask and answer the questions.

1 Do you follow anyone on _____ ?
2 Do you know how to upload videos to _____ ?
3 Do you prefer calling or _____ your friends?
4 Do you take many _____ ?

Listening

3 Work in pairs. Read the headlines. What do you think the stories are about? Write one sentence for each headline.

a Firm sacks workers by text

b YouTube or 'UFO-tube'?

d Email alert warns of traffic chaos

c How to enjoy tomorrow's eclipse of the sun

e Tweet your way around the world

4 ▶ 90 Listen to four conversations about the headlines. Write the number of the conversation next to the headline. There is one extra headline.

Unit 11 **Connections**

5 ▶90 Listen to the conversations again. Choose the correct option (a–c).

1 The journalist asks her followers _____ .
  a to meet her for breakfast
  b to send in photos
  c to suggest things to do
2 The website reminds readers _____ .
  a not to bookmark the eclipse page
  b not to use telescopes
  c to check the weather
3 The company told people _____ .
  a not to turn up for work
  b not to use text messages
  c to come to work early on Monday
4 The politician has invited aliens _____ .
  a to come to his house
  b to come to a meeting
  c to watch his video

Grammar reporting verbs

▶ **REPORTING VERBS: PATTERNS**

ask / tell / remind / invite	someone	(not) to + infinitive
promise / offer		(not) to + infinitive

For further information and practice, see page 176.

6 Look at the grammar box. Then answer the questions.

1 Underline the reporting verbs in the sentences in Exercise 5. How many verbs are there?
2 What follows the reporting verbs in the sentences in Exercise 5 – a verb, a noun or the word *that*?
3 Which verb form is used for the reported words?

7 Write the actual words the people used for the sentences in Exercise 5. Sometimes, more than one answer is possible.

1 Can you suggest things to do?

8 Match the words in these sentences with the reporting verbs in the grammar box. Then write sentences reporting what the people said.

1 Dinah to Amy: 'Don't forget to turn off your mobile.'
   Dinah reminded Amy to turn off her mobile.
2 Jared to Dinah: 'Can you set up my email account?'
3 Amy to Jared: 'Come and watch the film on our new flat screen TV.'
4 Dinah to Amy: 'Plug in the battery charger first.'
5 Jared to Dinah: 'I can put those photos on the computer for you.'
6 Amy to Jared: 'Don't worry, I'll switch it off when I'm finished.'

9 Read the reported comments. Write the actual words the people used.

1 Dinah invited me to join her group online.
2 I asked Dinah to send me a link with the address.
3 I reminded Jared to sign out of his account.
4 Dinah offered to help me synchronize my email accounts.
5 I told Jared to delete the tweet.
6 Jared promised to upload the video for me.

▶ **REPORTING VERBS: THOUGHTS**

Verbs like *realize, think, know* and *wonder* have the same pattern as *say + that* and *ask + if/whether*.
I thought you were coming earlier.
Jared wondered if/whether you had forgotten.

For further information and practice, see page 176.

10 Look at the audioscript on page 188. Underline reported thoughts with the verbs *realize, think, wonder* and *know*.

11 Pronunciation contrastive stress

a ▶91 Listen to these exchanges from two of the conversations in Exercise 4. Notice how the words in bold are stressed. Repeat the exchanges.

1 A: It's a great idea to use social media for something like that.
   B: I didn't realize social media could actually be useful for **anything**!
2 C: It says here there's an eclipse tomorrow. Did you know?
   D: Tomorrow? I thought it was **today**.

b ▶92 Listen to four other exchanges. Repeat the exchanges.

Speaking my life

12 Think of an offer, an invitation, a promise and a request for other people in the class. Write each one on a piece of paper. Make sure you include your name and the name of the other person.

from Francesca: I'll help Belinda upload her video.

13 Work in pairs. Exchange your pieces of paper. Then find the people and report what your partner said. Then report each person's reaction to your partner.

A: Hi, Belinda. Francesca **has offered to help** you **upload** your video.
B: Oh, great!

my life ▶ NEWS STORIES ▶ PERSONAL COMMUNICATION ▶ APPS FOR MOBILE PHONES ▶ TELEPHONE MESSAGES ▶ AN OPINION ESSAY

reading community journalism • critical thinking opinions • speaking apps for mobile phones

11c Spreading the news

Reading

1 Look at the photo and the caption. How many different things do you use your phone for?

2 Work in pairs. Are you familiar with these terms? What do you think they mean? Read the article quickly and underline the terms. Check your ideas.

internet access	community journalism
the digital divide	traditional media
media organizations	affordable technology

3 Read the article again. Find information about these things. Compare with your partner.

1 internet access in different places
2 mobile phone ownership in different places
3 *HablaGuate*
4 *CGNet Swara*

4 Answer the questions using information from the article.

1 What kind of technology is used by the community journalism projects described?
2 What kind of news stories don't usually appear in traditional news media?
3 What happens to the stories received by *CGNet Swara* before they are shared?
4 How successful is *CGNet Swara*?

5 Work in pairs. Find how these words are used in the article and decide if they are adjectives, nouns or verbs. Then try to think of another word that could replace them.

1 enables (line 27)   5 affairs (line 35)
2 links (line 28)   6 dial (line 44)
3 debate (line 29)   7 highlight (line 50)
4 rural (line 31)   8 issue (line 51)

6 Look at how the words in bold are used in these sentences. Which words in Exercise 5 have a similar meaning?

1 Living in a small **country** village, we are a long way from the city.
2 When you **call** the number, you hear a message.
3 Our class is going to **discuss** the main ideas of the film we watched today.
4 There are some serious environmental **problems** around the factory.
5 The motorway **connects** the two cities.
6 The news reports **emphasize** the fact that nobody was hurt in the accident.
7 There's a bus twice a day that **makes it possible for** us to get to school.
8 Following the expansion, everyone is hoping for an improvement in its financial **situation**.

7 Work in pairs. How is the community journalism described in the article different from traditional local journalism?

Critical thinking opinions

8 Look at the question in the title of the article again. Do you think the writer successfully answers this question?

9 Read these extracts from the article. The writer is expressing her opinion. Which words or phrases tell you this? What is her opinion in each case?

1 As a journalist myself, it seems clear that the digital divide is also a problem for media organizations.
2 Obviously, this has great benefits for rural communities.
3 Clearly, community journalism works.

10 Underline two places in the article where the author gives the opinion or view of other people. What two phrases does she use to introduce the opinion or view?

11 Which sentence (a–c) best summarizes the writer's view of the digital divide?

a The digital divide is a problem that needs to be solved as soon as possible.
b The digital divide doesn't exist any more, since so many people have mobile phones.
c The digital divide has resulted in successful alternative ways of connecting communities.

Speaking my life

12 Work in two pairs within a group of four. You are going to find out about new apps for mobile phones.

Pair A: Turn to page 153 and follow the instructions.

Pair B: Turn to page 154 and follow the instructions.

13 Tell the other students in your group about the most useful apps on your phone. Which one could you not live without?

SPREADING the news

Can we overcome the digital divide?

If these men in Kyrgyzstan had a signal, they could use their phones for more than just photos.

▶ 93

These days, the popular view is that we're all connected, all of the time, by the internet. But are we? On the one hand, we have people who live in cities. In many cities around the world, internet access is almost 100 per cent. On the other hand, we have those who live in rural areas. Even in richer countries, the number of rural households with internet access is much lower than 100 per cent. And in some rural areas of India, for example, it's less than one per cent. This situation is what's known as the digital divide – the gap between those who have and those who don't have the communications technology that gives them easy access to information. As a journalist myself, it seems clear that the digital divide is also a problem for media organizations.

Fortunately, the lack of internet access doesn't always mean that people can't connect to the wider world. That's because there is one type of technology that over three billion people do have access to – the mobile phone. And the great advantage of mobile phones is that you don't need the internet to use them. Mobiles connect people to their friends and family, but they can also help to connect whole communities. In fact, a whole new type of community journalism can exist thanks to mobile phone technology.

Let's look at Guatemala – a country of fifteen million people with twenty-two million registered mobiles. Guatemalan journalist Kara Andrade developed a project, *HablaGuate*, that enables people to send their stories to a community website from their mobiles. *HablaGuate* links communities, making it easier to debate and participate in the kind of local issues that don't usually make headlines in the traditional media. Obviously, this has great benefits for rural communities. Following its success in Guatemala, Andrade has adapted the idea for other countries in Central America. As she says, affordable technology like mobiles enables people to become active in local affairs that affect their lives.

Halfway across the world, another journalist had a similar idea. Shubhranshu Choudhary used to report for the BBC in his home country, India. According to Choudhary, the best people to report on local issues are local people. He set up *CGNet Swara*, a current affairs network based around news that is sent on mobiles. Since 2010, more than three hundred thousand stories have been sent to the network, of which about five thousand have been fact-checked and shared. To listen to the stories, users dial the number of the network and choose an option on a menu to hear audio clips. For example, one story was from a man who reported that elephants were causing problems for his village. Another audio clip was from a woman who called in with the news that a local company had finally paid its workers the wages that they were owed. This was a direct result of her previous story that highlighted the issue. What's more, the national media are now featuring some of the stories from *CGNet Swara*.

Clearly, community journalism works. And although the digital divide may be a problem for more traditional media organizations, some local communities have found ways of overcoming this problem.

my life ▶ NEWS STORIES ▶ PERSONAL COMMUNICATION ▶ APPS FOR MOBILE PHONES ▶ TELEPHONE MESSAGES ▶ AN OPINION ESSAY

11d Can I take a message?

Real life telephone language

1 ▶94 Listen to two telephone calls. Note down the information.

1 Who is the call for?
2 Who is the call from?
3 What's the call about?

2 ▶94 Look at the expressions for telephone messages. Listen to the telephone calls again. Tick the expressions the speakers use.

> ▶ **TELEPHONE LANGUAGE**
>
> **Introductions**
> This is a message for Anna Price.
> Could I speak to Jess Parker, please?
> Is Jess there?
> Can I take a message?
> I wonder whether I could leave a message?
>
> **Message content**
> Can you ask her to ring me?
> It's about the apartment.
> I'm returning her call.
> I'd like to speak to her as soon as possible.
>
> **Caller's details**
> I'm on 96235601.
> My number is 96235601.
> Can I take your name, please?
> Who's calling?
>
> **Endings**
> I'll try and call you later.
> I'll phone back.
> I'll let her know that you rang.
> She'll get back to you.

3 ▶95 Listen to the conversations about the phone calls. Answer the questions.

1 Who is going to call Roger back?
2 How many messages does the secretary give Jess?

4 Pronunciation polite requests with *can* and *could*

a ▶96 Listen to four requests. Notice how the speaker's voice rises at the end in order to sound polite.

b Work in pairs. Practise making requests with *can* and *could* and these ideas. Pay attention to sounding polite.

1 give me your name / number / address
2 leave my name / number / address
3 ask him/her to call me back / get in touch / give me a ring
4 make an appointment
5 call round

5 Work in pairs. Look at the audioscript on page 189 for the second telephone call in Exercise 1. Take a role each and prepare your role. Then close your books and practise the conversation. Change roles and repeat the conversation.

6 Work in pairs. You are going to leave a message for someone in your class. Use the expressions for telephone messages to help you.

Student A: Choose a classmate (Student C). Decide what your message is. 'Phone' Student B and leave the message for Student C.

Student B: Take the message for Student C.

Then change roles and repeat the telephone call.

7 Work in a new pair with the classmate you took the message for. Give this person the message.

writing an opinion essay • writing skill essay structure Unit 11 Connections

11e A point of view

Writing an opinion essay

1 Work in pairs. Look at the title of the essay. Discuss the question and make notes on at least two reasons to support your answer.

2 Read the essay and answer the questions.

1 Do you agree with the writer of the essay?
2 Does the essay include the ideas you had in Exercise 1?
3 What (other) ideas does the essay include?

DOES THE INTERNET MAKE IT EASIER FOR PEOPLE TO KEEP IN TOUCH?

1 These days, there are many different apps that allow you to communicate with other people. I think this makes it easier to stay in touch with friends and family, and also to make new friends.

2 Firstly, many people now have constant access to the internet via smartphones as well as tablets and PCs. This means that if you send someone a message, they will see it straightaway. I think that you stay in touch more easily when you can communicate quickly.

3 In addition, there are lots of different apps available. For example, you can share photos, videos and links with people as well as text messages. It's also very easy to have video chats. You can do all of these things either for a small charge or completely for free. Some people say it's not 'real' conversation, but I disagree. In my opinion, it's the same as writing letters used to be.

4 To sum up, I believe that the number of apps on the internet and the low cost make it very easy to keep in touch with people.

3 Writing skill essay structure

a Match the functions (a–d) with the paragraphs (1–4).

a additional opinions / other opinions / examples
b concluding statement referring to the ideas in the essay
c general statement and short response to the title
d statement to support your response

b Write the words and expressions from the essay that are used for these functions. Add a comma where necessary.

Starting a paragraph	
Giving your opinion	
Contrasting opinions	
Giving examples	

c Complete the essay with expressions from Exercise 3b. Remember to add a comma where necessary. More than one answer is sometimes possible. Compare with your partner.

¹_____ nearly everyone has a phone that lets them get online. I've read that experts think we spend too much time online and ²_____ we sometimes feel pressure to answer messages quickly. But ³_____ with both points.

⁴_____ there are many great reasons to go online. ⁵_____ you can use social media to connect with your friends. ⁶_____ being online gives you access to lots of information.

⁷_____ the advantages of being online outweigh the disadvantages.

4 Work in pairs. You're going to prepare an essay with four paragraphs. Choose one essay title. Write the introduction (paragraph 1) together. Look at your notes and decide which ideas can go together in paragraphs 2 and 3.

• Do people spend too much time online these days?
• Is it a good idea to have one day a week 'off' the internet?
• Do children under the age of ten need mobile phones?

5 Work on your own. Write paragraphs 2 and 3 to follow your introduction. Then write the concluding paragraph. Use expressions from Exercise 3b.

6 Use these questions to check your essay. Then exchange your essay with a new partner.

• Have you organized your essay correctly?
• Is your opinion clearly expressed?
• Have you used expressions from Exercise 3b correctly?

7 Work in pairs. Ask your new partner about one thing they wrote in their essay.

my life ▶ NEWS STORIES ▶ PERSONAL COMMUNICATION ▶ APPS FOR MOBILE PHONES ▶ TELEPHONE MESSAGES
AN OPINION ESSAY

11f Can you read my lips?

Learning sign language at school

Unit 11 Connections

Before you watch

1 Work in groups. Why do people use these three things? How much do you know about them?

1. a hearing aid
2. sign language
3. lip reading

2 Key vocabulary

a Read the sentences. The words in bold are used in the video. Guess the meaning of the words.

1. We used to play the same games every **recess** when I was a kid.
2. The art exhibition was also an **auditory** experience because each room had different music playing.
3. This note from Jim isn't very **legible** – I can't work out what he's written.
4. Some children **mumble** because they are too shy to speak loudly in front of a class.
5. Some people don't accept the concept of climate change, although I don't think it's hard to **grasp**.
6. We had to **wade** across a river, but luckily nobody fell in.

b Match the words in bold in Exercise 2a with these definitions.

a. describing sounds and hearing
b. a period of play between lessons at school (Am Eng)
c. to walk with difficulty through something wet
d. to understand something that seems difficult
e. words written clearly enough to be understood
f. to speak too quietly and not clearly enough to be understood

While you watch

3 ▶ 11.1 Watch the video. What is the girl, Rachel Kolb, saying at the end of the video?

4 ▶ 11.1 Work in pairs. Watch the first part of the video (00.00–01.10) again. Discuss what you think the video is demonstrating.

5 ▶ 11.1 Watch the second part of the video (01.11–02.22) again. Note down the things that can make lip reading difficult. Compare your answers with the class.

6 ▶ 11.1 Watch the final part of the video (02.23 to the end) again. Answer the questions.

1. Does Rachel Kolb prefer to lip read or to sign?
2. What does she say happens when lip reading works well for her?

After you watch

7 Work in pairs. What did you learn from this video?

8 Vocabulary in context

a ▶ 11.2 Watch the clips from the video. Choose the correct meaning of the words and phrases.

b Answer the questions in your own words. Then work in pairs and compare your answers.

1. Can you remember a time when something clicked for you?
2. How does it feel to launch into an explanation of something, then realize you don't really understand it?
3. Being successful in life isn't a given. Do you agree with this statement?

9 ▶ 11.1 Work in small groups. Watch the section of the video from 02.58 to 03.10 again. What do you think the girl is signing? Take turns to tell the group about something that has happened to you recently using only signs. How successful are you?

10 Look at the signs below. Practise spelling your name.

11 Work in pairs. Take turns to spell words for your partner to guess.

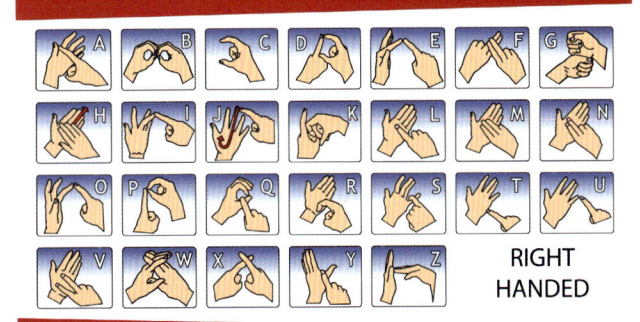

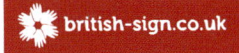

BRITISH SIGN LANGUAGE - FINGERSPELLING

RIGHT HANDED

british-sign.co.uk LEARN BRITISH SIGN LANGUAGE ONLINE AT WWW.BRITISH-SIGN.CO.UK

facial hair (n) /ˈfeɪʃəl ˌheə/ beards and moustaches
grade (n) /ɡreɪd/ a school year in the USA system
porcupine (n) /ˈpɔːkjəˌpaɪn/ a small animal covered in spikes
rely on (v) /rɪˈlaɪ ˌɒn/ depend on
swamp (n) /swɒmp/ an area of land that is a mixture of water, soil and plants

UNIT 11 REVIEW AND MEMORY BOOSTER

Grammar

1 Underline six reporting verbs in the news item. Write the words that were originally used.

Worries over lives lived online

The executive chairman of Google, Eric Schmidt, once said that there were only two states for children: 'asleep or online'. Recent studies claimed that vulnerable young people could become addicted to the online world and be unable to cope with the challenges of the real world. One study reported that teenagers who engaged with social media during the night could damage their sleep. The study said this would increase the risk of anxiety and depression in teenagers. Teenagers who tried 'switching off' for a week told researchers that they had enjoyed the break, but they were worried about conversations they had missed. Meanwhile, some organizations asked why the government wasn't looking at ways of educating young people more on this matter.

2 Read the news item again. Answer the questions.
1 What are the main risks associated with being online for young people?
2 How did some teenagers feel when they didn't go online for a week?

3 >> MB Work in pairs. Tell your partner about three stories you have read or heard recently in the news. Say:

- where you read or heard the stories
- why you remember them
- what people involved in the stories said

I CAN
report people's words (reported speech)
use appropriate verbs to report people's words (reporting verbs)

Vocabulary

4 Work in pairs. Give an example of the kind of story you would read about in these sections of a news website.

1 business section   5 national news
2 celebrity news   6 politics and society
3 entertainment   7 sports section
4 home page   8 world news

5 Match the beginnings of the sentences (1–4) with the endings (a–d)

1 I usually text
2 I've never followed
3 It's really easy to upload
4 My friend takes

a anyone on Twitter.
b my friends because it's quicker.
c photos of all her meals with her phone!
d videos these days.

6 >> MB Work in pairs. What do you think are the most usual ways of staying in touch with these groups of people? Why?

cousins	immediate family
current friends	old school friends
ex-work colleagues	people you met on holiday
grandparents	

I CAN
talk about news media
talk about communications technology

Real life

7 Work in pairs. Put the sentences from one half of a telephone conversation (a–e) into a logical order. Then act out the conversation, adding the other person's words.

a Thanks. I'll try and call him later, anyway.
b It's about the books he ordered. He asked me to ring him.
c OK. Well, could I leave a message?
d Yes, I'm on 548632 until about five this afternoon.
e Is Adam Meyer there, please?

I CAN
leave, take and pass on telephone messages

140

Unit 12 Experts

Sheep in the Scottish Hebrides islands

FEATURES

142 The man who ate his boots

Looking back at the mistakes of some British explorers

144 Experts in the wild

Listen to two stories about unexpected trouble

146 The legacy of the samurai

Find out about Japan's famous soldiers

150 Shark vs. octopus

A video about an encounter between a shark and an octopus

1 Work in groups. Look at the photo and the caption. What do you think the man's job is? What's he doing?

2 ▶ 97 Listen to an interview with a farmer from the Hebrides. Check your ideas from Exercise 1.

3 ▶ 97 Can you remember the answers to the interviewer's questions? Listen to the interview again and check.

   1 Why do you need to move the sheep like this?
   2 When do you bring them back?

4 Work in groups. Can you work out the solution to this farmer's problem?

A farmer has a fox, a chicken and a bag of grain. He needs to cross a river. He's got a boat, but he can only fit one other thing with him in the boat. Remember that foxes eat chickens and chickens eat grain. How does he get everything across the river?

my life ▶ DECISIONS ▶ WHERE DID I GO WRONG? ▶ GOING BACK IN TIME ▶ MAKING AND ACCEPTING APOLOGIES
▶ A WEBSITE ARTICLE

141

reading what explorers have to do to survive • grammar third conditional • speaking decisions

12a The man who ate his boots

Reading

1 You are going to read a review of a book about Arctic expeditions called *The man who ate his boots*. Work in pairs. Discuss the questions.

1 What kind of environment is the Arctic region?
2 What might go wrong on an expedition to the Arctic?
3 How much do you know about the lifestyles of people who live in the Arctic?

2 Read the first paragraph of the book review. Find the following information.

1 the reason for the British expeditions
2 what happened to the expeditions in the end
3 two words to describe the British explorers

3 Read the whole review. Are these sentences true (T) or false (F)?

1 The British explorers learned a lot from the local Inuit people they met.
2 Tents were an appropriate type of shelter for Arctic conditions.
3 The British wore adequate clothing for the weather in the Arctic.
4 The British pulled their own sledges rather than use dog teams.
5 The British had no supply of vitamin C to treat scurvy.

4 What do you think the title of the book refers to? Tell your partner.

▶ 98

The man who ate his boots is a fascinating account of expeditions that went wrong. The book tells the story of the nineteenth century British search for a route to Asia via the Arctic (the Northwest Passage). Author Anthony Brandt describes many attempts by both land and sea that ended in failure and tragedy, including the 1845 expedition led by Sir John Franklin. Brandt shows how these brave, yet sometimes foolish, British explorers would have avoided starvation, frostbite and even death if they'd copied the survival techniques of the local Inuit people. Some of the more surprising details the book reveals include:

Tents
The British had seen how the Inuit built igloos, but they still used tents. Tents freeze in sub-zero temperatures and don't keep the people inside them warm. If the British had built igloos, they would have been warm even in the worst Arctic weather.

Clothing
Frostbite was common among the British but rare among the Inuit. If the explorers had worn sealskin and furs like the Inuit, they wouldn't have suffered from frostbite.

Dog teams
Why didn't the British use dog teams to pull their sledges? British explorers pulled their sledges themselves right into the early twentieth century. It cost Scott and his men their lives on their return from the South Pole in 1912.

Salad
The British did get something right, however, when Captain Edward Parry grew salad vegetables in boxes on board his ship. It was known that fresh vegetables and fresh meat prevented scurvy, although at that time the reason for this – not enough vitamin C – hadn't been discovered. Parry's men wouldn't have stayed healthy if they hadn't eaten the salads.

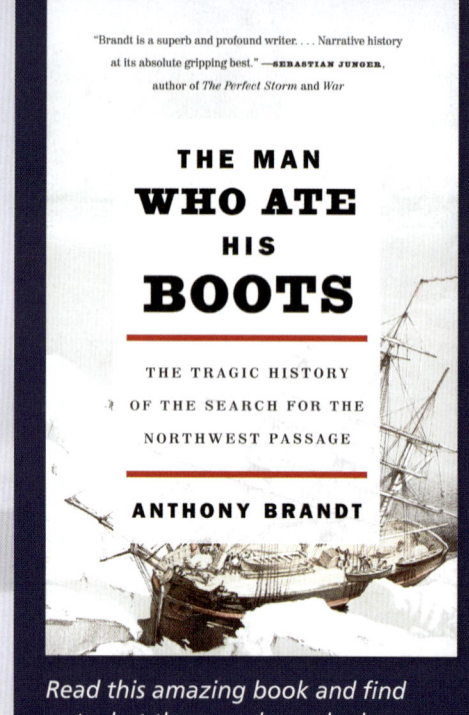

Read this amazing book and find out what these explorers had to do to survive.

frostbite (n) /ˈfrɒs(t)baɪt/ severe damage to the body caused by freezing conditions, usually affecting toes and fingers
scurvy (n) /ˈskɜːvi/ an illness affecting the mouth and teeth caused by lack of vitamin C
sledge (n) /slɛdʒ/ a wooden object for transporting people and things across snow
starvation (n) /stɑːˈveɪʃən/ death or loss of strength caused by not eating

Grammar third conditional

> **THIRD CONDITIONAL**
> 1 *If the British* **had built** *igloos, they* **would have been** *warm even in the worst Arctic weather.*
> 2 *Parry's men* **wouldn't have stayed** *healthy if they* **hadn't eaten** *the salads.*
>
> For further information and practice, see page 178.

5 Look at the grammar box. Which verb forms are used to make the third conditional?

6 Look at the grammar box again. Answer the questions.
1. a Did the British learn to build igloos?
   b Were they warm in the worst Arctic weather?
2. a Did Parry's men stay healthy?
   b Did they eat salads?

7 Find two more third conditional sentences in the book review.

8 Complete the sentences using the third conditional and the verbs in brackets.
1. If the British _____ (wear) furs, they _____ (not / get) frostbite.
2. The men _____ (not / be) exhausted if they _____ (use) dogs to pull their sledges.
3. If the men _____ (take) essential items only, the sledges _____ (not / be) heavy.
4. They _____ (not / become) ill if they _____ (know) their canned food was poisonous.
5. One expedition _____ (not / get) stuck on the ice if they _____ (speak) to local people.
6. If the expeditions _____ (follow) local customs, they _____ (be) successful.

9 Look at your completed sentences in Exercise 8. Say what actually happened.

1. *The British didn't wear furs. They got frostbite.*

10 Work in pairs. Match the pairs of sentences. Then write a new sentence using the third conditional.

1. We forgot to check our flight times.
   If we hadn't forgotten to check our flight times, we wouldn't have missed the plane.
2. We didn't ask anyone for information.
3. A local man gave us a map.
4. We didn't plan things very well.
5. The airline didn't let me take my bag on board.
6. We didn't get into the museum for free.
7. We didn't check the weather forecast.

a I packed too much.
b The holiday was a disaster.
c We found our way to the castle.
d We missed the plane.
e We didn't take a phrase book.
f We didn't take appropriate clothes.
g We didn't have our student cards with us.

Speaking my life

11 Think of three times in your life when you had to make a decision. They can be important or trivial decisions. Think about the answers to these questions.
1. Was it easy or difficult to decide what to do?
2. How did you decide?
3. What would have happened if you had done something different?

12 Work in pairs. Tell your partner about your decisions. Ask your partner follow-up questions. Would you have done the same things?

A: *When we were in Year 10 at school, we had to choose which foreign language to study.*
B: *Oh, so did we. What were your options?*
A: *French or German. And* **if I'd chosen** *German instead of French, …*

listening unexpected problems • grammar *should have* and *could have* • wordbuilding prefixes *in-*, *un-*, *im-* • speaking where did I go wrong?

12b Experts in the wild

Listening

1 Work in pairs. Discuss the questions.

1 Have you ever been camping? If so, what did you take with you? What was the experience like?
2 If you haven't been camping, would you like to go? Give your reasons.

2 Read about Emma Stokes and Beth Shapiro. Answer the questions.

1 What do they do?
2 What kind of places have they travelled to?
3 What kind of things could cause problems in those areas?

Emma Stokes is a wildlife researcher who has led projects to protect gorillas and tigers. She often has to cut paths through the forest and set up a camp. Her first-ever expedition was to the Central African forest, where she had an unexpected experience.

Beth Shapiro is a biologist and an expert on extinct mammal species. Much of her work is done on expeditions. She often goes to Siberia, where she hopes to find mammoth bones or tusks. On her first visit there, however, living animals caused the problem.

3 Work in pairs. You are going to listen to the stories of two difficult experiences Emma and Beth had. Before you listen, decide which story you think these words come from.

bones	mosquitoes
exhausted	remote
forest	rice
heavy steps	screaming

4 ▶99 Listen to the stories. Check your answers from Exercise 3.

mammoth (n) /ˈmæməθ/ an extinct animal, similar to an elephant
tracker (n) /ˈtrækə/ a person who shows you the way in a wild place
trumpeting (n) /ˈtrʌmpɪtɪŋ/ the noise made by elephants
tusks (n) /tʌsks/ two long teeth on the outside of the mouths of some animals

5 ▶99 Work in pairs. Look at the events from the two stories. Decide if they are about Emma (E) or Beth (B). Then listen to the stories again and put the events in order.

a She got her gear and got out of the tent.
b She had to take her mosquito net off her face to eat.
c She landed and set up camp.
d She was eaten alive by mosquitoes.
e The trackers woke her up by shouting.
f They made a meal of rice and fish.
g They made camp early one evening.
h When she went back, three of the tents were destroyed.

6 Work in pairs. What was the difficult experience in each case? What would you have done?

Grammar *should have* and *could have*

7 Read the comments. Who do you think said each one – Emma or Beth?

1 'We could have died.'
2 'We couldn't have avoided the insects.'
3 'We couldn't have imagined that would happen.'
4 'We should have checked the area before we camped.'
5 'We should have gone there at a different time of year.'
6 'We shouldn't have put up our tents there.'

8 Look at the sentences in Exercise 7 again. Match the sentences (1–6) with the meanings (a–d).

a This was the right thing to do, but we didn't do it.
b This was the wrong thing to do, but we did it.
c This was possible, but it didn't happen.
d This was impossible and it didn't happen.

> **SHOULD HAVE and COULD HAVE**
>
> should (not)
> could (not)   have + past participle
>
> For further information and practice, see page 178.

9 Look at the grammar box. Choose the best option to complete the sentences.

1 We *would / should* have brought more water – I'm really thirsty now.
2 The elephants came so close we almost *could / couldn't* have touched them.
3 We've run out of food – we *should / shouldn't* have known this would happen.
4 If I'd followed you, I *should / could* have got there more quickly.
5 I *should / would* have asked what was in the drink before I drank it.
6 If we'd taken the other road, we *wouldn't / shouldn't* have got lost.

10 Complete the story with *should (not) have, could (not) have* and past participle forms.

I'm an anthropologist and once when I was working in a remote area of Brazil, I ate something
¹ I _____ (eat). I was pretty sick.
² I _____ (feel) any worse, actually! I suppose
³ I _____ (have) some medicine with me, but I didn't. Anyway, the *curandeira* – the local healer – brought me the strongest of their local medicine.
⁴ I _____ (take) it straightaway, but I didn't because it smelled so bad. Of course, because of this I got much worse. So, the next day, I accepted the medicine. And after a few terrible days, I got better. Then I found out what the medicine was! I really think ⁵ I _____ (die) without it, though.

11 Pronunciation *should have* and *could have*

a ▶ 100 Listen to the sentences with *could have* and *should have* from Exercise 10. Notice the weak form of *have* /həv/.

b ▶ 100 Listen again and repeat the sentences.

Wordbuilding prefixes *in-, un-, im-*

> **WORDBUILDING prefix *in-, un-, im-***
>
> We can add *in-* and *un-* to the beginning of some adjectives to mean 'not'. We can also use *im-* before some adjectives which begin with the letter 'p'.
> *an inappropriate place, an unexpected experience, It was impossible.*
>
> For further practice, see Workbook page 99.

12 Look at the wordbuilding box. Replace the words in bold with an adjective beginning with *in-, un-* or *im-*.

1 We might see an elephant today, but it's **not likely**.
2 The guide is great even though he's **not experienced**.
3 In my country, it's **not polite** to speak while you're eating.
4 I hate sleeping in a tent – it's cold and **not comfortable**.
5 Don't worry about what to wear. The invitation says it's **not formal**.
6 My colleague is friendly, but he's **not patient**.

Speaking my life

13 Look at the problems you may have when doing some activities and write down one or two solutions for each one. Then talk to other students and find what advice they would give for one of the problems.

Activity	Problem
doing homework	couldn't find information
packed a suitcase	didn't have enough room
took photos	came out blurry
making a meal	burned everything
went to visit a friend	got lost

14 Work in pairs. Compare the advice you were given and decide which was the best advice.

my life ▶ DECISIONS ▶ **WHERE DID I GO WRONG?** ▶ GOING BACK IN TIME ▶ MAKING AND ACCEPTING APOLOGIES
▶ A WEBSITE ARTICLE

12c The legacy of the samurai

Reading

1 How much do you know about the samurai? Work in pairs. Try to answer the questions.
  1 Who were the samurai?
  2 Where were they from?
  3 When did they live?
  4 What did they do?

2 Before you read about the samurai, look at these words. Work in pairs and make connections between the words.

> army   duty   fighting   enemies
> generals   martial arts   opponents
> soldiers   sword   weapon

An army is made up of soldiers.

3 Read the article about the samurai. Check your answers from Exercise 1. Find the words in Exercise 2.

4 According to the article, are these statements true (T) or false (F)?
  1 The early samurai were similar to European knights.
  2 The samurai eventually died out following their defeat in battle.
  3 Samurai soldiers had a wide range of cultural interests.
  4 The military skills of the samurai have been lost.
  5 The legacy of the samurai has spread outside Japan.

5 Find these words in the article. Look at how they are used and try to guess their meaning. Then replace the words in bold in the sentences (1–6) with these words.

> battle-weary (line 29)   appeal (line 51)
> unarmed (line 39)   lone (line 53)
> overcoming (line 44)   fierce (line 61)

  1 I don't understand the **attraction** of war films.
  2 I think I'm **winning against** my opponent.
  3 That boxer is frightening. He's so **intense and aggressive**.
  4 The army was **exhausted after the attack**.
  5 We fought **without any weapons**.
  6 The police say they're looking for a **single, unaccompanied** gunman.

Critical thinking relevance

6 Which of these sentences could be included as additional information? Where should the sentences go in the article?
  1 His words might easily have been spoken by a Bushido master from three centuries ago.
  2 The samurai promised to be loyal to these men, who needed soldiers to protect and increase their power.
  3 In the late thirteenth century, a large Mongol army under the command of Kublai Khan, grandson of the Asian conqueror Genghis Khan, attacked Japan from the sea.
  4 Samurai also played *Go*, a board game about land conquest.
  5 The classic film *Seven Samurai* by Japanese director Akira Kurosawa has been described as one of the most influential films ever made.

Word focus *go*

7 Look at these extracts from the article. What do the expressions with *go* mean? Choose the correct option (a–c).
  1 The original samurai were soldiers **who went into battle** riding horses.
     a fought   b sat   c travelled
  2 Things **didn't go well** for the samurai.
     a didn't move   b were fine   c weren't good
  3 Samurai fighting skills **went into decline**.
     a improved   b influenced others   c weakened
  4 The 'samurai' is asked if he would like to **go back in time**.
     a return home   b return to the past   c start again

8 Work in pairs. What do the expressions with *go* mean in these sentences?
  1 The battle plan **went wrong** and ended in disaster.
  2 The battle **went on** for six days non-stop.
  3 The number of injured soldiers **is going up** daily.
  4 Suddenly, everything **went quiet**.
  5 We've decided to **go ahead** with our plan.
  6 I'm going to **have a go at** flower arranging.

Speaking my life

9 Would you like to go back in time and experience life in a different age and country? Or would you prefer to live in the future? Think about these points.
  - when and where
  - why that time appeals to you
  - your role or position in that society
  - opportunities
  - possible dangers

10 Work in groups. Ask questions to find out about your classmates' time-travelling choices. What is more popular – the past or the future?

The Legacy of the SAMURAI

Samurai history

The samurai (the word means 'one who serves') were the elite soldier class of Japan for nearly seven hundred years. In the tenth century, the rulers in Kyoto tried and failed to organize a conscript army. If the rulers had succeeded in this, the rich landowners might not have decided to employ private soldiers and the samurai might never have existed. The original samurai were soldiers who went into battle riding horses and fought their opponents following ancient traditions. Their customs would have seemed familiar to the European knights if they had ever met each other. Later, as the armies became larger and the fighting more violent, most samurai trained for hand-to-hand fighting. However, during a long period of peace in Japan things didn't go well for the samurai and eventually, in the 1860s, they lost their position of power in Japanese society.

Samurai identity

The sword of a samurai is a symbol of authority and luxury. It was both a weapon and an art object. This double identity mirrored the samurai themselves. As well as being soldiers, they used to socialize with artists, writers and philosophers. Samurai generals did flower arranging and went to the theatre. But of all their cultural activities, the tea ceremony was the most important. It was a slow and calm tradition. It took place in a small room where swords were forbidden, even to samurai, and it must have been very inviting to battle-weary soldiers.

Bushido

Bushido is the soldier's code. It was first written down as a kind of self-help manual during the long period of peace when samurai fighting skills went into decline. The martial arts tradition continues in Japan to this day. Millions of Japanese children still practise the classic skills of sword fighting (kendo), archery (kyudo) and hand-to-hand, unarmed fighting (jujitsu) at school. But Bushido is also a code of ethics: honour, loyalty and sacrifice. As Terukuni Uki, a martial arts teacher, explains, 'Here we teach the spirit of winning, but it's not so much defeating an opponent as overcoming one's own self. These days it seems everyone is looking for someone to blame rather than focusing on himself. Our message here is that if you try hard, at kendo or anything else, you will enjoy life.'

Samurai today

The continuing appeal of the samurai is due to a simple fact: he is one of the world's greatest action figures. He's the lone swordsman who kills dozens of enemies in the name of duty and individual glory. The samurai is the cowboy, the knight, the gladiator, and the Star Wars Jedi all rolled into one. The samurai have inspired hundreds of films, video games, comic books and TV dramas. In Japan, each spring, men put on samurai armour and act out famous samurai battles. These 'weekend' samurai look fierce and realistic, but, with their plastic goggles and swords, they wouldn't have been a threat to the real thing. One of the 'samurai' is asked if he would like to go back in time. 'Hmm,' he replies. 'They seem like better times, but I don't think they were, really. It was live or die.'

---

archery (n) /ˈɑːtʃəri/ the sport or fighting skill using bows and arrows
conscript (n) /ˈkɒnskrɪpt/ a soldier who is called up to fight by the authorities
ruler (n) /ˈruːlə/ the leader of a country
elite (adj) /eɪˈliːt/ the richest and most powerful people in a society
knight (n) /naɪt/ a soldier of a high status background

real life making and accepting apologies • pronunciation sentence stress

12d I'm so sorry!

Real life making and accepting apologies

1 Work in pairs. Do people apologize a lot in your culture? Would you apologize in these situations?

- arriving late for a meeting
- forgetting someone's name
- serving food a guest doesn't like
- not liking the food someone cooks for you
- taking someone's chair in a café
- asking someone to repeat something you didn't hear
- breaking something that belongs to someone else
- handing in some work after the deadline has passed at college
- losing something that belongs to someone else

2 You are going to listen to three conversations in which people make apologies. Look at the expressions for making and accepting apologies. What do you think the three conversations are about?

3 ▶ 102 Listen to the three conversations and check your ideas from Exercise 2.

4 ▶ 102 Listen to the conversations again. Then answer the questions.

1 What is the problem?
2 How is the situation resolved?

> ▶ **MAKING AND ACCEPTING APOLOGIES**
>
> **1**
> I'm really sorry you've gone to all this trouble.
> There's no need to apologize – it's not a problem.
> It's my fault. I'll make you something else.
>
> **2**
> I couldn't help it – I slipped.
> Don't blame me – this floor is slippery.
> Look, it was an accident! It could have happened to anyone.
> It's not your fault. Sorry I got upset.
>
> **3**
> I'm so sorry to keep you waiting.
> Don't worry about it – that service is terrible.
> Sorry about that!
> It's just one of those things – buses are unreliable!

5 Work in pairs. Do you think all of the expressions for making and accepting apologies would be appropriate in each of the three relationships? Why? / Why not?

6 Pronunciation sentence stress

a ▶ 103 Listen to the expressions for making and accepting apologies. Notice which word in black is stressed. Repeat the expressions.

b Work in pairs. Take turns to speak and respond using an appropriate expression. Pay attention to the words you stress.

1 Excuse me. This is a no smoking area.
2 I'm so sorry. I forgot to bring your book back.
3 Excuse me. That seat is taken.
4 You should have told me you didn't eat garlic!
5 Why is there no milk left?
6 I'm really sorry I didn't tell you I was coming!
7 Excuse me. Please wait until the waiter shows you to a table.
8 Sorry, we don't accept credit cards.

7 Work in pairs. Choose one of the problems in Exercise 1 or use your own idea. Decide what your relationship is and take a role each. Prepare a conversation which includes at least one apology.

8 Act out your conversation in front of another pair. Can they identify the situation and the relationship?

writing a website article • writing skill checking your writing

Unit 12 Experts

12e How to behave …

Writing a website article

1 Work in pairs. Have you ever spent time in an English-speaking country? Tell your partner three things (apart from the language!) you found strange or different there.

2 You are going to read an article from a website which arranges host families for foreign language students in the United Kingdom. What advice do you expect to find there? Tell your partner.

3 Read the article and see if your ideas are mentioned.

4 What do you think of the advice? Does any of it surprise you?

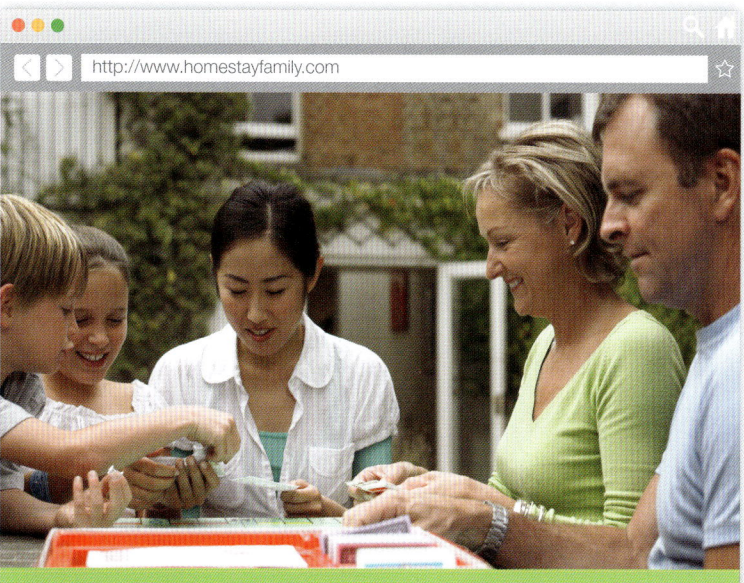

http://www.homestayfamily.com

How to behave with a **homestay family**

I've stayed with several families in Britain and Ireland and each of them has been different. But there are some key things I can pass on about getting the best out of your stay. I hope these things are useful!

Even though you are a paying guest in their home, take a small gift for your hosts. You'd expect a gift from a guest, I'm sure.

Your stay is not just about learning English. British and Irish people will expect you to show an interest in British and Irish culture.

Take some photos from home so that you can talk to your hosts about the photos. Taking the photos will also give you more opportunities to actually speak English too.

You're not a tourist, so don't behave like a tourist. Your host family will be getting on with normal life. Normal life is what you are there to experience!

And finally, remember the importance of being punctual (two o'clock means two o'clock!), polite (be careful with expressions you've picked up from pop music and movies!) and sociable (join in with things – at least the first time).

5 Writing skill checking your writing

a Look at this list of seven things which you should use to check your writing. Has the writer of the website article already checked all the things?

grammar	spelling
linking words	style
organization	vocabulary
relevance	

b The writer can improve the article by avoiding some words that are repeated. Look at the first line of the article. Who or what does *them* refer to?

c Replace the other highlighted words in the article with these words. There is one extra word.

| It | one | She | That | the same |
| their | them | there | they | This |

6 Work in groups. You are going to write an article for students coming to your country. Brainstorm ideas. Use these categories or ideas that are more relevant to your culture.

- celebrations
- dress
- food
- formality
- greetings
- house rules
- meal times
- money

7 Work on your own. Choose three to five ideas from your list in Exercise 6. Write an article of 150–200 words.

8 Use the list in Exercise 5a to check and revise your article.

9 Exchange articles with the other members of your group. Which were the most common topics?

my life ▶ DECISIONS ▶ WHERE DID I GO WRONG? ▶ GOING BACK IN TIME ▶ MAKING AND ACCEPTING APOLOGIES
▶ A WEBSITE ARTICLE

12f Shark vs. octopus

A giant Pacific octopus interacts with a scuba diver in the North Pacific Ocean.

Before you watch

1 Work in groups. Look at the photo and the caption. Discuss the questions.

1. What do you know about this animal?
2. How would you feel if you were the diver? Why?
3. Which animal would frighten you more: an octopus or a shark? Why?
4. What do you think might happen in a meeting between an octopus and a shark?

2 Key vocabulary

a Read the sentences. The words in bold are used in the video. Guess the meaning of the words.

1. We have a **tank** with eight different kinds of tropical fish in it. They're beautiful to look at.
2. Mice can be killed by several **predators**, such as foxes and birds, and of course, cats.
3. A tiger's stripes help to **camouflage** it as it moves through grass and bushes.
4. Polar bears are the same colour as their **surroundings** in winter, when everything is white.
5. Some animals **release** a strong smell when they are in danger.

b Match the words in bold in Exercise 2a with these definitions.
   a   to use patterns and colours so that it's difficult to be seen
   b   the place where you are and the things that are there
   c   to allow a liquid or gas to escape
   d   animals that kill and eat other animals to survive
   e   a large container of water to keep fish and similar animals in

While you watch

3 ▶ **12.1** Watch the video and check your ideas from Exercise 1 question 4. Are you surprised?

4 ▶ **12.1** Work in pairs, Student A and Student B. Watch the first part of the video (0.00–1.38) again. Make notes about your animal. Then tell your partner.

Student A: the spiny dogfish shark
1   usual food
2   how it gets its name
3   usual behaviour

Student B: the giant Pacific octopus
4   three ways it keeps itself safe from predators

5   usual food

5 ▶ **12.1** Try to complete the summary of what happened in the tank. Watch the video again to check your answers if necessary.

The spiny dogfish shark is a predator, but the octopus is not its usual prey. If it was, the aquarium staff wouldn't have put them in the same [1] _____. But then, dead [2] _____ started to appear at the bottom of the tank. The [3] _____ were worried. But then they discovered that the [4] _____ was attacking the [5] _____. Nobody had expected this to happen. The octopus was more dangerous than the sharks!

After you watch

6 Vocabulary in context

a ▶ **12.2** Watch the clips from the video. Choose the correct meaning of the words and phrases.

b Answer the questions in your own words. Then work in pairs and compare your answers.

1. What other words can you use to get someone's attention when you start to speak?
2. Think of some well-known inventions or products. Do you know how they got their names?
3. What kind of thing do people dine on in your country?

7 Work in small groups. Brainstorm as many animals as you can in two minutes. Then discuss the connections between them – which are predators and which are prey? How many animals can you connect into a 'food chain'?

---

aquarium (n) /əˈkweəriəm/ a type of zoo for fish and other sea animals
beak (n) /biːk/ the hard part of a mouth, usually on a bird
dismiss (v) /dɪsˈmɪs/ to reject or not consider something
prey (n) /preɪ/ an animal that is killed and eaten by a predator
sucker (n) /ˈsʌkə/ part of an animal's body that helps them hold things
welfare (n) /ˈwelfeə/ health or safety of people or animals

UNIT 12 REVIEW AND MEMORY BOOSTER

Grammar

1 Complete the article about the photo with the correct form of the verbs.

This photo is one of the most famous photos of the rare snow leopard. What makes this photo so extraordinary? Firstly, patience. The photographer, Steve Winter, spent ten months on this assignment. If he [1] _____ (be) in a hurry, he [2] _____ (not get) his shots. Secondly, dedication. Steve camped out for six weeks at 30 degrees below zero, conditions in which he [3] _____ (freeze) to death! Next, cooperation. Steve credited the knowledge of local experts Tashi Tundup and Raghu Chundawat, without whom he [4] _____ (not be able) to go ahead with the project. Finally, the animal itself. Steve says the photo 'was a real collaboration between the snow leopard and myself'. And it's true. Imagine how differently the photo [5] _____ (turn out) if the snow leopard [6] _____ (not go) hunting, slowly and silently, on that snowy night.

2 Read the article again. Which statements are true, according to the information given?

1 A combination of factors led to the success of the photo.
2 Steve Winter nearly died on this assignment.
3 Winter needed help to find the leopard.
4 The photo shows the leopard while it's hunting.

3 >> MB Work in pairs. Read the sentences about Steve Winter. Discuss what would/might/could have happened if the situations had been different.

1 His first camera was a gift from his father on his seventh birthday.
2 The snow leopard has a reputation for being impossible to find.
3 Steve didn't get any shots until he moved higher up the mountain.

I CAN
talk about things that did not happen (should have and could have)

talk about the hypothetical results of things that did not happen (third conditional)

Vocabulary

4 Write adjectives with the correct prefix which mean the same as:

1 not appropriate _____
2 not comfortable _____
3 not experienced _____
4 not formal _____
5 not likely _____
6 not patient _____
7 not polite _____
8 not possible _____
9 not unexpected _____

5 Write sentences with four of the adjectives from Exercise 4.

6 >> MB Work in pairs. Tell your partner about a time when:

- something went wrong
- you had a go at something new
- something went on for longer than you expected
- something went up in price or number very quickly

I CAN
use negative prefixes correctly

talk about things with expressions with go

Real life

7 Work in pairs. Complete the exchanges with these expressions. Then continue the conversations.

| Don't worry about it – | It's not your fault. |
| No, it's my fault. | Well, don't blame me – |

1 A: I'm so sorry I forgot to call you last night.
   B: _____ I wasn't at home anyway.

2 A: Oh, no. We haven't got any orange juice left.
   B: _____ I don't even drink it.

3 A: I'm really sorry about getting upset yesterday.
   B: _____ I shouldn't have shouted!

4 A: Sorry about the problem the other day.
   B: _____ You did nothing wrong.

I CAN
make and accept apologies

Communication activities

UNIT 3b Exercise 10, page 37
Pair A

Read the solution to puzzle A. Pair B will ask you questions to discover the answer to this puzzle. Then ask Pair B questions to discover the answer to puzzle B. Then turn back to page 37.

> **Solution to puzzle A**
> The people on the yacht decided to have a diving competition. When they were all in the water, they discovered they had forgotten to put a ladder down the side of the yacht. They couldn't get back into the yacht, so they drowned.

UNIT 9a Exercise 10, page 107
Student A

1 Complete the sentences with the passive form of the verb in brackets.

2 Read the sentences to your partner. Student B must decide if the sentences are true or false.

3 Listen to your partner's sentences. Decide if they are true or false. (Your sentence 3 is false.)

   1 Same-day shipping _____ by over 80 per cent of online shoppers nowadays. (*demand*, present simple)
   2 By 2030, a mobile device _____ by three out of four people globally. (*own*, future)
   3 By 2030, cash _____ no longer _____ in most stores in Europe. (*accept*, future)
   4 More and more brands _____ to show that their products are ethical and this will continue into the future. (*expect*, present continuous)
   5 In the next few years, over a quarter of all purchases _____ following recommendations on social media. (*make*, future)

UNIT 10a Exercise 9, page 119
Pair A

1 Think of one example for each of these categories. Write at least four clues for two of your examples using the second conditional.

   - a job
   - a famous person
   - an animal
   - a country

   job – airline pilot
   If we did this job, we'd spend a lot of time travelling.

2 Read the sentences to Pair B. They must guess your job, person, etc. Be prepared to give extra clues.

3 Listen to Pair B's sentences. Guess the job, person, etc.

UNIT 11a Exercise 10, page 131
Pair A

Read the news story. Write a short dialogue between the man and a rescuer. Practise your dialogue so that you are ready to act it out for Pair B. Then turn back to page 131.

> A walker who got lost in the hills was rescued this weekend after taking a photo with his phone and emailing it to the Volunteer Rescue Service. The man had fallen and was injured, but with no maps he couldn't tell the rescuers where he was. He took the photo after advice from the rescue team, who then recognized the location immediately.

UNIT 11c Exercise 12, page 134
Pair A

Read the notes. Practise describing the apps in your pair and make up a name for the app. Then tell Pair B about them. App 3 is the one that doesn't exist.

1 audio clips of different sounds – when you need to invent a reason to end a conversation
2 food app – tells you how many calories in food
3 clean clothes app – tells you when clothes are dirty and need washing

UNIT 1b Exercise 14, page 13
Pair A: The Blue Quiz

Ask Pair B the questions without the options. Give them 5 points if they can answer the question immediately. Give them 1 point if they need to hear the options. The correct option is in bold.

1 Where does the Blue-footed booby live?
   a in South Africa
   b in Australia and New Zealand
   c on the west coast of Central and South America
   The feet of adult female birds are darker than those of adult males or young birds. The colour comes from the fish the birds eat.

2 Who lives in the Blue House in South Korea?
   a the president
   b the king
   c the prime minister
   It's his official home and it's got a blue-tiled roof.

3 Do you know the name of the country where the Blue Nile begins?
   a Sudan
   b Ethiopia
   c Uganda
   It begins in Lake Tana and then joins the White Nile to form the Nile river.

4 Which part of the USA is famous for Blues music?
   a the west coast
   b the deep south
   c the mid-west
   Blues singers sing about their difficult life or bad luck in love. These people can be said to have the blues.

Communication activities

UNIT 3b Exercise 10, page 37

Pair B

Ask Pair A questions to discover the answer to puzzle A. Then read the solution to puzzle B. Pair A will ask you questions to discover the answer to this puzzle.

> **Solution to puzzle B**
> The man had fallen into the Dead Sea. This is actually a salt-water lake. The salt density is so high that you can easily float on the surface of the water.

UNIT 9a Exercise 10, page 107

Student B

1 Complete the sentences with the passive form of the verb in brackets.

2 Listen to your partner's sentences. Decide if they are true or false.

3 Read the sentences to your partner. Student A must decide if the sentences are true or false. (Your sentence 3 is false.)

 1 The amount of money which _____ by the middle classes around the world will triple by 2030. (*spend*, present simple)
 2 By 2030, over $500 billion _____ via mobile payments, compared to $75 billion in 2016. (*spend*, future)
 3 Larger and larger stores _____ to meet increasing demand from shoppers. (*build*, future)
 4 Delivery in 1–3 hours _____ by over 60 per cent of online shoppers nowadays. (*request*, present continuous)
 5 Personal information _____ with retailers by the majority of shoppers in the next few years. (*share*, future)

UNIT 10a Exercise 9, page 119

Pair B

1 Think of one example for each of these categories. Write at least four clues for two of your examples using the second conditional.

- a job
- a famous person
- an animal
- a country

job – airline pilot
If we did this job, we'd spend a lot of time travelling.

2 Listen to Pair A's sentences. Guess the job, person, etc.

3 Read your sentences to Pair A. They must guess your job, person, etc. Be prepared to give extra clues.

UNIT 11a Exercise 10, page 131

Pair B

Read the news story. Write a short dialogue between Adam and Corey. Practise your dialogue so that you are ready to act it out for Pair A. Then turn back to page 131.

> A message in a bottle which was put into the Atlantic Ocean in Florida has reached Ireland. Adam Flannery, aged 17, found the bottle which had been sent by high school student Corey Swearingen. The message gave Corey's contact details and asked the finder to get in touch with details of where the bottle ended up.

UNIT 11c Exercise 12, page 134

Pair B

Read the notes. Practise describing the apps in your pair and make up a name for the app. Then tell Pair A about them. App 2 is the one that doesn't exist.

1 how much sun cream? – tells you how sunny it is
2 late homework excuses – gives you different things to say to your teacher
3 positive messages – sent to your phone each day. 'I'm wonderful', etc.

UNIT 1b Exercise 14, page 13

Pair B: The Yellow Quiz

Ask Pair A the questions without the options. Give them 5 points if they can answer the question immediately. Give them 1 point if they need to hear the options. The correct option is in bold.

1 Where are yellow taxi cabs from originally?
  a **Chicago**
  b New York
  c Washington
  Mr Hertz started the Yellow Cab Company (in 1915) because yellow is easy to see from a distance.

2 Which yellow fruit does the Californian Fruit Festival celebrate?
  a the banana
  b **the lemon**
  c the pineapple
  There are lemon festivals in California every year.

3 Which sport gives a yellow jersey to the winner?
  a golf
  b horse racing
  c **cycling**
  More than 100 years ago, a newspaper gave money to pay for the Tour de France. The leader's jersey is the same colour as the paper the newspaper was printed on.

4 Can you tell me where the house that inspired Van Gogh's 'Yellow House' painting is?
  a in Holland
  b in Spain
  c **in France**
  Van Gogh spent the summer of 1888 in Arles, in the south of France.

UNIT 4d Exercise 8, page 52

Student A: Choose a number (1–12). You are going to make this request.

Student B: Look at your partner's number. Choose an appropriate situation (a–d) for this request. You are going to respond to the request.

Act out a conversation in this situation. Use the expressions on page 52 to help you. Take turns to make requests and respond.

Request
1 You want to sit down.
2 The phone number on a letter isn't clear.
3 You don't know where the company buildings are.
4 You want an application form sent in the post.
5 You haven't got a pen.
6 You need a taxi.
7 You need to know the time.
8 You want help with an application form.
9 You need a lift somewhere.
10 You want to leave your coat somewhere.
11 You want to wash your hands.
12 You want to use the phone.

Situation
a You're with a friend.
b You're in the reception area of a company.
c You're in an interview.
d You're on the phone.

UNIT 5 Review Exercise 9, page 58

Baklava
A rich, sweet pastry with chopped nuts and syrup or honey. From Turkey, the Caucasus and central Asia.

Borscht
A soup popular in many Eastern and Central European countries. Main ingredient: beetroot.

Coq au vin
A French chicken stew cooked with wine, mushrooms, herbs and garlic.

Couscous
From North Africa. A dish of semolina served with a meat or vegetable stew.

Fondue
Popular in Switzerland and France originally. Pieces of bread are dipped into a dish of melted cheese.

Goulash
A Hungarian meat soup or stew, flavoured with paprika.

Gravlax
Raw salmon cured in salt, sugar and the herb dill. From Scandinavia.

Kebab
Cubes of meat (or fish) on a skewer, cooked over an open fire. Originally from Central and Western Asia.

Lasagne
An Italian dish of pasta sheets layered with cheese, meat and tomato sauce and baked in the oven.

Paella
A rice dish originally from Valencia, Spain. Rice is cooked in a shallow dish with meat or seafood. Saffron flavours and colours the rice.

Sauerkraut
From northern Europe. Shredded cabbage is fermented until it has a sour flavour.

Tortilla
1 A type of flatbread made from corn or wheat in Central America.
2 A potato omelette from Spain.

UNIT 6a Exercise 2, page 70

Well, clearly the matches are to light the candle with and we know that drawing pins are for attaching things to other things. But what about the box? Yes, it's for holding the drawing pins. But you can also use it to hold the candle. And then you attach the box to the wall. Did you get it? Yes? Congratulations, you're a flexible thinker.

GRAMMAR SUMMARY UNIT 1

Present simple and present continuous

We use the present simple to talk about things which are permanent or generally true, such as facts, repeated behaviour, habits and routines.
*She **works** for the United Nations.*
*I usually **get** a new phone every year.*
*I **don't drive** to work. I always **walk** or go by bike.*

We use the present continuous:

- to talk about something in progress at the time of speaking.
*Wait a minute – I'**m** just **writing** an email.*

- to talk about things that are in progress around the time of speaking, but not necessarily at that exact moment.
*He'**s looking** for a new job at the moment.*

- to talk about a changing situation.
*Smartphones **are getting** more sophisticated all the time.*

▶ Exercise 1

Dynamic and stative verbs

Most verbs have dynamic meaning – they describe actions or things that happen. We can usually use dynamic verbs in both the simple and continuous form.
*I usually **read** books about travel and culture.*
*I'**m reading** a great book at the moment.*

Some verbs have stative meaning – they describe states such as thoughts and mental processes, the senses, emotions, qualities and existence. We usually use stative verbs only in the simple form.
***Do** you **know** Sue?* (not *Are you knowing Sue?*)
*I **don't understand**.* (not *I'm not understanding.*)

Common stative verbs include:

Thoughts and mental processes	admire, agree, appear, believe, care, depend, expect, feel, forget, hope, imagine, know, look (like), mean, mind, realize, recognize, remember, seem, sound, suppose, think, understand
The senses	feel, hear, see, smell, taste
Emotions, likes and desires	hate, like, love, prefer, need, want
Qualities and possession	come (from), consist of, contain, cost, deserve, fit, involve, measure, sound, suit, weigh belong, have (got), own, possess
Existence	be, be from, come from, exist

Some stative verbs can sometimes be used in the continuous form, especially in more informal contexts. We do this when we want to emphasize that the situation, feeling or attitude is at the moment, and is not permanent.
*I'**m feeling** much better today.*
*I'**m loving** this weather.*

Some verbs can be both stative and dynamic. The meaning changes if you use the continuous form.
*I **think** it's a good idea.* (stative: *think* = believe)
*Sssh! I'**m thinking**.* (dynamic: *think* = use your brain)

▶ Exercises 2 and 3

Question forms: direct questions

We normally form questions with auxiliary verb + subject + main verb.
***Are** you **leaving** now?* (*are* = auxiliary verb, *you* = subject, *leaving* = main verb)

Most tenses include an auxiliary verb. For the present simple and past simple, we add a form of the auxiliary verb *do*.
*Where **do** you live?*
***Did** you like the film?*

Some questions ask about a subject.
A: ***Who** wants a coffee?*
B: <u>***Valentina***</u> *wants a coffee.* (*Valentina* = subject)

When we ask about the subject of a sentence, we use the same word order as in a statement.
Who's seen *this film?* (not *Has who seen this film?*)

We don't use *do*, *does* or *did* for the present or past simple.
*Who **speaks** Arabic?* (not *Who does speak Arabic?*)
*What **happened**?* (not *What did happen?*)

▶ Exercises 4 and 5

Question forms: indirect questions

We use indirect questions to be less direct, because we want to be more polite or formal, or when we think the person we are asking may not know the answer.

Indirect questions begin with a question phrase such as *Do you know …* , *Can you tell me …* and *Could you tell me …* .
Do you know *where they are from?*

In *wh-* questions, we put the *wh-* word after the question phrase.
*Could you tell me **where** she lives?*

In *yes/no* questions, we put *if* after the question phrase.
*Do you know **if** we can book in advance?*

We use the same word order as in a statement. We don't need to add *do*, *does* or *did*.
*Can you tell me where **the museum is**?*
(not *Can you tell me where is the museum?*)
*Do you know where **she went**?*
(not *Do you know where did she go?*)

▶ Exercise 6

Exercises

1 Complete the exchanges with the present simple or present continuous form of the verbs.

1. A: They _____ (have) really good seafood here. It's what I usually _____ (eat) when I _____ (come) here.
   B: Oh, I'm vegetarian. I _____ (not / eat) seafood.
2. A: Oh no! It _____ (rain) again!
   B: Yeah, I'm afraid it _____ (rain) a lot here at this time of year.
3. A: You _____ (work) at the university, right?
   B: Normally, yes. But I _____ (not / work) there at the moment. I _____ (have) a break from teaching and I _____ (take) a year out. I _____ (write) a book, actually. I'm about halfway through.

2 Complete the sentences with the present simple or present continuous form of the verbs

1. I _____ (not / remember) my first day at school.
2. We _____ (prefer) the blue hats to the red ones.
3. Kate isn't sure about going to the conference, but she _____ (think) about it.
4. They're in the kitchen. They _____ (have) lunch.
5. Ben _____ (not / realize) what he _____ (need) to do.
6. I _____ (think) this jacket _____ (belong) to Lauren.

3 Choose the correct options to complete this extract from a book about the world's cultures.

The word 'culture' [1] *comes from / is coming from* the Latin 'colere', which [2] *means / is meaning* to cultivate and grow. Culture [3] *is / is being* the characteristics, knowledge and behaviour of a particular group of people. This [4] *includes / is including* language, religion, cuisine, social habits, music and arts. Today, cultural diversity across the planet [5] *increases / is increasing* faster than ever. This is because people [6] *move and mix / are moving and mixing* more easily and freely around the planet. At the same time, and as a result, more and more people, especially the younger generation, [7] *feel / are feeling* that they [8] *don't belong / aren't belonging* to a particular culture.

4 Write questions for these answers.

1. Where _____
   People wear white at funerals in East Asian countries.
2. When _____
   Hong Kong became independent from the UK in 1997.
3. How many _____
   About half the European countries use the euro.
4. What _____
   Ciao means both 'hello' and 'goodbye' in English.
5. Who _____
   The Chinese invented paper.
6. Which _____
   The two South American countries that don't have a coast are Paraguay and Bolivia.

5 Look at the interview with a travel writer. Write the questions.

1. _____
   I became a travel writer by writing about my travels on a blog. A magazine saw it and liked what I did and asked me to write for them.
2. _____
   The qualities and characteristics you need to be a travel writer are a love of travel, independent thinking and cultural sensitivity.
3. _____
   At the moment, I'm working on an article about some of the smaller ethnic cultures in South East Asia.
4. _____
   I usually choose my destinations. However, sometimes a magazine will ask me to go to a particular place.
5. _____
   I prepare for a trip by reading as much as possible about the place I'm visiting and getting advice from other authors who know the place.
6. _____
   What I find most exciting about my job is arriving in a new place for the first time.

6 Rewrite the direct questions as indirect questions.

1. What language do they speak in Mauritius?
   Do you _____
2. Where is Robert Fisher's office?
   Could you _____
3. Which terminal does the flight go from?
   Do you _____
4. Where did Julia go?
   Could you _____
5. Do people usually shake hands when they meet?
   Do you _____
6. Why do you need a new passport?
   Can you _____

GRAMMAR SUMMARY UNIT 2

Present perfect simple

Form

We form the present perfect simple with *have/has* + past participle. We normally use the contractions *'ve* and *'s* after pronouns.

*The record store **has closed**.*
*I **haven't bought** any CDs recently.*
*How many bands **have** you **seen**?*
*I**'ve read** that book.*

Many common past participles are irregular. They can be the same as an irregular past simple form (e.g. *buy – bought – bought*) or different to an irregular past simple form (e.g. *see – saw – seen*). For a full list of irregular past simple and past participle forms, go to the inside of the back cover.

Use

We use the present perfect simple:

- when we don't know exactly when an activity or situation started.
  *Millions of people **have bought** their music.*

- when an activity or situation started in the past and has an effect on the present.
  *It **has become** much easier to listen to music.*
  (= It became easier in the past and it's still easier.)
  *They**'ve released** a new album.* (= They produced it in the past, but it's new and available now.)

- to talk about activities and situations that started in the past and continue in the present.
  Use *for* to talk about a period of time.
  *I **haven't been** to a concert **for** years.*
  Use *since* to talk about a point in time.
  *They**'ve lived** here **since** 1960.*

- with superlatives.
  *I think that's the best song they**'ve written**.*

gone and been

The past participle of *go* is *gone*. It means 'go and stay away'.
*William**'s gone** to his brother's house.* (= He went there, and he's still there.)

But we also use *been* as a past participle of *go*. It means 'go and come back'.
*I**'ve been** to the shops.* (= I went there, and now I'm home again.)

▶ Exercises 1 and 2

already, just and yet

We often use the present perfect to talk about the recent past with *already*, *just* and *yet*.

- We use *already* in affirmative sentences and questions to say what has happened or is complete, often earlier than we expected.
  *I've **already** called Paul.*
  *Julie has **already** bought the tickets!* (= I didn't expect this.)

- We use *just* in affirmative sentences to say that something happened very recently.
  *He's **just** come back from work.* (= He came back a few minutes ago.)

- We use *yet* in questions to ask if something is complete.
  *Have you made lunch **yet**?*

We put *just* and *already* before the past participle. We put *yet* at the end of a question.
*Have you spoken to Mike **yet**?*
(not *Have you yet spoken to Mike?*)

▶ Exercise 3

Present perfect simple and past simple

We use both the present perfect simple and the past simple to talk about situations and events in the past.

We use the present perfect simple when we don't say when something happened.
*They**'ve played** concerts in over sixty different countries.*
*Robert**'s bought** a new car.*

We also use the present perfect simple with *ever* and *never* to talk about experiences in our whole life.
*Have you **ever** sung in front of an audience?*
*I've **never** listened to their music.*

We use the past simple when we say – or it is clear from the situation – when something happened.
*I **started** a new music course last week.*

With the present perfect, we use time expressions like *just, yet, already, for* and *since*. We also use the present perfect simple with unfinished time periods, like *today, this week, this month,* etc.

With the past simple, we use time expressions like *yesterday, last week, last month, in 2015, two weeks ago,* etc.

▶ Exercises 4, 5 and 6

Exercises

1 Complete the sentences with the present perfect simple form of the verbs in brackets. Use contractions where possible.

1 The concert _____ (start).
2 They _____ (make) lunch for us.
3 My sister _____ (not buy) any vinyl records.
4 _____ you _____ (finish) writing your report?
5 We _____ (know) each other since 2015.
6 _____ he _____ (see) this band play live before?
7 Our neighbours aren't here. They _____ (go) on holiday.
8 I _____ (not go) to a ballet for a long time.

2 Read the sentences (1–6). Choose the correct option (a–b) to explain each sentence.

1 I've broken my arm.
  a My arm is better.
  b My arm is still broken.
2 They've recorded three albums.
  a We know when this happened.
  b We don't know when this happened.
3 They've gone on holiday.
  a They're at home now.
  b They're on holiday now.
4 She's lived here for three years.
  a She lives here now.
  b She doesn't live here any more.
5 Sally's been to Mexico.
  a She's there now.
  b She's home now.
6 I've travelled a lot.
  a I'm talking about a general experience.
  b I'm talking about a specific time.

3 Put the word in brackets in the correct place in the sentences.

1 Have you eaten? (already)
2 The play has started. (just)
3 The train hasn't arrived. (yet)
4 He's had a coffee. (just)
5 We've seen this film. (already)
6 Has she woken up? (yet)
7 I haven't sent the message. (yet)
8 My brother has heard the album. (just)

4 Choose the correct option to complete the sentences.

1 I've lived in this part of Melbourne *for two years / in 2005*.
2 My sister been a music teacher *in 2000 / since 2000*.
3 I haven't seen my cousins *for 1995 / since 1995*.
4 We went to Japan *since three years / three years ago*.
5 Have you seen her *yesterday / today*?
6 I've worked in this office *since two years / for two years*.
7 We've started dance classes *last month / this month*.
8 My parents saw the show *in February / since February*.

5 Complete the sentences with the present perfect simple or past simple form of the verbs in brackets.

1 Our teacher _____ never _____ (go) to France.
2 My piano lesson _____ (start) at ten o'clock.
3 I _____ (not have) breakfast today.
4 _____ you ever _____ (see) a musical?
5 She _____ (not work) yesterday because she was very tired.
6 My brother _____ (get) married two weeks ago.
7 We _____ already _____ (read) this book.
8 _____ you _____ (go) to any concerts last month?

6 Complete the conversation with the present perfect simple or past simple form of these verbs.

| do | enjoy | go | not go | have | open |
| hear | not see | | | | |

A: What ¹_____ you _____ at the weekend?
B: I ²_____ to a concert.
A: Lucky you! I ³_____ a band play live for years.
B: This was a band called The Dotcoms. ⁴_____ you _____ of them?
A: No. ⁵_____ you _____ the concert?
B: Yes – it was amazing! I ⁶_____ a great time.
A: Wow! Where was it?
B: It was at the new concert hall. It ⁷_____ last month.
A: Oh, I ⁸_____ there. Is it nice inside?
B: It's great!

159

GRAMMAR SUMMARY UNIT 3

Past simple and past continuous

We use both the past simple and the past continuous to talk about situations and events in the past.

We use the past simple for:

- a short, completed action
  He **opened** the car door.

- a sequence of actions
  He **opened** the door, **got** out and **walked** towards the animal.

We use the past continuous for:

- an unfinished or continuing activity
  He **was trying** to switch on his camera.
  The lion **was looking** at them.

- a background situation
  It **was raining** and the trees **were blowing** in the wind.

Remember that we don't use the past continuous with state verbs, such as *like, love, need, own, want*.

We often use the past continuous and the past simple in the same sentence to talk about two things that happened at the same time. We often use *when* and *while* to link the two events in sentences like this.
  They **were driving** home when they **heard** a strange noise.
  We **got** lost while we **were walking** in the jungle.

We normally put *when* and *while* in the middle of the sentence. If we want to emphasize the first part of the sentence, *when* and *while* can go at the beginning. Remember to use a comma (,) in the middle of the sentence when this happens.
  While we **were walking** in the jungle, we **got** lost.

We don't normally use *while* with the past simple, but you can use *when* with the past continuous.
  I was swimming in the sea **when** I saw a dolphin.
  (not *I was swimming in the sea while I saw a dolphin.*)
  When I **was driving** home, I heard a strange noise.
  (or While I was driving home, …)

We often make questions in the past continuous to ask about activities at the time of a key event.
  What were you doing when you first saw the shark?

We often make questions in the past simple to ask about actions after a key event.
  What did you do when the shark swam away?

▶ Exercises 1, 2, 3 and 4

Past perfect simple

We form the past perfect simple with *had* + past participle. See the inside of the back cover for a list of common irregular past participles.

We use the past perfect simple when we need to make clear that one past action happened before another past action. For the action that happened first, we use the past perfect simple. For the action that happened second, we use the past simple.
  When they **got** to the station, the train **had left**.
             2   1

When we're telling a story, we sometimes also use the past perfect simple to describe events that happened before the start of a story.
  I visited Africa last year. I'd always **wanted** to go there. So I booked a holiday, and …

We only use the past perfect simple when we need to make it clear which action happened first. We don't need to use the past perfect simple when:

- the order of events is the same as the order of the verbs in the sentence.
  He **looked** down and **saw** a coin on the ground, so he **picked** it up.
  (not *… He had looked down and had seen …*)

- the order of events is clear.
  They **went** out on the boat after the storm **passed**.
  (not *… the storm had passed*)

We often use superlatives in sentences with the past perfect and the past simple.
  It was **the biggest** fish she'd ever seen.

▶ Exercises 5, 6 and 7

Exercises

1 Complete the story with the past simple or past continuous form of the verbs in brackets.

One weekend last summer, I ¹_____ (decide) to go for a walk in the mountains. It was a perfect day – the sun ² _____ (shine) and it wasn't too hot. But while I ³ _____ (walk), I suddenly ⁴ _____ (see) a huge bear on the path ahead of me. I was terrified! I ⁵ _____ (try) to decide what to do when the bear ⁶ _____ (turn) around and ⁷ _____ (run) away. I ⁸ _____ (not know) I was so scary!

2 Use the prompts to write questions with the tense in brackets.

1 What / he / do / when / saw the lion? (past continuous)

2 What / he / do / when / the lion walked towards him? (past simple)

3 Who / you / speak to / when / your phone battery ran out? (past continuous)

4 What / you / do / when / your phone battery ran out? (past simple)

5 What / they / do / when / the storm started? (past continuous)

6 Where / they / go / when / the storm started? (past simple)

3 Match the questions from Exercise 2 with these answers.

1 ☐   2 ☐   3 ☐   4 ☐   5 ☐   6 ☐

a He ran away!
b They were swimming in the sea.
c I was speaking to my boss.
d They went back to the hotel.
e I borrowed my friend's phone.
f He was sitting on the grass.

4 Complete the sentences with the past simple or past continuous forms of the verbs in brackets.

1 The sun _____ (shine) when we _____ (go) outside.
2 While I _____ (run) around the park, I _____ (lose) my phone.
3 They _____ (watch) TV when she _____ (arrive) at their house.
4 Thomas _____ (sleep) when the postman _____ (ring) the doorbell.
5 She _____ (drive) to work when she _____ (have) an accident.
6 While I _____ (wait) for the bus, I _____ (saw) my friend in her car.

5 Read the sentences and underline the action in bold which happened first.

1 He **sat down** and **watched** TV.
2 They **went out** on the boat after the storm **had passed**.
3 Before we **had** our ice creams, we **went** for a swim.
4 He **didn't have** his phone because he**'d lost** it.
5 The film **had finished** by the time we **arrived** at the cinema.
6 They**'d met** each other many times before they **started** their business.
7 Sophie **felt** very excited because she **hadn't been** to a ballet before.
8 By the time we **found** the shop, it **had closed**.

6 Complete the text with the past perfect simple form of these verbs. Use contractions where possible.

be	be	change	find	go	lose	spend

Dario and Federica ¹ _____ only _____ married for three days when Federica lost her wedding ring. It happened on the first day of their honeymoon. They ² _____ the whole day on the beach and then they ³ _____ back to the hotel. While Federica was getting ready for dinner, she realized that she ⁴ _____ her ring. She felt terrible because it ⁵ _____ very expensive. The young couple went back to the beach the next day, but they couldn't find the ring. Then Federica remembered something: the day before, she ⁶ _____ her clothes behind a big rock at the end of the beach. So she went back to the rock. Luckily, the ring was still there – she couldn't believe she ⁷ _____ it!

7 Complete the sentences with the past simple or past perfect simple form of the verbs in brackets.

1 Tania _____ (not go) to London before, so she _____ (be) really excited.
2 He _____ (not be) hungry because he _____ (eat) a big breakfast.
3 My cousins _____ (not come) to my birthday party because I _____ (forget) to send them an invitation.
4 The match _____ (already start) when we _____ (get) there.
5 I _____ (not want) to go to the cinema with my friends because I _____ (already see) the film.
6 Paco _____ (not know) the time because his watch _____ (stop) working.
7 The restaurant _____ (be) very busy, but luckily we _____ (book) a table.
8 By the time I _____ (realize) what _____ (happen), it was too late.

161

GRAMMAR SUMMARY UNIT 4

Predictions

We use *will*, *may* and *might* to make predictions.

Form

We use the same form of *will*, *may* and *might* for all persons (*I, you, he/she/it*, etc.) and we don't need to use a form of *do* to make questions or negatives. *Will*, *may* and *might* are always followed by the infinitive without *to*.

> Robots **will work** in our homes.

Note that *will* is normally contracted after pronouns.
> It**'ll** rain tomorrow. (or *It may rain …* and *It might rain …*)

The negative of *will* is *won't*. We never contract *may not* – it always stays as two words.
> It **won't** rain later. (or *It may not rain …* and *It mightn't / might not rain …*)

We don't form questions with *may*.
> **Will** it rain later? (or *Might it rain …*)

The most common way to ask somebody to make a prediction is *Do you think + will*.
> **Do you think** Jackie **will** like the present?

We don't normally ask questions about predictions using *may*.

Use

will/won't

We use *will* and *won't* when we are confident about a prediction. We often add adverbs like *certainly*, *definitely* and *probably* to make a prediction sound stronger. Adverbs like these normally come:

- after *will*
  My job **will definitely** be very different in the future.

- before *won't*
  Most people at my company **probably won't** have a job next year.

may/might

We use *may* (*not*) or *might* (*not*) when we are less confident about a prediction.
> The company **may** need to close the factory.
> They **might not** give me the job as I don't have much experience.

There is no difference in meaning between *may* and *might*, but *may* is more common in formal, written English.

We use *will/won't/might/might not + be able to* to make predictions about ability.
> She probably **won't be able to** come to the meeting.
> We **might be able to** get a discount.

▶ Exercises 1, 2 and 3

Future forms

We use different forms to talk about the future.

present continuous

We use the present continuous to talk about a fixed arrangement to do something at a specified (or understood) time in the future. We often use the present continuous when we have agreed to do something with another person, we have bought tickets for something, etc.
> I**'m meeting** my boss at 3.30. (= We both have the meeting in our diary.)
> She**'s flying** to New York next week (= She's already got her ticket.)

We often use the present continuous to ask people about their plans, especially when we want to make an invitation.
> A: **Are** you **doing** anything tonight?
> B: No, not this evening.
> A: Would you like to go and see a film?

will

We use *will* + infinitive without *to* for a decision made at the moment of speaking.
> A: Have you sent Martin the email?
> B: No – I**'ll do** it now.

going to

We use *going to* + infinitive for a plan or intention decided before the moment of speaking.
> I'm **going to look** for a new job. (= This is my intention. I decided this a few days ago.)
> Max has got a new job. We**'re going to organize** a party for him to say goodbye. (= This is our idea, but we don't have any fixed plans yet.)

The negative of *going to* is *not going to*. We don't normally make the infinitive negative.
> He**'s not going to** come. (not *He's going to not come.*)

To make questions with *going to*, we use *are you going to … , is she going to …* , etc.
> **Are** you **going to** send me the report soon?

We can say *going to go*, but some people prefer to say simply *going*.
> I'm **going to go** to the dentist later.
> (or *I'm going to the dentist …*)

present simple

We use the present simple for an event that follows a regular schedule or timetable, like the time of trains, flights, etc.
> My flight **leaves** at 6.34 am.
> My class **finishes** at 9.30 pm.

We don't normally use the present simple to talk about an arrangement with other people. We use the present continuous or *going to* instead.
> We're all **meeting** in the square at 8 pm.
> (not *We all meet in the square at 8 pm.*)

▶ Exercises 4, 5 and 6

Exercises

1 Correct the mistakes in these sentences.

1 They might to go out for a meal later.
2 James definitely will be late to the meeting.
3 She willn't spend a lot of money on my birthday present.
4 Some students mayn't pass their exams.
5 I think you'll to find a new job soon.
6 My parents won't probably like the film.
7 I'm sure you'll able to ski after a few lessons.
8 Robots'll help us with our household jobs.

2 Put the words in order to make predictions with *will / won't*.

1 snow / it'll / at the weekend

2 definitely / our meal / won't / my friend / pay for

3 be / will / open / the shop

4 forget / certainly / their holiday / won't / they

5 be able to / find / she / our house / won't

6 be able to / finish / the report / today / we'll

3 Chiara is starting a new job. Look at her predictions about the job and complete the sentences with *will/won't*, *may/might* or *may not / mightn't*.

confident	less confident
good things:	good things:
learn new things	good food in restaurant
meet new people	can travel abroad
can speak French	
bad things:	bad things:
can't walk to work anymore	have to work late
not know anyone there	tiring
not have many holidays	

1 My new job _____ be tiring, but I'm sure I _____ learn a lot of new things.
2 I _____ know anyone at first, but I _____ meet new people.
3 I _____ speak French and I _____ travel abroad for work.
4 There _____ be good food in the restaurant.
5 The office isn't near my home, so I _____ walk to work anymore.
6 I _____ have to work late and I _____ have many holidays.

4 Read the sentences (1–6). Choose the correct option (a–b) to explain each sentence.

1 I'm getting a new computer tomorrow.
  a I plan to buy a new one.
  b I've already chosen and ordered one.
2 I'll have some coffee, please.
  a I'd already decided to have this.
  b I've just decided that I want this.
3 He's going to retake his exam.
  a He's just decided to do this.
  b He plans to do this.
4 We leave at 6.45 tomorrow morning.
  a The train leaves at this time.
  b We plan to leave at this time.
5 He's moving abroad for work.
  a He plans to do this.
  b He's already got his contract.
6 I'll come to the shop with you after lunch.
  a I've just decided to do this.
  b We've already arranged to do this.

5 Choose the correct options to complete the email.

> Hi Rob
> I'm so excited because yesterday I booked a plane ticket for Australia! ¹ *I'm moving / I'll move* there for a year! ² *I'm working / I'm going to work* in Melbourne for the first six months, but I still need to find a job. Then, when I have some money, ³ *I'm going to travel / I'm travelling* around the country for six months. The only annoying thing is the time of my flight – ⁴ *it's leaving / it leaves* at 4 am! But there are hotels near the airport, so I think ⁵ *I'm booking / I'll book* a room on the internet. I hope everything's OK with you. ⁶ *Are you doing / Will do you do* anything this weekend? Would you like to meet up?
> Anders

6 Complete the conversations with the correct future form. Sometimes more than one form is possible.

1 A: Sorry, Adrien is busy right now.
  B: OK, I _____ (come) back later.
2 A: Do you want to go out tomorrow evening?
  B: Sorry, I _____ (go) to the theatre. I've already bought a ticket.
3 A: What are you doing this evening?
  B: I _____ (study) because I have an exam soon.
4 A: Are you hungry? How about going out for a meal?
  B: No, it's OK – I _____ (make) something to eat.
5 A: When do you need to be at the station?
  B: My train _____ (leave) at 8.23, so I need to be there at about 8.15.
6 A: Let's go to the cinema this evening.
  B: No, we can't. We _____ (meet) Lucy and Mark, remember? I arranged everything yesterday.

GRAMMAR SUMMARY UNIT 5

Modal verbs (1)

Form

We use modal verbs like *must*, *can* and *should* with the infinitive without *to*. We use the same form for all persons (*I*, *you*, *he/she/it*, etc.) and we don't need to use a form of *do* to make questions or negatives.

You **can** leave your bag here.
You **mustn't** leave your bag here.
Should I leave my bag here?

Have to and *be allowed to* have similar meanings to modal verbs, but they do not have the same grammar. We use a form of *do* to make questions and negatives with *have to*.

Do we **have to** sit here?
You **don't have to** come.

With *be allowed to*, we make questions and negatives in the same way as other forms with *be*.

Are we **allowed to** come in?
You **aren't allowed** to make phone calls in here.

Use

Obligation

To say there is an obligation, we use *must* or *have to*.
You **have to** leave everything in the oven for two hours.
Restaurants **must** make their prices clear.

We do not normally ask questions about obligation with *must*. We use *have to* instead.
Do I **have to** take my shoes off?
(not *Must I take my shoes off?*)

There is no past form of *must* to talk about obligation. We use *had to* to talk about obligation in the past.
We **had to** be at work at six o'clock this morning!

To say there is no obligation, we use *don't/doesn't have to*.
We **don't have to** be there until 8 pm.

Prohibition and permission

To talk about prohibition (to say 'don't do it!'), we use *mustn't*.
You **mustn't** talk here.

To give permission, we use *can*.
You **can** pay for your drinks when you leave.

To say somebody doesn't have permission, we use *can't* or *cannot*.
You **can't** sit in this part of the restaurant. (or You cannot sit …)

We also use *allowed to* and *not allowed to* talk about permission.
Are we **allowed** to take our food outside?
You**'re not allowed** to park there.

Advice and recommendation

Should doesn't express a rule. We use *should* and *shouldn't* to give advice and recommendations.
You **should** try to eat some fruit every day.
You **shouldn't** eat too much before you go to bed.

must and *have to*

The modal verbs *must* and *have to* have very similar meanings. We normally prefer to use *have to* in spoken English to talk about obligation. In formal, written English, we prefer to use *must*. But *mustn't* and *don't have to* have very different meanings. *Mustn't* expresses a rule – we use *mustn't* to say 'don't do this'. *Don't have to* doesn't express a rule – we use *don't have to* to say 'it's not necessary to do this'.

Customers **must not** enter the kitchen. (= Don't do this!)
The restaurant is huge. You **don't have to** book a table. (= This isn't necessary.)

▶ Exercises 1, 2 and 3

First conditional

We use the first conditional to talk about future possibility and things which are generally true. The form is usually:
If + present simple, + *will/won't*

If I **have** time, I**'ll call** you tonight. (= future possibility)
If you **don't eat** healthily, you **won't feel** good. (= generally true)

Note that we never use a future form in the *if* clause.
If it **it's** a nice day tomorrow, we'll go for a picnic. (not *If it will be a nice day …*)

Conditional sentences have two parts: the *if* clause and the main clause. The main clause describes the result of the situation in the *if* clause.

If you're late, **we'll go** without you. (we'll go … = main clause = result)

When the *if* clause comes first, we use a comma between the two clauses. When the main clause comes before the *if* clause, we don't add a comma between the two clauses.

If you're late, we'll go without you.
We'll go without you if you're late.

▶ Exercise 4

when, as soon as, unless, until, before

We also use *when*, *as soon as*, *unless*, *until* and *before* to talk about the future. We always use a present tense, not a future form, after these expressions. We often use the expressions in a sentence with *will*.

When I **finish** my work, I'll get something to eat
I won't eat there again **unless** they **start** using less salt.
As soon as we **arrive**, I'll give you a call.
You won't lose weight **until** you **improve** your diet.
I'll have a shower **before** we **go** out.

As with the first conditional, we put a comma when the clause with the time expression comes first.

▶ Exercises 5 and 6

164

Exercises

1 Correct the mistakes in these sentences.

1. She hasn't to go to work today.
2. I can to make you a drink.
3. Do I should come back later?
4. Has he to go to the meeting?
5. We aren't allowed park here.
6. You don't must use your phone here.
7. You mustn't help me with the dishes. I can do them myself.
8. He shouldn't has salt on his food.

2 Read the signs. Complete the sentences with the correct modal form. Write all the possible answers.

1. **TICKETS NEEDED BEFORE ENTRY**
   You _____ / _____ buy a ticket before you enter.
2. **TABLETS AND PHONES ALLOWED ON THIS FLIGHT**
   You _____ switch off your tablets or phones on this flight.
3. **NO PARKING**
   You _____ / _____ / _____ park here.
4. **THIS FILM IS NOT RECOMMENDED FOR CHILDREN**
   Children _____ see this film.
5. **EXAM IN PROGRESS: BE QUIET!**
   You _____ / _____ speak quietly.
6. **SERVICE INCLUDED: TIP NOT NECESSARY**
   You _____ leave a tip in this restaurant.
7. **NO ENTRY EXCEPT FOR CYCLISTS**
   You _____ / _____ / _____ ride your bicycle here.

3 Complete the text with modal verbs and the verb in brackets. Use affirmative and negative forms of the modal verbs.

School dinners are very popular in the UK. Most children [1]_____ (pay) for school dinners, but they don't cost a lot. However, poorer families [2]_____ (pay) – the school dinners are free.

There are strict rules about school dinners. For example, every meal [3]_____ (include) meat or fish, fruit and vegetables and bread, potatoes and other cereals. Another rule is that school canteens [4]_____ (sell) food and drinks with a lot of sugar and salt.

Children [5]_____ (eat) school dinners if they don't want to. They [6]_____ (bring) a 'packed lunch' from home. There are many recommendations for the types of food to give children in their packed lunches. For example, children [7]_____ (eat) fruit every day and they [8]_____ (have) junk food like crisps and chocolate.

4 Choose the correct option to complete the first conditional sentences.

1. If he *does / will do* more exercise, *he gets / he'll get* fitter.
2. If the train *doesn't / won't* arrive soon, *I'm being / I'll be* late for work.
3. *You feel / You'll feel* better if *you eat / you'll eat* healthier food.
4. They *don't go / won't go* on holiday if they *don't find / won't find* cheap plane tickets.
5. *Do you / Will you* come out tonight if *you finish / you'll finish* your homework?
6. If you *have / will have* enough money, *do / will* you buy some new shoes?

5 Match the beginnings of the sentences (1–6) with the endings (a–f). Then complete the endings of the sentences with the correct form of the verbs in brackets.

1. If she doesn't leave soon,
2. They'll have a picnic in the park next to their house
3. You can't go out
4. You'll feel sick
5. Can you call me
6. I think he'll drive to the station

a. if there _____ too much traffic. (not be)
b. until you _____ all your homework. (finish)
c. as soon as you _____ this message? (get)
d. she _____ her bus. (miss)
e. if you _____ all that chocolate! (eat)
f. unless it _____. (rain)

6 Complete the conversation with the correct form of these verbs.

| eat | exercise | follow | go | lose | not do |
| not feel | not lose | | | | |

A: How are you?
B: I'm fed up! I'm trying to lose weight, but nothing's working!
A: Well, I'm sure if you [1]_____ healthy food, you [2]_____ some weight. And you need to exercise too.
B: I try to eat healthily, but I never have time to exercise!
A: But you [3]_____ weight if you [4]_____ any exercise.
B: Alright! I'll go on my exercise bike before I [5]_____ to bed this evening.
A: No, that's the worst time to do exercise! If you [6]_____ in the evening, you [7]_____ sleepy afterwards. And sleep is also important for losing weight …
B: OK, so I'll go for a run at lunchtime instead.
A: Great. But remember – unless you [8]_____ a regular fitness programme, you'll never lose weight.

GRAMMAR SUMMARY UNIT 6

Grammar purpose: *to ...* , *for ...* and *so that ...*

We use *to*, *for* and *so that* to explain why people do something or the purpose of an object. Phrases with these words answer the questions *Why?* or *What for?*

to + infinitive

We use *to* + infinitive to say why we do something.
> She's doing a course **to improve** her communication skills.
> I used an old piece of plastic **to fix** the hole in the bath.

We often use *to* + infinitive to answer questions with *why*.
> A: Why did you call me?
> B: **To ask** if you want to come to the cinema.

We only use *to* + infinitive if the subject of the sentence is the same as the subject of the infinitive.
> I went to the library **to get** a book. (= **I** went to the library. **I** got a book.)

for + noun

We also use *for* + noun to say why we do something.
> She went there **for a job interview**.
> They stopped at a café **for some lunch**.

We never use *for* with a verb form to say why we do something. Use *to* + infinitive instead.
> I bought this book **to have** something to read on the plane. (not *I bought this book for to have something ... / for having something ...*)

for + -ing

We use *for* + -ing to talk about the purpose or function of an object.
> A: What app are you using?
> B: It's a game. It's **for improving** your memory.

so that

We also use *so that* to say why we do something. We often use this:

- with the modal verbs *can*, *could*, *will* or *would*.
  > I'll call Sam **so that** he'**ll know** where to go.
  > We got to the cinema earlier **so that** we **could** get a good seat.

- when the result is negative.
  > I want to buy an ebook reader **so that** I **don't have to** carry lots of books with me.

We only use *so that* when we do something to get a specific result. To talk about a result on its own, we use *so* without *that*. Note that we use a comma before *so* which introduces a result.
> I didn't wake up on time, **so** I missed my flight.
> (not *... on time so that I missed ...*)

We often use *so* instead of *so that* in informal English.
> She drove me to the shops **so** (**that**) I didn't have to walk.

▶ Exercises 1, 2 and 3

Certainty and possibility

We use the modal verbs *must*, *might (not)*, *may (not)*, *could* and *can't* to talk about certainty and possibility.

We use *must* when we think that something is probable.
> Her flight was at four in the morning. She **must** be very tired.

We use *might*, *may* and *could* when we think that something is possible.
> Paul **might** be able to help you.
> Hotel Tourist **may** have a room free.
> There **could** be a problem with the trains.

We can make *might* and *may* negative with this meaning, but not *could*.
> Stephanie **might** not want to eat out.
> (not *Stephanie could not want ...*)
> I **may** not have the correct address.
> (not *I could not have ...*)

We use *can't* when we think that something is impossible.
> A: Is that Mike in the café?
> B: No, it **can't** be him. He's on holiday in Greece!

When we're talking about things we're totally sure about, we don't use modals at all.
> Stefan lives near here. (= I know this. I've been to his house.)
> Esther doesn't eat meat. (= I know this. She told me.)

▶ Exercises 4 and 5

In the present and in the past

We use modal verb + infinitive to talk about certainty and possibility in the present.
> You **must be** hungry. (= It's probable that you're hungry now.)

We use modal verb + *be* + -ing if the action is in progress.
> He's not answering his phone. He **might be driving**.
> (= I think he's driving now.)

We use modal verb + *have* + participle to talk about certainty and possibility in the past.
> His plane **must have arrived** by now. (= It's probable that his plane has arrived.)
> A: Where are they?
> B: I don't know. They **may/might/could have got** lost.
> (= It's possible that they got lost.)
> A: I saw Sara this morning.
> B: You **can't have seen** her. She's on holiday in Morocco!

We can also use *couldn't have* instead of *can't have*:
> A: I think I left my phone on the plane.
> B: No, you **couldn't have left** it there – we checked really carefully.

▶ Exercise 6

Exercises

1 Match the beginnings of the sentences (1–7) with the endings (a–g). Then complete the endings of the sentences with the infinitives of these words.

ask buy catch get give see watch

1 I've joined a gym
2 She's going to the supermarket
3 He bought some flowers
4 I went to the station
5 We opened the box
6 I switched on the TV
7 Emilia called

a _____ what was inside.
b _____ more exercise.
c _____ my train.
d _____ me a question.
e _____ some food for dinner.
f _____ to his wife.
g _____ my favourite series.

2 Rewrite six of the sentences in Exercise 1 with *so that*. With which sentence can't you use *so that*?

1 _____
2 _____
3 _____
4 _____
5 _____
6 _____
7 _____

3 Choose the correct options to complete the conversation.

A: You look tired!
B: Well, I'm waking up at 5.30 am these days.
A: Why?
B: [1] *To do / For doing* yoga before I go to work.
A: I'm not surprised you're tired! Well, you should go to bed early [2] *for / so that* a good night's sleep.
B: I'd like to, but I'm always too busy in the evening to have an early night. For example, I've also started an online language course [3] *for improving / to improve* my German! I'm always up until late doing exercises.
A: Maybe you're doing too much. I've got a great app on my phone that could help you. It's [4] *for organizing / to organize* my day.
B: Sounds interesting. Can you show me it [5] *for / so that* I can see how it works?
A: Sure, but I haven't got time now. My phone's just told me that I've got to take the car to the garage [6] *to / for* a check. See you soon. Bye!

4 Read the sentences (1–4). Choose the correct option (a–b) to explain each sentence.

1 John must be asleep.
  a I'm sure John is asleep.
  b It's possible that John is asleep.
2 That can't be my phone. Mine's in my pocket.
  a It's impossible that it's my phone.
  b It's possibly not my phone.
3 Your keys might be in your bag.
  a Your keys are definitely in your bag.
  b It's possible that your keys are in your bag.
4 That woman with Frank could be his wife.
  a I'm certain that she's Frank's wife.
  b I think it's possible that she's Frank's wife.

5 Read the pairs of sentences. Rewrite the first sentence using a present modal verb.

1 It's impossible that that's Martin's car. His car is in the garage.
That _____ .
2 I'm sure it's cold outside. It's snowing!
It _____ .
3 It's possible that they aren't at home. Their car isn't outside their house.
_____ .
4 I'm sure you know each other very well. You've been friends for a long time.
You _____ .
5 It's possible that she's a doctor. She's wearing a white coat.
She _____ .
6 I'm sure the bill isn't right. I only had a salad!
This bill _____ .

6 Choose the correct options to complete the conversation.

A: Are we close to the castle ruins yet?
B: I think we [1] *may go / may be going* the wrong way. What did the guidebook say?
A: It said the ruins are near a small lake.
B: Oh – we passed a lake about five minutes ago!
A: So, we [2] *must drive / must have driven* past the road we need to take!
B: OK, oh look – there's the lake. We [3] *can't be / can't have been* far away now.
B: What's the name of the road we're looking for?
A: Old Hill … Oh, hold on – it [4] *might be / might have been* this one.
B: No, that's Field Lane.
A: Well, we're near the lake, so the road [5] *must be / must have been* close.
B: Look at the top of that hill. I can see something. I'm not sure, but it [6] *might be / must be* part of the ruins. Drive up that way!
B: OK. … Hmm – we [7] *must go / must have gone* the wrong way again. That's a petrol station!
A: Maybe the guidebook is wrong! There [8] *can't have been / might have been* a castle here!

167

GRAMMAR SUMMARY UNIT 7

used to, would and past simple

used to

We use *used to* to talk about past habits and states.
> We **used to** go on holiday to California every year when I was a kid. (= past habit)
> They **used to** have a really tiny flat in the city centre. (= past state)

Used to is always followed by the infinitive. We use the same form for all persons (*I, you, he/she/it*, etc.). In negatives and questions, we use *use to* not *used to*.
> There **didn't use to** be so much traffic here.
> **Did** you **use to** live near the sea?

We often use adverbs of frequency and other time phrases with *used to*.
> We used to eat there **every week**.

We often use *used to* to describe past actions and states that aren't true any more.
> I used to live in Germany. (= I don't live there now.)
> She used to watch a lot of TV. (= She doesn't watch much TV any more.)

We sometimes use frequency adverbs with *used to*. They come before *used to*.
> We **always** used to go to the seaside in the summer when I was a child.

To talk about habits in the present, we use the present simple with *usually*.
> We **usually** go for a walk in the park every day. (not *We use to go for a walk …*)

We don't normally use *used to* for repeated actions that lasted a short period of time. We use the past simple instead.
> I **cycled** to work every day last week. (not *I used to cycle to work every day last week.*)

▶ Exercise 1

would

We also use *would* + infinitive to talk about repeated past actions. In spoken English, *would* often becomes *'d*.
> **I'd** spend every day in summer outside when I was a child.

We only use *would* to talk about repeated actions in the past. We don't use *would* to talk about states.
> We **used to** own a really nice house in the countryside. (not *We'd own a house …*)

We sometimes use frequency adverbs with *would*. They come after *would*.
> I'd **always** do my homework at the last minute when I was at school.

When we talk about the past, we often start with *used to* and then continue with *would*.
> When I first moved to London, I **used to** go out a lot. **I'd** visit museums and go to concerts. **I'd** eat out at least once a week …

▶ Exercises 2 and 3

Comparison: adverbs

more/less + adverb

To make comparative forms of adverbs, we use *more* + adverb (*that*).
> This room gets warm **more quickly** than the rest of the house.
> You can live **more cheaply** in other parts of the city.

The opposite of *more* + adverb is *less* + adverb.
> You clean the flat **less often** than me.

Some comparative adverb forms are irregular. They have the same form as the comparative adjective. For example, *well → better, badly → worse, far → further, fast → faster, high → higher, early → earlier, late → later, soon → sooner*.

▶ Exercise 4

(not) as + adverb + as

To make comparisons, we also use *(not) as* + adverb + *as*. *Not* normally goes with the verb.
> Martina can run **as fast as** Silvia. (= Martina and Silvia can run at the same speed.)
> I **don't** go out **as often as** I did in the past. (= I used to go out more often.)

▶ Exercise 5

Comparison: patterns

To say that a situation is changing, we use comparative + *and* + comparative. We can use a comparative adjective or a comparative adverb in this structure.
> It's getting **colder and colder** – it's probably going to snow. (comparative adjective – one syllable)
> Things are becoming **more and more expensive** in this country. (comparative adjective – longer adjective)
> I've got so much work that I'm going to bed **later and later**. (comparative adverb)

Remember that we add *-er* to most one-syllable adjectives, and we put *more* before longer adjectives to make the comparative adjective form.

We often use *more and more* + noun.
> **More and more people** cycle to work these days.

To say that two things change at the same time, we use comparative + clause, *the* + comparative + clause.
> The harder you work, the more success you have. (= If you work hard, you'll be more successful.)
> The worse the weather is, the more traffic there is. (= When the weather is bad, the traffic gets bad too.)

We sometimes use this structure with only a noun phrase instead of a clause, or with only a comparative form.
> The taller the mountain, the greater the difficulty. (= Tall mountains are more difficult to climb.)
> The more the merrier. (= When there are lots of people, everyone is happier.)

▶ Exercise 6

Exercises

1 Complete the sentences with the correct form of *used to* and these verbs.

do	drive	listen	live	love	own
not be	not feel				

1. I _____ in Lima when I was young.
2. What _____ you _____ at the weekends when you were a child?
3. We _____ going to the theatre when we lived in London.
4. There _____ any houses here when I was young – it was all fields.
5. I _____ worried when I had an exam at school.
6. We _____ a lovely house by the sea.
7. _____ people _____ more before they built a metro here?
8. She _____ to rock music before she went to university.

2 Tick the sentences in which *used to* can be replaced by *would*.

1. I didn't use to like classical music when I was a teenager, but now I love it.
2. We used to visit Los Angeles often before we had children.
3. Their music used to sound very different before the new guitarist joined the band.
4. When I was younger, I used to believe in UFOs, but I don't any more.
5. Sean used to play basketball every day when he was a teenager.
6. My family used to go to the same holiday resort every year when I was a child.

3 Complete the conversation with the *used to*, *would* or the past simple form of the verbs in brackets.

A: You've been to Hamburg, haven't you?
B: Yes, I ¹_____ (go) there often for work when I was living in Germany. Are you going to visit?
A: Yeah, next month. Any recommendations?
B: Well, I ²_____ (leave) Germany in 2012. Things might be different now. But, I remember we ³_____ (eat) in a great Italian restaurant. It was by the river. I can't remember the name, but they ⁴_____ (make) fantastic pizza.
A: OK, I'll look for it. Anything else?
B: Well, I remember I once ⁵_____ (visit) the modern art gallery with my company. It was excellent. I think they always ⁶_____ (take) visitors there.
A: OK, thanks. Any other advice?
B: Yes – walk everywhere! The city centre is quite small. I never ⁷_____ (use) public transport when I was there.

4 Complete the sentences with the correct comparative form of the adverbs in brackets. Sometimes, you will need to use irregular comparative forms.

1. Jack always wins when they race. Jack runs _____ than John. (quickly)
2. Ruth is the laziest person in her family. Ruth works _____ than her brothers. (hard)
3. Your motorbike is really noisy. Your motorbike runs _____ than mine. (quietly)
4. The last flight is the Fastair flight. The Fastair flight arrives _____ than all the others. (late)
5. Katy is a very slow worker. Sarah doesn't work _____ than Katy. (slowly)
6. Mike exercises once a week, but Martin exercises every day. Mike exercises _____ than Martin. (often)
7. Julie's exam result was better than the other students' results. Julie did _____ in the exam than the others. (well)

5 Complete the sentences so that they mean the same as the sentences in Exercise 4. Use (*not*) *as … as* and the verbs and adverbs in brackets.

1. John _____ Jack. (run quickly)
2. Ruth _____ her brothers. (work hard)
3. Your motorbike _____ mine. (run quietly)
4. The other flights _____ the Fastair flight. (arrive late)
5. Katy _____ Sarah. (work quickly)
6. Martin _____ Mike. (exercise often)
7. The other students _____ Julie in the exam. (do well)

6 Match the statements (1–6) with the replies (a–f).

1. I could only find this birthday cake. Is it too big?
2. I want to get fit, but jogging is so hard!
3. There's so much traffic on the roads these days.
4. What time shall we go for lunch?
5. The price of flats is so high here at the moment.
6. Why are you doing another course?

a. I know – more and more people are driving.
b. It's fine – the bigger, the better!
c. The earlier the better – I'm already feeling hungry!
d. Yes, it's getting harder and harder to buy somewhere to live.
e. The more qualifications you have, the easier it is to get a job.
f. The more you run, the easier it'll get.

169

GRAMMAR SUMMARY UNIT 8

Verb patterns: -ing form and to + infinitive

When we put two verbs together in a sentence, the form of the second verb depends on the first. After many verbs we use the *-ing* form.
*I **love** travelling abroad.*
*I **can't stand** waiting in queues.*

Other common verbs followed by the *-ing* form: *adore, avoid, can't help, can't stand, describe, don't mind, enjoy, fancy, finish, imagine, keep, mention, miss, practise, recommend, spend (time/money), suggest.*
The negative of the *-ing* form is *not + -ing*.
*I **enjoy not getting** up early at the weekend.*

After many other verbs, we use a verb in the *to +* infinitive form.
*I **hope to see** you later this year.*
*It **seems to be** a good destination.*

Other common verbs followed by the *to +* infinitive form: *agree, arrange, ask, can't afford, choose, decide, expect, fail, hope, intend, learn, manage, need, offer, plan, pretend, promise, refuse, seem, threaten, want, would like, would love, would prefer.*

The negative of *to +* infinitive is *not + to +* infinitive.
*I promise **not to be** late.*

These verbs can also be followed by both the *to +* infinitive and *-ing* form, with no difference in meaning: *begin, continue, hate, like, love, prefer, start.*
*I **began reading** the book.* (or *I **began to read** …*)

▶ Exercises 1 and 2

Other uses

We use the *-ing* form when we use a verb as the subject of a sentence.
***Travelling** can be very educational.*

We also use the *-ing* form when a verb follows a preposition.
*I'm usually good **at finding** cheap hotels.*
*We often **think about** travelling for a year.*

We often use *to +* infinitive after an adjective.
*It was **amazing to visit** Chile for the first time.*

▶ Exercise 3

Present perfect simple and continuous

Form

We form the present perfect simple with *have/has +* past participle of the main verb. (See the inside of the back cover for a list of common irregular past participles.)
*I've just **got** back from holiday.*

We form the present perfect continuous with *have/has + been + -ing* form of the main verb.

For example: *I've been waiting, he's been doing, they haven't been reading.*

▶ Exercise 4

Use

We use both the present perfect simple and the present perfect continuous to talk about something that started in the past and continues in the present. We use:

- the present perfect simple to talk about a state that started in the past and continues in the present.
*I've **loved** Turkey since I first visited in 2005.*

- the present perfect continuous to talk about a long action or a repeated action that started in the past and continues in the present.
*I've **been waiting** for your email since last week.* (long action)
*We've **been coming** here for years.* (repeated action)

We also use both the present perfect simple and the present perfect continuous to talk about actions in the past that have an effect on the present. We use:

- the present perfect simple to talk about short actions that are complete and that have an effect on the present.
*Joel **has broken** his arm.* (= it's still broken)

- the present perfect continuous to talk about long actions in the past that have an effect on the present.
*We've **been walking** in the forest all morning.* (= and now we're hungry and tired)

We often use the present perfect continuous to emphasize the duration of a longer past activity and the present perfect simple to talk about its final result.
*I've **been researching** holidays all morning. I think I've **found** the perfect one for us.* (*researching* = longer activity, *found* = result)

For other uses of the present perfect simple, see Unit 2.

Remember that we don't normally use stative verbs in the continuous. See Unit 1.

▶ Exercise 5

How long … ?

We make questions with *how long* to ask about duration. We use:

- *how long +* present perfect simple to ask about a state which started in the past and continues in the present.
***How long** have you known David?*

- *how long +* present perfect continuous to ask about an action or a repeated action which started in the past and continues in the present.
***How long** have you been doing conservation work?*

- *how long +* past simple to ask about a state or action that is now finished.
***How long** did you live in Africa?*

We use *for* in answers to questions in all three tenses, but we can't use *since* with the past simple.
I lived in Africa for ten years. (not *… since 2002.*)

▶ Exercise 6

170

Exercises

1 Choose the correct option to complete the sentences. Sometimes, both options are possible.

1 Do you fancy *going / to go* to the cinema tonight?
2 He's pretending *being / to be* sick so that he doesn't have to go to work.
3 She'd prefer *not speaking / not to speak* to anyone at the moment.
4 I love *to swim / swimming* in the sea at night.
5 Can you imagine *having / to have* as much money as a famous actor?
6 I hate *to have / having* to rush in the morning.
7 I recommend *visiting / to visit* the history museum. It's fascinating.
8 They've chosen *not having / not to have* a party for their wedding anniversary.

2 Complete the conversation with the correct form of the verbs in brackets.

A: I'm going on holiday soon!
B: Oh, you're so lucky. I'd really love ¹_____ (go) away somewhere! Where are you going?
A: To Spain. I'm going to spend all day ²_____ (lie) on a beach! What are you going to do in the summer holidays?
B: Well, I can't afford ³_____ (travel) very far, but I'm hoping ⁴_____ (go) camping somewhere near here.
A: At least you won't have to get on a plane. I can't stand ⁵_____ (fly)!
B: Really? Well, when you're on the plane, just avoid ⁶_____ (think) about where you are. Just relax and imagine ⁷_____ (sit) on a beach.
A: I'll try. Well, anyway, I'm going to enjoy ⁸_____ (not work) for a few weeks!

3 Complete the text with the correct form of these verbs.

drive	eat	get	take	use	visit	walk

If you're keen on ¹_____ a break from modern life, then La Posada del Inca Eco-Lodge may be the place for you. It's on one of the most beautiful islands on Lake Titicaca, in Bolivia. ²_____ here is impossible because it is a car-free island. This means it's great ³_____ if you enjoy ⁴_____, especially as the views are spectacular. It is possible ⁵_____ all your meals in the hotel; the food is simple but delicious. The rooms don't have fridges, TVs or wi-fi, but they do have hot water and heating. It is difficult ⁶_____ an internet connection on the island, but if you really need ⁷_____ the internet, then you'll have to climb up to the restaurants near the top of the hill.

4 Write sentences and questions with the present perfect continuous form.

1 I / live / here / since / 2015.
2 She / not wait / long.
3 you / work / all day?
4 They / swim / for / about an hour.
5 I / not listen / to the radio.
6 he / play computer games / all morning?

5 Choose the correct option to complete the sentences.

1 I've already *eaten / been eating*, so I don't need any dinner.
2 We've *come / been coming* to this island since I was a child.
3 He's *had / been having* that car for ages.
4 I haven't *seen / been seeing* Jack for three years.
5 She's *studied / been studying* all afternoon and now she needs a break.
6 Sorry, have you *waited / been waiting* for ages?
7 We haven't *known / been knowing* each for long.
8 I travel a lot. I've *visited / been visiting* ten countries.

6 Complete the conversation with the present perfect simple or present perfect continuous of the verbs in brackets. Sometimes both forms are possible.

A: You look tired. What ¹_____ (you / do)?
B: I ²_____ (search) on the internet for hours for a holiday destination. And I still ³_____ (not find) anywhere!
A: What about the usual place you go?
B: Oh, I ⁴_____ (go) to that resort for the last five years. I'm bored with it!
A: Well, why don't you go on a cycling holiday?
B: A cycling holiday?! I'm not sure … ⁵_____ (you / go) on one before?
A: Yes. I went an organized tour around Rajasthan last year. It was the most amazing holiday I ⁶_____ ever _____ (have)!
B: Really? It sounds very tiring!
A: It was fun! And I made new friends. We ⁷_____ (stay) in touch since our holiday. I ⁸_____ (already book) my next cycling holiday with the same company.
B: How long ⁹_____ (it / do) these tours?
A: Oh, for a long time. They're very good. You should come with me! You'd love it!
B: Well, yes, but I ¹⁰_____ (not have) much time to exercise recently.
A: That's OK. I'm going in six months. You can start cycling tomorrow!

171

GRAMMAR SUMMARY UNIT 9

Passives

Verbs can be active or passive. We normally use the active form when the focus of the sentence is on the 'agent' – the person or thing that does an action.
*   ***All kinds of people** buy products like these.* (focus = all kinds of people)

When we use the passive, a sentence isn't about the agent any more. The passive emphasizes the action.
*   ***Products like these** are bought by all kinds of people.* (focus = products like these)

Form

When we use the passive, the object of the active sentence becomes the subject of the passive sentence.

All kinds of people buy <u>products like these</u>.
OBJECT

<u>*Products like these*</u> *are bought by all kinds of people.*
SUBJECT

We form the passive with a form of the auxiliary verb *be* and the past participle of the main verb.

Tense	Active	Passive
Present simple	buy	is/are bought
Present continuous	is/are buying	is/are being bought
Past simple	bought	is/was bought
Past continuous	was/were buying	was/were being bought
Present perfect	has/have bought	has/have been bought
Past perfect	had bought	had been bought
Modal verbs	can buy will buy etc.	can be bought will be bought etc.

We can use *by* + noun to say who does or did the action in a sentence with a passive verb. This makes the information sound new or important.
*   *The new farmers' market was opened **by a local businessman** last month.*

▶ Exercise 1

Use

We often use the passive:

*   when it's obvious who does an action
    *The letter **was delivered** this morning.* (= obviously by the postman)

*   when it's unimportant who does an action
    *When I complained to the company about the camera I bought, I **was sent** a new one.* (= it doesn't matter who sent it)

*   when we don't know who does an action
    *My bag **was stolen**.* (= I don't know who stole it)

*   when we don't want to say who does an action
    *The house **hasn't been cleaned** again.* (= I don't want to say who hasn't cleaned the house.)

▶ Exercises 2 and 3

Articles

We use *a/an* the first time we mention something.
*   *I've just bought **a** new washing machine.*

We use *the* when we mention something which is known (because it has already been mentioned, for example and when there is only one of something.)
*   *I bought a shirt and a tie. **The** shirt was quite cheap.*
*   *It was warm and **the** sun was shining.*

We use no article (**zero article**) to talk in general about uncountable or plural nouns.
*   ***Tourism** brings a lot of money to the country.*

▶ Exercise 4

Quantifiers

We use *a lot of*, *lots of*, *loads of* and *plenty of* with uncountable and plural nouns to talk about large quantities. We often use *plenty of* to mean 'more than enough'.
*   *There are **a lot of** food shops in my neighbourhood. We don't need to go to the supermarket. There's **plenty of** food in the fridge.* (= more than enough food)

We also use *many* + plural noun in more formal, written English to talk about a large quantity.
*   *There are **many** ways to save money on your shopping.*

We don't normally use *much* in affirmative sentences. However, we use *too much* with uncountable nouns and *too many* with plural nouns in both spoken English and formal writing to say there is more than we want.
*   *There's **too much** noise here – I can't work.*

We also use *much* and *many* to ask questions about quantities.
*   *Were there **many** nice clothes in the sale?*

We use *some* to talk about neutral, non-specific quantities with uncountable and plural nouns.
*   *I've got **some** food.* (= not a lot, not a little)

We use *several*, *one or two*, *a couple of* and *a few* to talk about smaller quantities with plural nouns. We normally use *several* to refer to larger quantities than *one or two*, *a couple of* and *a few*.
*   *We've got **one or two** questions about the offer.*
*   *I've been to **several** nice cafés by the river.* (= five or six)

We use *a little* and *a bit of* to talk about smaller quantities with uncountable nouns.
*   *We've got **a little** money left. Let's get some ice cream.*

We use *not any* with plural and uncountable nouns to talk about zero quantity. We also use *any* when we ask questions about uncountable and plural countable nouns.

We use *little* + uncountable noun and *few* + countable noun to say 'not much' and 'not many' in formal, written English. They have a more negative meaning than *a little* and *a few*.

▶ Exercises 5 & 6

172

Exercises

1 Are the sentences correct? If not, correct any mistakes with the passive.

1. My new book can found online or in bookshops.
2. Is the building being painted this week?
3. The hole in the roof still hasn't be repaired!
4. Your order was been sent to you ten days ago.
5. The show is watched from millions of people all over the world.
6. Our friends' food being brought to the table when we arrived.
7. Will the meeting be finished before lunch?
8. I hadn't was told about the party.

2 Choose the correct options to complete the text.

> **Great meal at Rexo!**
> This new Mexican restaurant ¹ *has advertised / has been advertised* quite a lot on the radio recently, so I decided to try it. I love Mexican food anyway! We arrived at around 8 pm. It was really busy, but we ² *gave / were given* a table after just five minutes. While our table ³ *was prepared / was being prepared*, we ⁴ *looked / were looked* at the menu. There's a great selection and the prices are good.
> After ⁵ *we'd ordered / we'd been ordered*, our food ⁶ *was brought / brought* quickly. Everything was delicious. We only had one complaint. We'd asked for a bottle of tap water. But when we paid, we saw that $2 ⁷ *had added / had been added* for the bottle. This didn't seem fair – tap water is free in all the other restaurants in town! But overall, I'm sure Rexo will be a success and their delicious food will ⁸ *enjoy / be enjoyed* by everyone!

3 Rewrite the information in the passive. Don't include the agents in brackets.

1. The supermarket has just delivered the shopping.
   The shopping _____ .
2. (The technician) is fixing my computer.
   My computer _____ .
3. Will (you) invite Sonia to the party?
   _____ Sonia _____ to the party?
4. (We) didn't finish the work.
   The work _____ .
5. (You) can't use mobile phones here.
   Mobile phones _____ here.
6. The manager had called the police.
   The police _____ .
7. Do (you) accept credit cards?
   _____ credit cards _____ ?
8. (People) don't use the new shopping centre.
   The new shopping centre _____ .

4 Complete the text with *the*, *a(n)* or – (zero article).

¹_____ cash machine in ²_____ New York had to be switched off because it was giving out too much money. ³_____ machine, in one of ⁴_____ busiest underground train stations, was giving ⁵_____ ten-dollar notes instead of ⁶_____ five-dollar notes. As soon as ⁷_____ people realized what was happening, ⁸_____ queue developed. Within thirty minutes, news of what was happening appeared on ⁹_____ internet, and even more people arrived. But not long after, ¹⁰_____ employee from the bank came to switch it off.

5 Complete the second sentences with these quantifiers so that they mean the same as the first sentences.

| a couple of | a little | how much | loads of |
| plenty of | several | too much | |

1. There's more traffic than we want in this town.
   There's _____ traffic in this town.
2. There are one or two good shops in this street.
   There are _____ good shops in this street.
3. I have some money left, but not very much.
   I have _____ money left.
4. There are a lot of good offers in that shop.
   There are _____ good offers in that shop.
5. We won't be late – we've got more time than we need.
   We won't be late – we've got _____ time.
6. Four or five new restaurants have opened near my flat.
   _____ restaurants have opened near my flat.
7. How many bottles of juice do we have?
   _____ juice do we have?

6 Choose the correct options to complete the conversation.

A: Right, we've spent ¹ *a lot of / much* money now. Let's go home.
B: Not yet. I still need to get ² *a couple of / loads of* things – just a new dress and some shoes.
A: Really? You've already got ³ *many / plenty of* pairs of shoes at home – more than you need, in my opinion.
B: Yes, but I ⁴ *don't have any / have not any* shoes that match my new coat!
A: I see. Well, ⁵ *how much / how many* time do you need? I'm getting hungry. I only had ⁶ *a bit of / a couple of* breakfast.
B: I won't be long – I promise. Why don't you go to the café over there? Then I can have ⁷ *a little / little* time to myself.
A: Alright. I'll see you in ⁸ *a few / few* minutes.

GRAMMAR SUMMARY UNIT 10

Second conditional

We use the second conditional to talk about unreal situations in the present or future. The form is:
If + past simple + *would* + infinitive
> *If I **liked** science, I'd **read** more books about space exploration.*
> *If we **had** to live on Mars, it **wouldn't** be easy.*

We can also use *might* in the main clause when we are less sure about the result.
> *If you **saw** the film, you **might** like it.*

We often use *could* in the main clause to talk about ability and possibility.
> *If we lived by the sea, we **could** go swimming every day.* (= we would be able to go swimming)

When the *if* clause comes first, we use a comma between the two clauses. When the main clause comes before the *if* clause, we don't add a comma between the two clauses.
> ***If** we wanted to, we could do more to protect the planet.*
> *We could do more to protect the planet **if** we wanted to.*

We don't normally put *would* in the *if* clause. We normally use a past tense.
> *If I **had** more time, I would go travelling more often.* (not *If I would have more time, ...*)

When we put *be* in the *if* clause, we can use *were* instead of *was*. We normally do this when we use the phrase 'If I were you' to give advice.
> ***If I were you**, I wouldn't take the job.*

We also use *were* in this way in other sentences. This normally sounds more formal, but some people consider it more correct.
> *If I **were** richer, I'd become a space tourist.*
> *If he **were** more careful, he wouldn't have so many accidents.*

▶ Exercises 1, 2 and 3

Defining relative clauses

We use defining relative clauses to say exactly which person, thing, place or time we are talking about.
> *That's the doctor **that I saw last month**.* (relative clause tells us which doctor)

that, *which* and *who*

To introduce a relative clause, we use a relative pronoun or relative adverb after a noun. The choice of relative pronoun depends on the type of noun:

- for things, use *that* or *which*
  *This is the finger **that/which** hurts.*

- for people, use *that* or *who*
  *The people **that/who** spoke to us are here.*

We can leave out *that*, *which* and *who* when they are the object of the verb in the relative clause.
> *She loves **the flowers (that/which)** you brought.* (*that/which* = object of *brought*)
> *The person **(that/who)** you know isn't here.*

We can't leave out the relative pronoun if it's the subject of the relative clause.
> *That's **the film that** won five Oscars last year.* (not *That's the film won ...*)

▶ Exercise 4

whose, *when* and *where*

We use the relative pronoun *whose* to talk about possession.
> *Sonia has a daughter **whose** dream is to become a doctor.*

We also make relative clauses with the relative adverbs *where* and *when*. They mean the same as preposition + *which*.
> *That's the hospital **where** I was born.* (= the hospital **in which** I was born)
> *Do you remember the moment **when** you decided to become a nurse?* (= the moment **in which** you decided to become a nurse)

▶ Exercises 5 and 6

Exercises

1 Match the beginnings of the sentences (1–8) with the endings (a–h).

1 If I were you,
2 People wouldn't feel so stressed
3 If my sister didn't buy so many things,
4 Which sport would you do
5 If Paul didn't drink so much coffee,
6 If my parents lived closer,
7 I wouldn't have to use public transport
8 If space travel were cheaper,

a I could visit them more often.
b she'd have more money.
c if you had more free time?
d I'd find another flat.
e if they didn't work so much.
f he might sleep better at night.
g would more people try it?
h if I had a car.

2 Choose the correct form to complete the sentences.

1 If you *were / would be* a millionaire, what *would / did* you buy first?
2 People would *feel / felt* happier here if it *were / would be* sunnier.
3 If we *lived / would live* in the countryside, *we'll / we'd* be able to see the stars at night.
4 If I *hadn't / didn't have* so much work to do, I'd *go / I went* to bed earlier.
5 I *can / could* buy a new car if *I'd save / I saved* more money.
6 My dad *would have / had* more friends if *he'd be / he was* more friendly.
7 *Would / Did* you take a job for less money if it *was / would be* closer to home?
8 If *I lived / I'd lived* nearer my work, I *could / might* walk there.

3 Complete the sentences to make second conditionals.

1 I don't exercise, so I'm not very fit.
  If I _____ more, I _____ fitter.
2 She doesn't have his number, so she can't call him.
  If she _____ his number, she _____ him.
3 You're tired because you don't get enough sleep.
  You _____ tired if you _____ enough sleep.
4 He doesn't study, so he won't pass his exams.
  If he _____, he _____ his exams.
5 I'm ill, so I can't go to work.
  If I _____ ill, I _____ to work.
6 She often gets headaches because she uses her computer so much.
  She _____ headaches so often if she _____ her computer less.

4 Circle the correct relative pronoun or pronouns. Then cross out the relative pronoun(s) that can be omitted.

1 Is that the athlete *that / which / who* won the gold medal?
2 Those are the books *that / which / who* I borrowed from the library.
3 This is the website *that / which / who* has a lot of good recipes.
4 My boss doesn't like the report *that / which / who* I wrote for him.
5 I've just seen someone *that / which / who* I know.
6 This is the TV programme *that / which / who* got good reviews.

5 Complete the sentences with a relative clause.

1 This is a hotel. Leo is staying here.
  This is the hotel _____ .
2 The doctor has already seen those people.
  Those are the people _____ .
3 This man is Will. His wife likes running ultramarathons.
  Will is the man _____ .
4 The first woman won a gold medal at the Olympic games in 1900.
  1900 was the year _____ .
5 I told you about that man. He's my old school teacher.
  That man's the old school teacher _____ .
6 I got a lovely present from my sister. This is it.
  This is the lovely present _____ .

6 Complete the text with the phrases (a–f) and an appropriate relative pronoun or adverb.

a she grew up
b she was attacked
c story has inspired people
d was based on her life story
e lost her arm
f was living in a hotel nearby

Bethany Hamilton is an American professional surfer ¹ _____ in a shark attack at the age of just sixteen and ² _____ all around the world. On October 31, 2003, Bethany was surfing at a local beach in Hawaii when she was attacked. She lost sixty per cent of her blood on the way to hospital, but luckily she was saved by the medical team there, including one doctor ³ _____ . The attack was terrible, but Bethany was surfing again within a month, and in 2005, less then two years after the day ⁴ _____ , she won her first national surfing competition. Bethany became well known around the world when a film ⁵ _____ came out. Bethany is now married and has a child. Her wedding was by the sea on an island in Hawaii ⁶ _____ .

175

GRAMMAR SUMMARY UNIT 11

Reported speech

Statements

We can use direct speech or reported speech to say what someone else said.

　　Direct speech: *He said, 'I'll see you later.'*
　　Reported speech: *He said that he'd see me later.*

We can leave out *that*, especially in informal, spoken contexts.

　　She said she'd go. (or *She said **that** she'd go.*)

When we use reported speech, we normally make some changes to the words the person actually said. We normally change the tense of the verb.

Direct speech	Reported speech
Present simple Paul said, 'I **want** to give you something.'	Past simple Paul said (that) he **wanted** to give me something.
Present continuous Maria said, '**I'm waiting** for the train.'	Past continuous Maria said (that) she **was waiting** for the train.
Past simple Paul said, 'I **sent** you a message.'	Past perfect Paul said (that) he **had sent** me a message.
Present perfect simple Maria said, 'I **have** just **arrived** home.'	Past perfect simple Maria said (that) she **had** just **arrived** home.
will Paul said, '**I'll** call you.'	would Paul said (that) he **would** call me.
can Maria said, 'I **can't** come.'	could Maria said (that) she **couldn't** come.

The modals *might* and *would* don't change in reported speech.

　　'You **might** like it.' → Paul said I **might** like it.
　　'We**'d** love to visit.' → Maria said they**'d** love to visit.

When we report words that are still true at the time of reporting, we don't need to change the verb form.

　　'It**'s** a great film'. → Nic said it**'s** a great film.
　　'I**'ve** lost my phone.' → Max said he**'s** lost his phone.
　　(= He still hasn't found it.)

We normally need to make changes to pronouns and adjectives, and words and expressions about time and place when we report.
pronouns: *I* → *he/she*, *we* → *they*
adjectives: *my* → *his/he*, *our* → *their*, *this* → *that*
time: *now* → *then*, *today* → *that day*, *tomorrow* → *the next day*, *yesterday* → *the previous day*
place: *here* → *there*

　　Seb said, '**We'll** see **you here tomorrow**.'
　　→ Seb said **they'd** see **me there the next day**.

However, if the sentence is reported on the same day it was said, we don't need to change the verb form, the place or the time.

　　Seb said, '**We'll** see **you here tomorrow**.'
　　→ Seb said **they'**ll see **me here tomorrow**.

▶ Exercise 1

Questions

We normally use the verb *ask* to report questions. To report a *wh-* question we use normal word order (subject before verb). We don't add *do*, *does* or *did*.

　　'Where do you work?' → She asked where I worked.

To report a *yes/no* question, we add *if* or *whether* before the subject in the question.

　　'Did you read the article?' → She asked **if** I had read the article. (or She asked **whether** I had read …)

▶ Exercises 2 and 3

Reporting verbs

Patterns

To report statements, we use *say* and *tell*. With *tell*, we always use an object before the reported speech. The object is often a pronoun.

　　'I can't help.' → She told **them** (that) she couldn't help.

With *say*, we never use an object before the reported speech.

　　'We don't want to come.' → They said that (they) didn't want to come. (not *They said me …*)

We also use many other verbs to report speech and thoughts. We use *ask, tell, remind, invite* with an object + *(not) to* + *infinitive*. The object is usually a person.

　　'Can you hold my bag?'
　　→ She **asked** me **to hold** her bag.
　　'Don't sit down.' → He **told** us **not to sit** down.
　　'Remember to bring the present, Marcos.'
　　→ She **reminded** Marcos to bring the present.

We use *promise* and *offer* + *to* + infinitive. We do not use an object with these verbs.

　　'I won't be late again.'
　　→ He **promised not to be** late again.
　　'Would you like me to drive you to the station?'
　　→ She **offered to drive** me to the station.

We can also use *promise* + *(that)* + clause.
　　He **promised that he wouldn't be** late again.

▶ Exercise 4

Thoughts

To report thoughts, we use the verbs *realize, think* and *know*. They are followed by *that* + subject + verb. We sometimes leave out *that* after these verbs, especially in informal, spoken contexts.

　　I **realized** (that) I had forgotten my wallet.
　　She **thought** (that) it looked like a nice restaurant.
　　He **knew** (that) it wasn't the right house.

We use the verb *wonder* to say 'ask yourself'. It is followed by *if/whether* or a question word.

　　'Has Julia come home yet?' → He **wondered if** Julia had come home yet. (or He wondered whether …)
　　'Where can I leave my car?' → I **wondered where** I could leave my car.

▶ Exercises 5 and 6

Exercises

1 Choose the correct option to complete the reported speech sentences.

1 'I love the hotel.'
He said *he loved / he'd loved* the hotel.
2 'We arrived late.'
They said *they were arriving / they'd arrived* late.
3 'You might not enjoy the film.'
She said I *might not enjoy / might not have enjoyed* the film.
4 'We're leaving soon.'
They said they *were leaving / left* soon.
5 'I can't come.'
He said he *couldn't come / can't came*.
6 'We've just got home.'
They said *they just got / they'd just got* home.

2 Put the words in order to make reported questions. There is one extra word that you don't need.

1 Jo asked (had / seen / if / the film / been / I)
She asked _____ .
2 Barbara asked (did / lived / I / where)
She asked _____ .
3 Tina asked me (Luke / if / was / had / to / I / spoken)
She asked me _____ .
4 Enzo asked (leaving / why / were / being / we)
He asked _____ .
5 Jaime asked (was / where / hungry / I / if)
He asked _____ .
6 The men asked us (whether / wanted / we / did / something)
They asked us _____ .

3 Complete the story with the reported speech form of the direct speech.

I was on the train last week when I saw my old boss. I said 'hi'. He asked ¹_____ . I told him that ²_____ , but that we ³_____ for years. He said that ⁴_____ and asked me ⁵_____ . I said ⁶_____ , but that ⁷_____ . He asked me ⁸_____ . I said that ⁹_____ , but that ¹⁰_____ . In the end, he gave me a job!

1 'Do I know you?'
2 'We worked together.'
3 'We haven't seen each other for years.'
4 'I remember.'
5 'How are you?'
6 'I was fine.'
7 'I'm looking for a job.'
8 'Would you like an interview today?'
9 'I can't.'
10 'I'll be free tomorrow.'

4 Complete the sentences with these reporting verbs.

| asked | invited | offered | reminded | said |
| told | | | | |

1 'I can lend you some money.'
She _____ to lend me some money.
2 'Would you like to go to the theatre?'
He _____ me to go to the theatre.
3 'Do you need some help?'
She _____ if I needed some help.
4 'Don't forget to call me later.'
I _____ him to call me later.
5 'It's a nice film.'
He _____ that it was a nice film.
6 'I don't want to stay.'
I _____ her that I didn't want to stay.

5 Choose the correct option to complete the sentences. Both options are possible in one sentence.

1 He asked *me to help / that I help* to fix his car.
2 They reminded *us to / that we* bring our dictionaries.
3 I wondered what *to cause / was causing* the delay.
4 He realized *to leave / that he'd left* his bag at home.
5 We invited *to go / them to go* on holiday with us.
6 She promised *to call / that she'd call* straight away.

6 The direct speech in these sentences is spoken to you. Complete the reported speech. Use the past simple form of the reporting verbs in brackets.

1 'Don't leave your bag there.' (tell)
She _____ there.
2 'Did I forget my passport?' (wonder)
I _____ passport.
3 'I'll never lie to you again.' (promise)
She _____ again.
4 'Oh dear. We've left the map at home.' (realize)
They _____ at home.
5 'Can you give me your email address?' (ask)
He _____ email address.
6 'Would you like me to carry your bag?' (offer)
He _____ bag.
7 'Don't forget to close all the windows.' (remind)
She _____ all the windows.
8 'Maria will love the present.' (know)
I _____ the present.

GRAMMAR SUMMARY UNIT 12

Third conditional

We use the third conditional to talk about unreal situations in the past. The form is:
If + past perfect + *would* + *have (not)* + past participle

We use a negative verb if the past event happened and a positive verb if the event didn't happen.
If you'd worked harder, you wouldn't have failed the exam. (= You didn't work hard. You failed the exam.)
If Tina hadn't helped me, I wouldn't have been able to finish the project. (= Tina helped me. I finished the project.)

When the *if* clause comes first, we use a comma between the two clauses. When the main clause comes before the *if* clause, we don't add a comma between the two clauses.
If you'd invited me, I'd have come to the party.
I'd have come to the party if you'd invited me.

We use the contraction *'d* in spoken English and more informal writing. It can replace either *had* or *would*.
If I'd (= had) had more time, I'd (= would) have visited the castle again.

We don't normally put *would* or *have* in the *if* clause. We normally use the past perfect.
If those people had known the area, they wouldn't have needed a map.
(not *If those people would have known ...*)
They wouldn't have needed a map if they'd known the area. (not *... if they'd have known the area.*)

▶ **Exercises 1, 2 and 3**

should have and *could have*

We use *should (not) have* + past participle to talk about regrets about past actions. We use:

- *should have* when something was the right thing to do, but we didn't do it.
  *I **should have called** you to tell you where I was.*
  (= I didn't call you. I regret that.)

- *shouldn't have* when something was the wrong thing to do, but we did it.
  *I **shouldn't have brought** such a heavy bag on holiday.*
  (= I brought a heavy bag. I regret it.)

We also use *should/shouldn't have* to criticize people's past actions.
*You **shouldn't have** shouted at me. It was very rude.*

▶ **Exercise 4**

We use *could (not) have* + past participle to say whether something that didn't happen was possible or impossible. We use:

- *could have* when something was possible but it didn't happen.
  *You **could have** really hurt yourself!* (= You didn't hurt yourself, but it was possible.)

- *couldn't have* when something was impossible and it didn't happen.
  *We **couldn't have** come earlier – the traffic was terrible.* (= We didn't come earlier and it wasn't possible because of the traffic.)

We also use *could have* to say something was possible in the past and we're not sure if it happened.
He could have got lost. (= It's possible he got lost. But I don't know what happened.)

▶ **Exercises 5 and 6**

Exercises

1 Read the sentences (1–5). Choose the correct option (a–b) to explain each sentence.

1 If you'd called me, I would have helped you.
   a   You didn't call me.
   b   I helped you.
2 If I hadn't been so rude, we wouldn't have had an argument.
   a   We didn't have an argument.
   b   I was rude.
3 I wouldn't have gone to Scotland if you hadn't recommended it.
   a   I went to Scotland
   b   You didn't recommend Scotland.
4 We would have missed our flight if we'd left when you wanted to.
   a   We didn't miss our flight.
   b   We left when you wanted to.
5 You wouldn't have been so cold if you'd brought a warm coat.
   a   You brought a warm coat.
   b   You were cold.

2 Match the beginnings of the sentences (1–6) with the endings (a–f). Then complete the main clauses with *would have* or *wouldn't have*.

1 If I'd had my umbrella with me,
2 If you hadn't bought that expensive new car,
3 If I'd known how boring this job was,
4 If you'd been more careful,
5 If they hadn't booked such a cheap hotel,
6 If we hadn't forgotten to bring the map,

a   we _____ been able to afford a holiday.
b   you _____ broken the window.
c   they _____ had a better holiday.
d   I _____ got wet.
e   I _____ come to work here.
f   we _____ got lost.

3 Complete the sentences to make third conditionals. Use contractions where possible.

1 We didn't pay attention and we got lost.
   If we _____ lost.
2 We saw lots of plants when we visited the park.
   If we _____ plants.
3 We didn't take more water because we didn't know how hot it was.
   If we _____ more water.
4 My phone didn't work, so I couldn't call for help.
   If _____ for help.
5 I went to Kenya. I met my husband there.
   If _____ my husband.

4 Complete the sentences with *should have* or *shouldn't have* and these phrases. Use the correct form of the verb.

buy a ticket	invite so many people
check it more carefully	stay up so late last night
have a bigger breakfast	tell us earlier

1 Your report was full of mistakes.
   You _____ .
2 Our house is a mess after the party.
   We _____ .
3 John just called to say he can't come.
   He _____ .
4 I was already hungry at 11 am.
   I _____ .
5 We all feel exhausted this morning.
   We _____ .
6 I got a parking fine last week.
   I _____ .

5 Complete the sentences with *could have* or *couldn't have* and the correct form of the verb in brackets.

1 Why didn't you wear a helmet when you went skiing? You _____ (hurt) yourself.
2 It's normally very hot at this time of year. We _____ (know) it would be so bad.
3 I think he _____ (win) the race, but he hadn't trained hard enough.
4 Thanks for all your help organizing the trip. I _____ (done) it without you.
5 I've been waiting an hour for you! You _____ (call) to say you'd be late.
6 I did my best, but I didn't pass the exam. I _____ (try) any harder.

6 Complete the conversation with *could have*, *couldn't have*, *should have* or *shouldn't have* and the correct form of the verbs in brackets.

A: Did you read about the woman who survived in the wild for a week after her car broke down?
B: Yes, I saw that. She was twenty kilometres from the nearest village. And she walked into the forest to find help and then got lost. I think it was a mistake to leave the car. She [1] _____ (stay) there. They [2] _____ (find) her more quickly that way.
A: I agree. And I think she [3] _____ (leave) home without telling her friends and relatives where she was going. The article says nobody knew where she was!
B: OK, but she [4] _____ (know) her car would break down.
A: I always tell someone if I'm going on a long journey. She [5] _____ (tell) at least one person – that's obvious.
B: OK. But even then, it [6] _____ (take) a long time to find her. She was really in the middle of nowhere.
A: That's true.

Audioscripts

Unit 1

▶ 1

When we look at people and cultures all around the world, we find similar things. For example, people need a sense of group identity. Look at this Wanapum girl with her horse. She's taking part in a traditional meeting of Native Americans in the state of Oregon. It's a special occasion that happens every September. Horses are very important in Native American culture and many children learn to ride a horse before they learn to ride a bike. In the past, they helped people hunt for food and helped people carry things from camp to camp. And horses eat grass, so they are easy to feed. The girl's clothes are also important. The colours of Native American traditional dress mean different things to different tribes. For example, red can mean earth or blood, and white can mean winter or death. Around the world people wear traditional dress, uniforms or the colours of our favourite sports team to say the same thing – we belong to this group.

▶ 3

A: Do you want to do this quiz with me?
B: OK. What's it about?
A: Colours and what they mean around the world. For example, look at this photo. Where are the women going?
B: I don't know. To a party?
A: No, they're guests at a wedding in India. The guests and the bride herself wear bright colours. OK, here's your next question. Do you think red means different things in Eastern and Western cultures?
B: Yeah, I think it does. I always associate red with strong emotions like love or anger.
A: Let me check the answers … that's right. And in Eastern cultures red often means luck. Oh, and bravery too. OK, next: Do you know where yellow means knowledge?
B: Well, a yellow jersey means the winner of the Tour de France to me!
A: Well, there are two options. Do you think it's China or India?
B: I think it's … oh, China.
A: Let's see … no, you're wrong, it's India. And in China, yellow means power. So maybe you should wear yellow when you finish your studies!
B: Well, I didn't know that. What's the next question?
A: OK … which colour means happiness in Japan? Orange or pink?
B: Oh I know this, it's orange.
A: Yes, it is! How did you know that? Amazing! It's happiness and love. OK, the next one's about the colour blue. Do Mexicans wear blue to a funeral?
B: I've got no idea. I'd say people usually wear black for funerals, but is it different in Mexico?
A: Yes it is. It says here that blue is associated with death. That's a bit sad.
B: Are there any more questions?
A: Yeah, the last one is, who uses green as their symbol? There are two options, but I'm not going to tell you them. It's too easy.
B: Green? Something to do with nature … ? Oh yes, it's international really. Environmentalists and conservationists … that sort of thing.
A: Of course it is! Now, here's a quiz all about the colour green. Do you want to have a go?

▶ 6

1
P = Paola, C = Colin
P: Good morning! Allow me to introduce myself. I'm Paola Iannucci.
C: How do you do. My name's Colin Burke.
P: It's a pleasure to meet you, Colin. I see you work for an advertising agency.
C: Yes, erm … Paola. I'm the art director at Arrow Agency. I mostly work on web adverts.
P: Do you? That sounds interesting.
C: It is. We're developing some really great ideas for advertising. The internet is vital to an advertising campaign nowadays.
P: Oh, I agree, Colin. I know exactly what you mean – I'm in sales.
C: Oh, are you?
P: Yes, I work for an electronics company. Online sales is very important to our business.
C: Really? Well, Paola, why don't I give you my card? Here you are.
P: Thanks. It's been good talking to you. Let's stay in touch.

2
L = Lucy, Y = Yuvraj
L: Hello, how are you. I'm Lucy.
Y: I'm very pleased to meet you. I'm Yuvraj Singh. I work for 'Get fit' – it's a chain of gyms.
L: Oh yes, my brother goes to 'Get fit'.
Y: Does he? Great. We're building a big new gym in the town centre here. It's nearly ready to open, in fact.
L: Is it? That's great.
Y: Yes, we're all really excited about it. Erm, what about you?
L: I'm looking for a new job at the moment, actually.
Y: OK, well, thanks for your time. Let me give you my card. Don't forget to check out our new gym when it opens.

Unit 2

▶ 8

1 I love going to the theatre and I especially love seeing new drama, but I think a lot depends on the director. Sometimes, you can get marvellous actors and a great play. But if the director is wrong, then the whole thing can be disappointing. We usually go a couple of times a month if we can. We take turns choosing what to go and see.

2 I've never been to anything like it before, but I have to say I really enjoyed myself. They recorded it for television and there were ten different choirs in the competition. The standard of the singing was excellent. Honestly, they were as good as professional even though they were all amateurs who just sing in their free time. It's on every year, so I am definitely going back next year.

3 I love all the colour and movement, and energy and excitement of events like this. When there's a big audience, the atmosphere is brilliant. I think it's really important to keep traditional dancing alive, as well. So it's great when young people join in, like they do here.

▶ 12

Bruce Daley is the owner of a dance studio in London. He runs dance classes for all ages. He spoke to us about his work.

'I adore dancing and I can't imagine doing anything else with my life. I've taught hundreds of people to dance – it's wonderful. I opened the studio when I retired from dancing professionally. My first students were young kids, but these days it has all changed. Everyone wants to dance. A lot of older people began coming when the big TV shows started. They say it makes them feel young. It's wonderful to watch them. Many people have found a new social life here and made new friends. Two of my older students even got married last year!

One of the great things about dancing is it can really change your mood. I've seen how dancing can affect people. Traditional ballroom dancing became

180

fashionable a few years ago. It was really popular with young professional people. Once, a very angry and stressed-out young man came to class. After a couple of hours, he left with a smile. The class changed his mood completely. Dancing has been my life, really. And starting this school was the best thing I've ever done. My injuries ended my career as a dancer ten years ago. But opening the school gave me a new career as a teacher.'

▶ 13

Bruce has been my teacher for about two years now. I started coming here during a bad period at work. Bruce's classes are great – I've never had so much fun! I've met all kinds of people here. Some of them have become really good friends. At first, I didn't know how to dance. But I soon realized that you can't get embarrassed – you just have to dance! Everyone here has felt the same way at some point.

▶ 14

1 Bruce has been my teacher for about two years now.
2 Some of them have become really good friends.
3 You just have to dance!
4 Everyone here has felt the same way at some point.

▶ 16

L = Lesley, R = Richard

L: Do you feel like going out tonight?
R: Yeah, why not? We haven't been out for ages. What's on?
L: Well, there's a film about climate change. Do you like the sound of that?
R: Oh, not really. It doesn't really appeal to me! What's it about? Just climate change?
L: I think it's about how climate change affects everyday life. I wonder how they make it entertaining?
R: Well, it sounds really awful. It's an important subject, I agree, but I'm not in the mood for anything depressing. What else is on?
L: There's a Flamenco festival.
R: Oh, I love dance. That sounds really interesting.
L: Apparently, it's absolutely brilliant. Let's see what it says in the paper: 'Aida Gómez leads in a thrilling production of the great Spanish love story *Carmen*.'
R: OK then. What time is it on?
L: At 7.30.
R: Well, that's no good. We haven't got enough time to get there. Is there anything else?
L: There's a comedy special on.
R: Where's it on?
L: It's at the City Theatre. It's a kind of comedy marathon for charity with lots of different acts. It looks pretty good. The critic in the local paper says it's the funniest thing he's ever seen. It says here: 'Roger Whitehead is absolutely hilarious as the embarrassing host to a night of comedy gold.'
R: Hmm, I'm not keen on him. He's not very funny.
L: Are you sure you fancy going out tonight? You're not very enthusiastic!
R: Perhaps you're right. OK, let's go and see the Flamenco – but tomorrow, not tonight.
L: Great. I'll go online and book the tickets.

Unit 3

▶ 18

Coming up in today's programme, we look at some more active alternatives to simply lying around on the beach this summer. Jason reports on a kayaking trip around the beautiful Pacific Ocean coastline of Australia – a more relaxing activity than water-skiing or jet-skiing but just as much fun. Jenna has been to the Red Sea to try diving and snorkelling for the first time, so we'll find out how she got on. And we also talk to people here in the UK to find out whether windsurfing on a lake is different to windsurfing at the seaside, as well as the best rivers to experience the thrill of real white-water rafting. But first, the latest travel news from Anya.

▶ 19

1 I live in Zambia and we have fantastic rivers here. I love rafting on the Zambezi River, it's one of the best white-water runs in the world. On my very first trip, we had a real surprise! We were coming down fast from a section of rapids and we could see calm water ahead. Then I saw a big hippo near the river bank. It's best to avoid hippos if you can! We started moving away quickly because it was coming towards us! And then, we were going around a small island in the middle of the river, when suddenly …

2 I began diving when I was about twelve. I actually learned to dive while I was on holiday in Mexico. My parents went there to explore the underground lakes – or cenotes, as they're called here. My brother and I were just sitting around on the beach, getting bored, so we took a diving course. Then we did our first dive in the 'easy' cenotes while my parents were exploring the dangerous stuff. It wasn't very deep underground and the sun was shining in through an opening in the roof of the cave. It was really calm and beautiful. I felt like staying there all day! I was concentrating on doing everything right. I didn't notice that …

▶ 20

1 And then, we were going around a small island in the middle of the river, when suddenly we surprised an eight-metre crocodile. It was lying in the sun on the other bank. It jumped into the water about a metre away from our boat – it nearly landed in the boat! Fortunately, it didn't take much interest in us so we got away! Maybe it wasn't hungry!

2 I was concentrating on doing everything right. I didn't notice that I was swimming into an area that was only for advanced divers. There were ropes and signs to stop you going into some tunnels where it was easy to get lost. Luckily for me, my mum realized pretty quickly that I was missing and she came after me. I still had no idea where I was going!

▶ 22

1 They tried to get away.
2 We rowed down the river.
3 What happened to you?
4 The crocodile looked dangerous to me.
5 We arrived too late.
6 We walked ten kilometres along the beach yesterday.

▶ 25

1
A: Did I ever tell you about the time my goldfish learned to fly?
B: What? No, I don't think so.
A: Well, we had these two goldfish. They were really huge. And they lived in a fish tank above the kitchen sink. But these two fish were really active. They loved to jump in the air. Especially when someone was doing the dishes.
B: No way!
A: Seriously! After we saw it the first time, we put a lid across the top of the tank. So, a couple of weeks later, I came into the kitchen one morning and the tank was empty.
B: Oh, no!
A: Oh, yes! During the night, the fish had jumped out of the tank! They were lying in the sink! Fortunately, there was some water in it!
B: That's incredible!

Audioscripts

2

C: I remember once, a couple of years ago, we were looking after this friend's parrot when he was on a business trip. Anyway, after a few days, I realized that this parrot knew how to open its cage.

D: Really?

C: Oh yes! It happened a couple of times. When I went out, the parrot was in its cage. And when I got back home, it had got out. So one day, I was at work and all of a sudden I remembered that I hadn't filled up the bird's food and water. I immediately rushed back home … and there it was … the empty cage again. I searched everywhere. I was going round the house calling 'Polly! Polly, come on Polly'. But I couldn't find it.

D: What happened then?

C: Well, the next thing was, I started to panic. So I went into the kitchen to make the tea, and guess what? There was the bird. It was having a bath in my teacup!

D: That's unbelievable!

▶ **26**

1 Especially when someone was doing the dishes.
2 They were lying in the sink!
3 we were looking after this friend's parrot
4 I was going round the house calling 'Polly'!

Unit 4

▶ **27**

1 When I was little I wanted to be a superhero, like in my comic books. I wanted to save the world. When I realized that superheroes aren't real people, I decided to be a fireman. It seemed like a very exciting job. Now, of course, I realize that it's dangerous, dirty and extremely challenging. So I'm glad I decided to work in an office – I'm not really very brave!

2 When I was a child, my ambition was to drive a train. My uncle was a train driver and I wanted to be just like him. I liked the idea of being in charge of the train and being responsible for all the passengers. I'm actually an accountant! It's not a very exciting job – but it's not as boring as many people think it is.

3 I was really into sports when I was a kid, especially football. My bedroom walls were covered in posters of my favourite footballers. I wanted to be just like them – the best footballer in the world. Footballers were well-paid and famous. But I'm not likely to be a footballer now. I'm training to be a nurse – which is not well-paid and is quite stressful! But in the end I think nursing will be enjoyable. I hope so!

▶ **29**

1 **Devi is from West Sumatra in Indonesia**

D: I didn't stay on at school, because generally girls don't here. But then I got this job. I'm the first girl in my family to work outside the home. Since the economic crisis, more women have jobs. I feel very different about my future now. I'm going to change my job. I don't want to stay in this one forever. I want to train as a nurse, so I've applied to college. I hope to get a place on the next course. It starts in January. I'm taking the entrance exam next month. I'm very nervous about it. I haven't told my boss. I suppose I'll tell him soon.

2 **Elisabeth is from Bruges in Belgium**

E: I work in a factory. It's a good job but the company is making people redundant. So I'm going to take the redundancy package because it's an opportunity to start again. I got married very young and had a family, so I didn't finish my education. But I've just finished evening classes in business studies, and now I'm going to start my own business. It's something I already do as a hobby, I make and sell speciality cheeses. Just a moment, I'll get you some. Here you are, taste this. Do you like it? Well, I'm meeting the bank manager on Wednesday to discuss my business plan. And hey, maybe I'll take some cheese for him to taste as well!

3 **Sahera is from Kabul in Afghanistan**

S: It's very difficult to study at university level here. Many girls get no education at all. But we have managed to complete our degrees and graduate from the department of language and literature. Now we're thinking about the next step. Many of the graduates are going to work as teachers. My friend is going to continue her studies in the United States. I'm going to stay here in the city, because my family is here. I guess I'll take some time off and visit my parents. And I want to spend time with my friend because she's leaving next week.

▶ **31**

R = Rudi, M = Mark

R: This looks interesting – this assistant researcher job for a TV company.

M: I know, the only thing is the experience. They want two years, but I've only worked part-time for a year, really.

R: One or two years experience it says, and anyway you meet the other requirements. You're good under pressure and with deadlines – you always hand your essays in on time at college!

M: That's not the same thing!

R: Of course it is. And you're really well-organized, hardworking, highly motivated …

M: OK, OK, if that's what you think … is it all right if I give you as my referee?

R: Hmm, I'm not sure about that. I don't think you can just put down your friends' names.

M: I know, shame! But seriously, do you mind helping me with my CV? I need to make it look a bit more professional.

R: Of course not. Are you going to apply for this job, then?

M: Yeah, I think I will. But I'll need my CV anyway, whichever job I apply for.

R: OK, print it out and I'll have a look at it.

M: Will you be able to do it today?

R: Yes, I will. But what's the hurry?

M: The closing date for applications is in a couple of days. Oh, can you have a look at my covering letter too?

R: Have you already written it?

M: No, but I'll do it this afternoon and then I can send everything off tonight. Hey, they might ask me to go for an interview this week!

R: Yeah, they might.

M: But I haven't got any smart clothes! Would it be OK to borrow your suit?

R: Sure, no problem.

Unit 5

▶ **34**

Really, the first thing to say about food is that everyone has different needs. That means we can't say 'a portion should be this size'. What you have to do is eat for the size that you are. So, children obviously need to eat less than adults, and most women need to eat less than most men. How do you know how much to eat? Use your body as a guide. So for a typical adult woman,

182

Audioscripts

the amount of cereal or rice in a portion is the same size as your clenched fist. Notice I say *your*, not *a* fist. It's the size of *your* hand that matters. If you're eating a piece of meat, then make sure it's no bigger than the palm of *your* hand. For snacks like popcorn, the biggest portion size is two of your own handfuls. And for cakes, which we all know we need to be careful with, then the portion should be the size of two of your fingers. That doesn't sound like very much? Exactly!

▶ 36

1
- **A:** I've never tried durian. Have you? Apparently, it tastes much better than it smells.
- **B:** No, I haven't tried it. But I know that it smells so much that you aren't allowed to take it on buses in Singapore.

2
- **C:** What's fugu? F– U– G– U?
- **D:** Oh, I know what it is. It's a kind of fish they eat in Japan. It's actually poisonous, so only qualified chefs are allowed to prepare it in restaurants. If you eat the wrong part, it can kill you!

3
- **E:** Can you eat shark meat?
- **F:** Yes, it's popular in lots of countries. Sometimes, you have to ferment it first because the fresh meat is bad for you. That's what they do in Iceland. It's called hakarl there.

4
- **G:** Are you going to boil those potatoes like that, without peeling them?
- **H:** Yeah, why? You don't have to peel potatoes before you boil them.
- **G:** Yes, you do. At least that's what we do in my house!

5
- **I:** I love eating oysters, but I can never remember when it's safe to eat them.
- **J:** The rule is you mustn't eat them in the warm summer months, but I don't know why not.

6
- **K:** I feel a bit sick. I wonder if it was the mayonnaise on my salad?
- **L:** Was it fresh mayonnaise? You should avoid using raw eggs in mayonnaise, didn't you know? They can make you ill.

7
- **M:** Are you making chilli con carne?
- **N:** Yes, but the recipe says you must boil red beans for fifteen minutes or they aren't safe to eat. Do you think that's right?

8
- **O:** What's this on the menu? Steak tartare? Is that raw steak?
- **P:** Yes, you can eat steak raw. It's cut into very thin pieces. You should try it.

▶ 39

L = Lin, J = Jack
- **L:** Hi, Jack. Have you read this item on imaginary eating?
- **J:** Hi, Lin. Yes, I saw it this morning. What a load of rubbish! I've never heard anything so ridiculous. If we think about eating food, we'll lose weight, it said.
- **L:** Not exactly. It said if you think about eating food, you stop wanting to eat it so much. So if you don't eat it, then you might lose weight. I thought it made sense.
- **J:** No, it's rubbish. I'll believe it when I see it! You can't 'think yourself thin'.
- **L:** Well, I'm not so sure. I think willpower is really important, especially where food is concerned. Imagine you are overweight and you want to lose a few kilos. If you don't train your mind, you won't be able to lose weight. I reckon you can achieve anything if you believe you can do it.
- **J:** You mean like 'mind over body'? Well, OK, mental attitude is important when you're trying to change something in your life. But I don't think that's the same as what the news item said. So are you going to do this imaginary eating thing, then? Do you really think it'll work?
- **L:** Yeah, why not? I won't find out unless I try.
- **J:** And what exactly are you going to do, then?
- **L:** OK, let's think. I eat too many crisps and snacks, right? So, when I want to eat a snack, I'll try just imagining that I'm eating it. Hey, you know what? This could be amazing. I'll never need to buy chocolate again if this technique works!
- **J:** Well, I can't believe my ears!
- **L:** Hey, as soon as it starts working, I'll let you know. Self-belief, that's what's important.
- **J:** I'm going to buy you some chocolate just in case. I think you'll need it.

▶ 41

W = waiter
- **W:** Are you ready to order?
- **A:** Erm, not quite.
- **W:** No problem. Would you like something to drink while you decide?
- **A:** Yes, please, just water's fine for the moment.
- **B:** Oh, this menu looks interesting. I love trying new dishes. What are plantain fritters?
- **A:** Well, plantain is a kind of banana and a fritter is a fried dish – in this case, fried, mashed banana balls.
- **B:** Do you mean like a sweet, dessert banana?
- **A:** No, plantain is a type of savoury banana you eat as a vegetable. It's quite a bland flavour, really.
- **B:** OK. What about akkra? What's that made from?
- **A:** It's made from a kind of bean called black-eyed peas. They're fritters too.
- **B:** Hmm. What do they taste like?
- **A:** Well, akkra's usually pretty hot and spicy.
- **B:** Sounds good! I think I'll try that. Now, what's this – ackee and saltfish?
- **A:** Where's that?
- **B:** In the main courses, at the top of the list.
- **A:** Ah yes. I think ackee's a kind of fruit that's traditionally served with saltfish.
- **B:** And saltfish?
- **A:** That's dried salted cod. You have to soak it in water before you cook it, but then it's a bit like fresh cod. It doesn't taste salty when it's cooked.
- **B:** OK. I might try that. What are you going to have?
- **A:** I can't make my mind up. Oh, here comes the waiter again.
- **W:** Can I take your order now?
- **A:** Yes, please. I'll have the akkra to start with.
- **B:** And I'll have the same.
- **W:** And for your main course?
- **A:** I'd like to try the ackee and saltfish. Does it come with vegetables?
- **W:** Yes, with plantain.
- **A:** And how's that cooked? Is it fried?
- **W:** No, it's boiled.
- **A:** OK, that sounds fine.
- **W:** And what about you, sir?
- **B:** Can I have the goat curry, please?
- **W:** Certainly.
- **A:** I've never tried goat.
- **B:** You can try some of mine when it comes. It's like lamb, but the flavour's a bit stronger.
- **A:** OK, great.

Unit 6

▶ 43

- **W:** What a photo! It's like a dream. Is it real? I mean, do you think the photographer photoshopped it?

183

Audioscripts

M: No, it's totally genuine according to the website. It was taken on a really hot day, so maybe that's why it looks a bit strange.

W: But I don't really understand where the cows are.

M: They're on a beach. It says here the photographer was driving along a coast road in Andalusia and saw some cows lying on the empty beach. He couldn't get close in his car, so he had to park and walk along the beach in 35 degrees Celsius heat.

W: That sounds horrible. I don't think I'd do that just to get a shot.

M: I know. I'm surprised he didn't frighten them – it's hard to get close to animals.

W: But what's going on in the background? I can't make it out.

M: It looks like people on the beach. I think they're parasailing. It's a really popular sport there. It's always windy on that beach.

▶ 44

I have two questions for you today. The first: how good are you at flexible and creative thinking? And the second: does the promise of a reward make you work harder?

So, let's test your flexible thinking. I'm going to give you a task. You have a candle, a box of drawing pins and some matches. The task is to attach the candle to the wall so that the wax doesn't drip on the floor below. How do you do it? Well, clearly the matches are to light the candle with and we know that drawing pins are for attaching things to other things. But what about the box? Yes, it's for holding the drawing pins. But you can also use it to hold the candle. And then you attach the box to the wall. Did you get it? Yes? Congratulations, you're a flexible thinker.

Now, let's turn to the second question. Imagine I offer half of you some money to do this task more quickly. Not a lot of money, but a fair amount. It's work – and we all work for money, don't we? And I tell the other half of you that I'm going to see how long it takes you so that we can find out the average time. What do you think will happen? The people with the reward of money will be quicker, right?

Well, I can tell you the results of this experiment. And it's the same result every time. The people in the first group – the ones who are offered some money – need more time to find the answer – usually about three minutes longer, in fact. That's right. It's a mystery. You offer someone a reward, and they work more slowly. What's going on?

▶ 46

The Nasca lines are enormous drawings on the ground, in the Nasca desert in southern Peru. Most of the lines are just shapes, but about seventy are animals such as a spider, different types of birds, a monkey, or a dog. There are human figures as well. And they are huge – the biggest of the drawings is about two hundred metres across. Altogether, there are hundreds of these drawings and they are in an area of about eighty kilometres across.

The lines were made by the Nasca people over a period of time starting about two thousand years ago. They moved the brown stones that cover the desert and so showed the white ground underneath. You can still see the stones along the edges of the lines.

▶ 47

The mysterious thing about the lines is that they only became clear about one hundred years ago when air travel began. But the Nasca people couldn't have seen the patterns from above. So the question is how, and indeed why, did they make them?

One of the first people to study the lines was an archaeologist called Maria Reiche. She became convinced that the lines must have been a type of calendar. Other people thought they may have been ancient Inca roads. The strangest idea was that they could have guided creatures from space!

One of the other mysterious aspects of the Nasca people is that although this region of Peru is one of the driest places on Earth, they built a successful society there. How could they have done this without water? Well in fact, there is a river in the mountains. It goes underground for many kilometres before it reappears on the surface. Some people think that this might have seemed mysterious to the Nasca people, and so the lines were part of traditional or religious beliefs linked to the water. Whatever the explanation, one thing is for sure: the Nasca people can't have known that the lines would still be visible centuries later.

▶ 51

1
A: Did you hear that story about the sheep?
B: No, I don't think so. What was it about?
A: Apparently, they reflect the sun back into the atmosphere, because they're so white.
B: Oh yeah?
A: And then the heat from the sun gets trapped, so it makes everything hotter. So they think sheep cause global warming.
B: Come off it!
A: Well, that's what it says in the paper today.
B: You're having me on!
A: It does – here, look.
B: Hmm, that can't be right! Hang on a minute, what's the date today?

2
C: Let me have a look at those twenty-euro notes for a moment.
D: Why?
C: The blue ones are no good – they're forged.
D: You must be joking! All twenty-euro notes are blue!
C: Not the real ones.
D: Are you sure?
C: I'm absolutely positive. The girl at the travel agent's told me. It was on the news last night.
D: They must have made a mistake … oh no, and we've just changed all this money! What are we going to do?
C: I don't know … but it is 1 April today…

3
D = daughter, F = father
D: Oh, honestly! I really believed you!
D: Dad, did you see the news about petrol prices? They've gone down to almost half the price.
F: Really? How come?
D: I don't know. But anyway, I've put petrol in the car.
F: Great … hold on … did you say petrol?
D: Yeah.
F: Are you serious? The car uses diesel, not petrol!
D: I know, but petrol is so much cheaper!
F: Yes, but …
D: I'm sorry, did I do something wrong?
F: Diesel engines don't work with petrol, you must know that! Oh, this is going to cost me a fortune.
D: Dad?
F: Yes?
D: How do you suppose I managed to drive the car home, then? April Fool! It's 1 April!

Unit 7

▶ 54

1 We're a big family, and it's quite a small house. I share a bedroom with my two older brothers. My

184

grandparents live with us too. It's cramped and noisy, but at least there's always someone around. It's the only house I've ever known. I love living with my family, we all get on so well. I suppose I'll move out when I get married. I don't know when that will be!

2   I had to move to London when I started work. I saw an advert in the paper for a room in a shared house. Well it's a flat on the first floor of a big house, actually. My flatmates are away working quite a lot, so it's just like living on my own a lot of the time, really … especially during the week. Weekends are different. I have to say that living with friends is more difficult than I thought it would be. For one thing, nobody ever wants to do any housework.

3   I'm in my last year at college and I'm really looking forward to finishing and going abroad or getting out of this town! I can't wait to get away from here and be independent. It's going to be brilliant. My sister and I have shared a room all our lives. My family's lovely, but I'd like to have the chance of my own space – preferably in a lovely sunny country somewhere.

▶ 56

1   As an architect, I'm interested in everything about house design. But we can learn so much from traditional buildings and designs. Traditional houses usually survive bad weather conditions better than modern ones, so the question is, what can we copy from those houses when we build new houses? Like the rock homes, you know? They heat up less quickly than brick houses, which is great in hot climates.

2   Well, a shelter is a lot less permanent and more basic than a house. The igloos that people build with ice in the Arctic region are a perfect example of a shelter. A shelter just protects you from the weather, but a home has several spaces with different uses.

3   I'd say a ger is both a shelter and a home. It's organized around a fire in the centre with a chimney, and it has separate areas for men and women. A ger isn't as solid as a brick or wooden house but you can take it down and put it up much faster, which is what nomadic people in Mongolia need.

4   Well, it all depends on the local weather. I mean, if you live in an area that has regular floods, it's a good idea to live in a house on stilts. That way, you can live much more safely above the water and you don't have to worry every time it rains a lot! And the higher the stilts, the safer you are!

5   I think that modern homes are fairly similar wherever they are in the world, which doesn't always mean that they are the best design for every situation. In our crowded cities, modern houses are getting smaller and smaller so that they can be built more cheaply. Unfortunately, sometimes modern houses are also built badly. They don't work as efficiently as traditional houses – they need central heating in winter and air conditioning in summer.

▶ 58

A = estate agent, C = customer
A: Good morning.
C: Hi, I'm interested in any properties you have in the town centre.
A: OK, and is that to rent or to buy?
C: Oh, it's to rent. I've just started a new job here, so I think I'd rather rent than buy, for now anyway.
A: Right, well we have quite a few flats on our system, from one-bed studios to four-bedroom apartments.
C: I'd prefer something small, but not too small. I imagine I'll get a lot of friends staying with me. So, two bedrooms, and preferably with a lift. I cycle a lot and I don't want to carry my bike up lots of stairs!
A: Well, most of the modern buildings have lifts, but a lot of the properties in the centre are quite old. Would you rather look at new places or older ones?
C: I don't mind, at this stage I'm just getting an idea of what things are like here.
A: OK … so you're new to the area?
C: Yeah, I lived in a little village up near the mountains until recently.
A: Oh, that sounds lovely.
C: To be honest, I prefer towns to villages. The problem with a village is that everyone knows your business. Maybe I'm unfriendly, but I like the way that in a town you don't know everyone.
A: Ah yes, I've heard a few people say that! To be honest, I prefer living here. I suppose I like my privacy too. Right, erm, what about garage space? Do you need that?
C: No, I haven't got a car, I prefer to walk or cycle. It keeps me fit.
A: Of course, you mentioned your bike!
C: Yeah! And anyway, in my experience, driving in town is a nightmare!
A: I know, and it's getting worse. OK, well, the next thing to consider is your budget and the rental period.

Unit 8

▶ 61

1   A couple of years ago I went on a round-the-world trip with a friend. What an experience! The best bits were when we took local buses and trains – you know the kind of thing. They stop everywhere and it takes ages to get to where you're going. On the other hand, we met some really interesting people on the buses in Peru. We learned a lot about the history of Peru. But I took far too much luggage with me – I couldn't carry it easily and I worried about losing it. Just take a small backpack with the essentials, that's my advice.

2   I haven't travelled very much in the last few years. I've been on a few day trips to Liverpool and I've had a couple of weekends away to Scotland this year. I don't go far any more. I'm more interested in the place I'm going to than in the journey. Edinburgh and Glasgow are fascinating cities. But in my experience, the key to a good trip is good planning. Don't leave anything to chance!

3   I work in IT and I travel a lot – too much – for my job. I spend a lot of time on planes and in my car on the motorway, travelling to the projects I'm working on. I don't particularly enjoy it, especially when there are delays, but it's part of my job. I often get a very early flight from Gatwick and delays can mean I lose a whole working day. I have to go on business trips abroad several times a year. My travel tip? Once the flight starts, take your watch off and relax. You have no control over the time you arrive, so why get stressed?

▶ 63

R = Rose, M = Matt
R: Hi there, I'm Rose.
M: Hi, I'm Matt.
R: Is this your first time in Corfu?
M: No, actually. We come every year. We love staying here.
R: So do we. We keep coming back year after year. It's hard to find somewhere with everything you need for a holiday – great beaches, fantastic weather and something for everyone to do.
M: I know. Actually, there's a paragliding class later – I fancy trying that.
R: My friends want to do that too! To be honest, lying by the pool is my idea of a holiday.
M: Oh, I get a bit bored with doing that after the first day or two. I need to move around and do things.

185

Audioscripts

R: Well, why not? It's a different way of relaxing, I suppose.
M: Yes, that's right. Well, if you decide to go paragliding with your friends, we'll see you there!

▶ 65

When you've walked across half of Africa and you've walked up the west coast of North America, where do you go next? On tomorrow's show my guest is a man who can give us the answer. I'm talking about the conservationist Mike Fay – a man with a very personal way of saving what he calls the last wild places on Earth. For those of you who don't know Mike Fay, he does some unusual things in his work with the Wildlife Conservation Society. For instance, he's spent more than two years of his life trekking through some of the toughest places on the planet. And he often just takes a T-shirt, a pair of shorts and a pair of sandals on these treks. Fay says he has only slept in a bed about fifty times in ten years. The last time he was on the show, he'd just finished a survey of giant redwood trees on the west coast of the United States. What has he been doing since then? Well, he hasn't been taking it easy! In fact, recently he's been walking again, this time across Canada. In western Canada, mining companies have been looking for gold and oil. To do this, they've been digging up enormous areas – they've destroyed hundreds of square kilometres of wilderness. You can hear what Mike Fay feels about this in tomorrow's show. And we'll also find out what's been happening to national parks in Gabon since Fay was there. We know that people have been trying to set up mines near the parks and the Gabonese government has stopped at least two mining operations. Hear more tomorrow in my interview with Mike Fay, and find out what he thinks a population of seven billion people might do to our planet.

▶ 67

T = tourist, G = guide

1
T: I wonder if you could help us. Our luggage hasn't arrived.
G: Right. Are you with SunnyTimes tours?
T: Yes. Mr and Mrs Cameron.
G: And which flight were you on, Mrs Cameron?
T: The FastJet flight from Manchester. I think it's FJ2498. We've been talking to some of the other passengers and their luggage has come through, no problem.
G: Ah, yes. It seems some bags have gone to another airport. Flight FJ2498?
T: Yes, that's right. Do you know which airport our bags have gone to?
G: Yes, I'm afraid the luggage has gone to Rome.
T: Rome? How did that happen?
G: I'm not sure, but all the missing bags are coming on the next flight.
T: But when's the next flight?
G: It's tomorrow morning. Don't worry, we'll arrange everything. Which hotel are you staying at? Your bags will go there directly.
T: But all our summer clothes are in the suitcases.

2
G: Hello, Mr Jones. Is anything wrong? Can I help?
T: Well, it's about my wife, actually. She hasn't been feeling well for a couple of days.
G: I'm sorry to hear that. Is it something she's eaten, do you think? Or just travel sickness?
T: I don't know. She's had a temperature all night, but she feels cold.
G: OK, … erm, how long has she been feeling like this?
T: A couple of days? Yes, since the boat trip on Tuesday. Is there anything you can do?
G: Well it's probably nothing to worry about. But I'll ask the hotel to arrange for a doctor, just in case.
T: That's great, thank you.

Unit 9

▶ 70

R = researcher, S = shopper

1
R: Hi, do you mind if I ask you some quick questions about your shopping today?
S: Not at all, no.
R: Lovely. Well, first, can I ask what you've bought?
S: Oh yes, I've bought the latest Iphone.
R: Is it for you?
S: No, for my mum. For Mother's Day, next Sunday. She's really into gadgets and technology.

2
R: Hello, you look happy. Have you bought something nice?
S: Emm, I've got a couple of nice shirts in the sale, actually. That's all I came in for.
R: And who did you buy them for?
S: Just for myself. I buy all my clothes in the sales.
R: OK!

3
R: Hi, have you got time to answer a quick question or two?
S: Yes, I think so. We need a break!
R: Have you been spending a lot of money?
S: No, that's the problem! We're looking for some nice jewellery, earrings or a gold chain maybe … but we can't find anything we like.
R: And who is it for?
S: It's just for ourselves. We usually buy each other something special for our anniversary every year. It's a little tradition we have.
R: Well, good luck!

▶ 73

D = Dan, S = Samira

D: So, Samira, have you read any interesting articles this week?
S: Yes, I have, Dan. Several websites have articles about impulse buying. They're based on a study by the BBC.
D: And impulse buying is … ?
S: OK, have you ever gone to the shops to buy just one or two items – like bread and milk – and come back with loads of things you hadn't intended to buy? Well, that's impulse buying. Buying things just because you see them, without really thinking about it.
D: Oh, that sounds like me.
S: Well, don't worry, you're not alone. We've probably all done it at one time or other. And in fact, the study says that about five per cent of us have even spent more than £500 on a purchase that wasn't necessary!
D: But sometimes you see special offers or good deals on things. Especially on electrical goods like TVs or tablets. If we can save a bit of money, that's good isn't it?
S: OK, but as it says in a couple of the articles, the fact that something is good value for money doesn't matter if you can't afford it! You should always have a budget – work out how much you can spend and then stick to that amount. Anyway, there are some points in the research I thought were really interesting. The study divided people into two groups – men and women.
If you're female and under twenty-one, you're more likely to buy on impulse. Apparently, many women, but few men, use shopping as a way of managing their mood when they're unhappy. Also, if you go shopping when you're hungry, you're more likely to buy loads of food.

D: Oh, that explains why I spend too much money at the supermarket! So I just need to make sure I have a snack before I go?

S: Yes, that and make a list. Actually, there are plenty of simple things you can do to avoid impulse buying. You just need to take a little time to plan your shopping and you'll save money.

▶ 77

A = assistant, C = customer

1
A: Can I help you at all?
C: Yes, can I have a look at this silver chain?
A: This one?
C: Yes, please.
A: It's lovely, isn't it? Is it for you?
C: No, for my sister.
A: It's in the sale actually – it's got twenty per cent off.
C: Oh? I like it, but it's a bit heavy. I was looking for something lighter.
A: How about this?
C: Yeah, that's great. That's just right, I think. Erm, can she return it if she doesn't like it, though?
A: Yes, she can exchange it within ten days.
C: OK, good.
A: That's as long as she's got the receipt, of course.
C: I'll take it then. Can you gift-wrap it for me?
A: Well we don't actually do gift-wrapping, but we have some nice gift boxes for sale, over there.
C: Right.

2
C: Excuse me, are you in this department?
A: Yes, can I help you?
C: Well, I'm looking for a sofa that I saw on your website, but I can't see it here.
A: OK, do you have the reference number or the model name?
C: Yes, it's Byunk. The number is 00 389 276.
A: Right, let me see if it's in stock.
C: The website said 'available' this morning …
A: Yes, here we are. Do you want it in red, grey or blue?
C: Blue, if you've got it.
A: Yes, there are plenty in stock. Just give them this reference number at the collection point.
C: OK. What about delivery? How much do you charge for delivery?
A: Can you tell me your postcode? The charges go by area.
C: NE4 6AP
A: That would be £55.
C: Wow… OK.
A: If you go to the customer service desk, they can take your details and arrange the delivery date.
C: And do I pay here or … ?
A: The tills are by the collection point. You can pay by card or in cash.
C: Right, thanks for your help. Erm, how do I get to the tills, sorry?
A: Just follow the yellow arrows.

Unit 10

▶ 80

This man is Steve Holman. He's 52 years old and his friends think he's crazy. Why? Because he's running 200 kilometres in the Sahara desert. And he has to carry all his food with him, in a backpack that weighs twelve kilos. With the temperature hitting 38 degrees, he struggles up enormous sand dunes, sometimes crawling on his hands and knees. This is the annual *Marathon des Sables*, one of the key events on the ultrarunning calendar. Any race longer than a regular 42-kilometre marathon is called ultrarunning, but there is more to this kind of running than simply the distance. Ultrarunners push the human body to incredible limits and learn that it's stronger than you'd imagine. Another ultrarunner is Leslie Antonis, who ran 160 kilometres in 34 hours at the age of 47. It's amazing what the human body can do!

▶ 82

P = Peter, G = Gail
P: Now I'm sure most of us are amazed when we watch the Paralympics and we see athletes who run a marathon on blades or play rugby in a wheelchair. Tonight on Channel 10, there's a documentary which features some famous Paralympians. Gail, you've seen a preview of the programme.
G: Yes, Peter. The programme is a fascinating look at how medical science is changing people's lives right now. The Paralympians you mentioned use blades and wheelchairs, but these are devices that don't actually give them extra power. We also see some athletes whose devices are bionic.
P: And what's the difference, exactly?
G: I suppose the simplest explanation of a bionic device is one that uses electronics in some way. Sometimes they have their own power. And in sports, this means you can improve your performance.
P: So you mean bionic hands or arms?
G: Yes, and bionic legs too. Now there are also wheelchairs which are controlled electronically by the user.
P: So bionics is great news for patients who have lost the use of a limb.
G: Absolutely. And the range of bionic devices the programme describes is growing all the time. Let me tell you about a woman whose life suddenly changed after a skiing accident. Her name's Amanda Boxtel – she lost the use of her legs and didn't walk for over twenty years. Now she can use a robotic structure which supports her body so that she can walk. The structure she uses is called an exo-skeleton. Amanda used to be an athlete, but these days she works with an organization that promotes bionic technology.
P: And I believe there are already devices that help blind people to see and deaf people to hear.
G: That's right. It seems as if there's no limit to the things bionic devices will be able to do. So don't forget to watch the programme on Channel 10 tonight at 9.30.

▶ 86

1
A: What on earth has happened to you? There's blood all down your leg!
B: Oh, it's nothing. I tripped up when I was out running. I fell on a bit of tree or something.
A: Let me see. Oh, that looks nasty! It's quite a deep cut. You'd better wash it straightaway.
B: Yeah, I will.
A: You know, if I were you, I'd go down to A and E. I'd get it looked at.
B: It doesn't hurt. It's just a cut, really. I'm not going all the way to the hospital about a cut on my leg.
A: Hmm, it might need stitches, though. I would keep an eye on it if I were you.
B: OK, if it doesn't stop bleeding, I'll give the surgery a ring and see if the nurse is there.
A: Good, because I don't think we've got any plasters big enough!

2
C: Is my neck red? I think I've been stung or something.
D: A bit, yeah. It looks a bit swollen. Is it itchy?
C: Not exactly. It's painful rather than really itchy. How funny, I don't usually react to insect bites and stuff. Oooh, I feel a bit sick, actually.
D: You should put some antihistamine cream on it and see if it gets better.

Audioscripts

C: Have you got any?
D: Yes, I'm sure I've got some somewhere. You'll have to check the date on the tube, though. I'm not sure how long I've had it.

3

E: Ow!
F: Is your wrist still hurting you?
E: Yeah, actually it is. It hurts when I move it.
F: It might be worth getting it X-rayed. It's been, what, three days now? I wouldn't just ignore it, you might have broken something.
E: No, you're probably right. But I'm sure it's just a sprain, from when I fell against the table …
F: Even so, it's probably best to get it looked at.
E: Hmm.
F: Why don't you go and see Rosana in reception? She's the first-aid person. She'll know.
E: Good idea.

Unit 11

88

I = interviewer

1
I: Do you follow the news?
M: Yes, most of the time. I get the headlines direct to my mobile so that I can keep up with business news. I never buy a paper. I just catch up with the news online. Every couple of days, I have a quick look through the world news or at the comment and analysis sections, and I bookmark an article if it looks interesting.

2
I: How often do you read or buy a newspaper?
W: Oh! I don't read the papers, I haven't got time. I can see the news on my tablet, but I don't usually click on headlines unless they're about celebrities. If there's a video clip, then I might have a quick look at that. I prefer that to reading.

3
I: What kind of news stories interest you?
M: I like stories about my town, so I follow a couple of local websites. Also, celebrity interviews are always fun to read, but I don't believe everything I read because journalists sometimes change people's words. But I usually read the gossip column when I'm on the bus rather than the serious news.

4
I: How often do you share news stories you see online?
W: I sometimes send a story to friends if it's something that makes me laugh. I wouldn't share the big headline stories because they're probably reading about them anyway. I mean, we've got 24-hour news on TV and live streams of news online all day, haven't we?

90

1
A: I like this Twitter travel idea.
B: What's that?
A: It's this travel journalist, Rita Shaw. She goes off to different places and asks her followers on social media to suggest things to do. You know, 'I've just got off the train in Paris and I'm feeling hungry. Where can I get a good breakfast?' That sort of thing.
B: OK. And then what happens?
A: And then she writes about it. It's like a travel guide by the people who live in places – they're the ones who really know what's good. It's a great idea to use social media for something like that.
B: I didn't realize social media could actually be useful for anything!

2
C: It says here there's an eclipse tomorrow. Did you know?
D: Tomorrow? I thought it was today.
C: No, tomorrow. We should be able to see it from here. I'm just looking at this weather website. It's reminding people not to look at it with telescopes.
D: Yeah, I know.
C: It's quite a good website, actually. It tells you all sort of things.
D: I know. I've got it bookmarked.
C: Oh, I wondered if you had.

3
E: Wow, that's terrible. Have you seen this? It's bad enough to lose your job, but finding out from a text!
F: I saw that story. The company sent about 200 employees a text message. They told them not to turn up for work on Monday.
E: I didn't think that you could do that.
F: Me neither, but there you go …

4
G: Oh, that's hilarious!
H: Hmm … ?
G: You know that weird politician, the one who believes in UFOs?
H: Oh yeah, I can't remember his name, but I know who you mean.
G: He's posted a video on the internet. He's invited 'all friendly aliens' to come to a meeting in the Houses of Parliament.
H: No way! I didn't know you followed him online.
G: I don't, but there's an article about it in the paper. Look!

94

1

A = answerphone, R = Roger

A: The person you are calling is not available. Please leave a message after the tone.
R: Hi, this is a message for Anna Price. It's about the apartment for rent in the town centre, the one advertised in the Town Hall. OK, er, my name is Roger, I'm on 96235601. So, I'll try and call you later if I don't hear from you first. Thanks.

2

R = Roger, S = secretary

S: P and Q Associates, good morning.
R: Oh, hello. Could I speak to Jess Parker, please?
S: I'm afraid she's not in the office at the moment. Can I take a message?
R: Actually I'm returning her call. She left me a message this morning.
S: OK, I'll let her know that you rang. Who's calling?
R: It's Roger Lee. She has my number.
S: OK well, I'm sure she'll get back to you as soon as she comes in, Mr Lee.
R: Right, thanks.

95

1

T = Tony, A = Anna

T: Morning, Anna!
A: Oh, hi Tony. Oh, someone called about the apartments in the town centre. He called my number, but it should go to you really. You're handling those apartments, aren't you? Let me see, his name's Roger and his number is 96235601, but he said he'd call back.
T: OK, thanks. I'll give him a ring.

2

J = Jess, S = secretary

J: Hi, I'm back.
S: Hi, Jess. Just a moment, there were a couple of calls for you while you were out. Suzy … she said she would call back … and a guy called Roger said he was returning your call.
J: OK, thanks. Any more?
S: No, that's all.

Audioscripts

▶ 96
1 Could I speak to Jess Parker, please?
2 Can you give her a message?
3 I wonder whether I could leave a message?
4 I wonder if you could tell her I called?

Unit 12

▶ 97

I = interviewer, F = farmer

I: I'm here on the Isle of Lewis, in the Hebrides. It takes almost three hours to get here on the ferry from the Scottish mainland, so obviously it's not a journey people do every day. The traditional industries in the Hebrides include farming sheep and fishing. I'm with Alistair, a Hebridean farmer. Alistair, you were telling me about moving sheep by boat. That sounds like a difficult task! I've never heard of putting sheep in a boat before.
F: Well, it's not as hard as it sounds. It's normal practice for us.
I: Why do you need to move the sheep like this? Where do you take them?
F: We move them over to a small island for the summer, where there's plenty of grass for them to eat. The thing is, we can only fit a few in the boat, so we have to go back and forward a few times.
I: And when do you bring them back?
F: We normally go and get them to bring them back to the main island for the winter. We fetch them before the bad weather starts, usually in September. So, do you want to come across to the island with me one day?
I: OK! Why not? It should be interesting.

▶ 99

E = Emma, B = Beth

(The words of Emma Stokes are spoken by an actor.)

E: The first real eye-opener I had of what life was like in the African forest was on my first-ever expedition. It was the first day and we ended up making camp early that evening. I was exhausted and I fell fast asleep straightaway.
About four hours later, I was woken up by a lot of screaming and shouting and the words NJOKO, NJOKO! It was the local trackers shouting. Then I heard loud trumpeting and sounds of heavy steps. Basically, we'd put our tent in the middle of a giant elephant path. We couldn't have picked a more inappropriate place!
By the time I'd managed to get all my gear and get out of the tent, all of the trackers and all of the local guides had already disappeared into the night. When we came back, three of the tents were completely destroyed. That was my first taste of where not to set up a camp in the forest.

(The words of Beth Shapiro are spoken by an actor.)

B: A couple of summers ago we went to Siberia. We were looking for mammoth bones and tusks, and even hoping to find some mammoth mummies. We flew in on a small plane. It's pretty remote and there are no people there. When you land and get out of the plane, you look around and there's nothing there. And you set up your camp and there's still nothing there. And you're sitting there, relaxing, in total silence and there's nothing … Then all of a sudden, you're joined by ten million mosquitoes. I remember we made this kind of rice and fish dish for dinner, and we were sitting there, trying to enjoy this rice and fish meal … being eaten alive by mosquitoes. We had nets over our heads, but they were totally inadequate. The mosquitoes could still bite you. And you had to take the net off in order to eat. Every time you did that, hundreds of mosquitoes landed all over your face. They got in the food as well. It was just one part rice, one part fish and one part mosquito! You could go mad after just a few days of that!

▶ 102

1
A: Is everything OK with your food?
B: Yes, yes, it's lovely. But, erm, I should have told you that I don't eat meat.
A: Oh! Oh dear!
B: I'm really sorry you've gone to all this trouble.
A: There's no need to apologize – it's not a problem.
B: No, I should have said something earlier.
A: It's OK. I should have asked you if there was anything you couldn't eat. It's my fault. I'll make you something else.
B: No, please don't. The vegetables are delicious and there's plenty to eat.
A: Are you sure?
B: Yes, really. I'm enjoying this. I'll just leave the meat if that's OK with you.
A: OK.

2
C: Oh, my goodness! What was that?
D: I dropped the tray of glasses!
C: Oh, those nice glasses from Italy …
D: I couldn't help it – I slipped.
C: Are you OK? Let me help you up. You are clumsy, though.
D: Don't blame me – this floor is slippery.
C: Yes, but if you'd been more careful …
D: Look, it was an accident! It could have happened to anyone.
C: I know, I know. It's not your fault. Sorry I got upset.
D: It is a shame about those glasses, though. We've only just got them!

3
E: I'm so sorry to keep you waiting. The bus didn't come!
F: Were you waiting for the number 46?
E: Yes, it was supposed to come at half past five.
F: Don't worry about it – that service is terrible. It's always late.
E: I tried to phone you, but I couldn't get through.
F: Ah, I think my phone is switched off! Sorry about that!
E: Goodness, I'm almost an hour late!
F: It's OK. It's just one of those things – buses are unreliable! Anyway, you're here now and that's the main thing.